The Corporate Alibi

The Corporate Alibi

CAPITALISM AND THE CULTURAL POLITICS OF US INVESTMENTS IN AFRICA

Amy Elizabeth Stambach

UNIVERSITY OF CALIFORNIA PRESS

University of California Press
Oakland, California

© 2025 by Amy E. Stambach

Library of Congress Cataloging-in-Publication Data

Names: Stambach, Amy, 1966– author.
Title: The corporate alibi : capitalism and the cultural politics of U.S.
    investments in Africa / Amy Elizabeth Stambach.
Description: Oakland, California : University of California Press, [2025] |
    Includes bibliographical references and index.
Identifiers: LCCN 2025001878 (print) | LCCN 2025001879 (ebook) |
    ISBN 9780520394414 (cloth) | ISBN 9780520394421 (paperback) |
    ISBN 9780520394438 (ebook)
Subjects: LCSH: Investments, American—Africa, Sub-Saharan. |
    Corporations, American—Africa, Sub-Saharan. | Foreign subsidiaries—
    United States. | Social responsibility of business—United States. |
    United States—Foreign economic relations—Africa, Sub-Saharan |
    Africa, Sub-Saharan—Foreign economic relations—United States.
Classification: LCC HG5822 .S73 2025 (print) | LCC HG5822 (ebook) |
    DDC 332.67/367—dc23/eng/20250401
LC record available at https://lccn.loc.gov/2025001878
LC ebook record available at https://lccn.loc.gov/2025001879

GPSR Authorized Representative: Easy Access System Europe,
Mustamäe tee 50, 10621 Tallinn, Estonia, gpsr.requests@easproject.com

34   33   32   31   30   29   28   27   26   25
10   9   8   7   6   5   4   3   2   1

Contents

Illustrations

Preface

The Goose and the Common

> *The law locks up the man or woman*
>   *Who steals the goose from off the common*
>   *But leaves the greater villain loose*
>   *Who steals the common from off the goose.*
>
> *The law demands that we atone*
>   *When we take things we do not own*
>   *But leaves the lords and ladies fine*
>   *Who take things that are yours and mine.*
>
> *The poor and wretched don't escape*
>   *If they conspire the law to break;*
>   *This must be so but they endure*
>   *Those who conspire to make the law.*
>
> *The law locks up the man or woman*
>   *Who steals the goose from off the common*
>   *And geese will still a common lack*
>   *Till they go and steal it back.*
>
> —Anonymous, "The Goose and the Common"

If more people realized how much of our world is controlled by corporate America, how deep its reach is worldwide, and the detrimental impact it has on our air, water, land, food, jobs, and education, I suspect we might have a twenty-first-century version of the Boston Tea Party. If this seems far-fetched, hear me out.

Corporations influence governments, take over public healthcare systems, hoodwink small farmers into selling family lands, and control what foods we eat, the quality of the air we breathe, and even what computers or books teachers use. Corporations invest in food banks and agricultural services that channel corporate products into impoverished communities. They build on wetlands, destroy wildlife, and then sometimes promise to "restore" sites' natural habitats. They avoid or minimize the taxes they pay to governments while using taxpayer-funded public services such as roads, utilities, and telecommunications. They often hire "cheap" labor, asserting that people need to work, but they rarely support trade unions, workers' associations, or collective bargaining practices.

America's corporate CEOs make millions—even billions—of dollars, fly into space, travel on personal jets, buy mansion-size yachts, and spend more in a day on personal services and security than many of their hourly employees earn in a year. While millions struggle to make ends meet, a select few enjoy extravagant lifestyles and unimaginable wealth; their industries not only contribute to this stark inequality but also destroy the planet—one breath of fresh air, one plant cell, and one drop of water at a time. Year after year, the world's one hundred largest companies emit more than 60 percent of the world's total greenhouse gas emissions, and dozens of the top one hundred US toxic water polluters routinely violate US federal environmental regulations.[1]

When US corporations destroy communities' drinking water and wetlands in the United States, various state and federal laws and regulations can check and censure corporations.[2] But when US corporations destroy communities' water overseas, those corporations may not be accountable to anyone. How can this be? How can corporate America destroy other people's resources and cover up their actions outside the United States? And why don't those of us in the United States hear about the nefarious overseas operations of American firms? For the past thirty years, I have been conducting anthropological research in various regions of Africa, where I have witnessed firsthand the effects of US corporations and their actions. I see two main reasons why many Americans do not know about US corporations' operations in Africa.

First, US corporations work through overseas brokers and subsidiaries: They *outsource* their harms. Corporate America hires subcontractors and private companies to do its dirty work. When these subsidiaries broker shady deals and are found out and held accountable, those subsidiaries, not corporate America, take the blame for adverse consequences. In the United States, courts have determined that even if a subsidiary's actions violate US law, those subsidiaries cannot be held liable in the United States. Americans rarely hear about the impact of US investors' projects on African communities because US entities are technically not legally responsible for their overseas subsidiaries' actions.[3]

The second reason is that corporate America often employs misleading tactics to hide or minimize offenses related to environmental protection, labor, and safety regulations. In law, an *alibi* is a claim or evidence indicating that a person was elsewhere at the time of a crime and, therefore, is not implicated. Businesses use alibis to evade accountability for offenses in which they are involved. These alibis can take many forms and serve many purposes. They may involve economic or social maneuvers, such as giving gifts or making charitable donations to divert attention from the harm inflicted on individuals or the environment. In other cases, these tactics might focus on the environment, emphasizing "sustainable" aspects of a company's operations while engaging in ecologically destructive practices. Additionally, corporations might exploit gaps or ambiguities in the law to evade responsibility when one of its subsidiaries faces local legal challenges.

Many Americans may be unaware of corporate America's destructive impact on the land and lives of people overseas because corporate media and influencers promote half-truths and alibis. Or, having the information, some Americans may nonetheless ask, Who cares? Africa's a million miles away; why should Americans care about what's happening around the world? However, there are three important reasons to pay attention: democracy, the planet, and people.

Democracy faces significant challenges worldwide, including in Africa. Supporting diplomacy and fostering economic interdependence can promote democracy; however, multinational corporations often prioritize shareholder returns over transparency and shared market interests. This focus can lead to the erosion of independent regulatory frameworks, a decline in fair resource distribution, and a weakening of judicial systems. While governments can enforce fair labor laws, implement environmental protections, and promote community engagement, overseas governments often encounter obstacles when trying to litigate against US companies. The US Supreme Court has ruled that legal claims against American companies operating overseas must be filed in the United States because doing otherwise would extend US law beyond US boundaries.[4] Yet, in certain situations—especially those involving the protection of human rights and the environment—holding US corporations accountable for their actions abroad may ensure that they do not exploit weaker regulatory environments and prevent corporate malfeasance.

Then there is the planet. Corporations setting their own environmental goals often prioritize profits over ecological protections. While some companies may adjust their operations under pressure to address environmental issues, some changes merely replace one problem with another. For example, during a recent drought in Cape Town, South Africa, Coca-Cola's subsidiary responded to municipal water rationing requirements by transporting water from unaffected regions to Cape Town instead of reducing water usage,[5] increasing fossil fuel consumption in the process. Although Coca-Cola's PR team later highlighted that the company reduced its water footprint from two liters to one liter for each bottle of Coke, this fact pertained to changing to plastic bottles, which reduces the need for water to wash glass or aluminum containers. At the same time, plastics production and recycling contribute to industrial air pollution, which has surged by 66 percent globally since 2000 and today is one of the most significant risk factors for premature death in Africa.[6] Substituting one environmental threat for another is ethically questionable. Water and air know no boundaries. Caring about the effects of climate change anywhere means caring about accountability everywhere.

The primary reason we should pay attention to US corporations' activities across various regions in Africa is their impact on people. Practices that would be unacceptable in the United States are often carried out by US companies or their subsidiaries in Africa and other parts of the world.[7] Occasionally, companies use Africa as a testing ground for their products, which can involve employing questionable labor practices, conducting business in unethical ways, or even trialing new medications on people. The information gathered from these trials can then be used to enhance products and production processes in the United States.

Exploitation manifests in taking advantage of workers in countries with weaker health and safety regulations. Corporations may actively influence governments to prevent the implementation of meaningful regulations, allowing them to engage in questionable practices or pay starvation wages that would not be acceptable in the United States. Meanwhile, some companies frame this outsourcing as a means of creating jobs and alleviating poverty. In 2022, for example, Silicon Valley's ChatGPT paid Kenyans less than $2.00 per hour for "content moderation," which involves reviewing user-generated content on online platforms to find and remove illegal items, scams, instances of violence, hate speech, and sexual abuse before they enter AI-generated systems and reach the eyes of consumers. In 2024, US media ran several exposés about ChatGPT's practices.[8] But ChatGPT had an alibi ready: It said it was not responsible for any abusive labor conditions imposed by its subsidiaries in Kenya. But why did ChatGPT outsource this practice?

The answer is not just that the cost of labor is higher in the United States but that Americans demand more humane treatment of people hired for this kind of traumatizing "content moderation" job. But should Kenyans not also be guarded from the distressing sounds, words, and images? ChatGPT's San Francisco–based subsidiary described itself as an "ethical AI company" that was lifting people out of poverty. Yet calling such a wage "livable" or an "anti-poverty contribution" in Kenya is deceitful and unethical. In addition to exploiting workers through meager wages and harming them through mental trauma, such labor practices also contribute to lower expectations about standards of living everywhere.[9]

If environmental laws and labor regulations are to have any real value in the United States, they must govern US entities operating overseas. Yet, when corporate America is involved in legal proceedings involving overseas actions, its lawyers make sure the corporations evade accountability. For example, Apple, Dell, Google, Microsoft, and Tesla all source cobalt from the Democratic Republic of the Congo to manufacture lithium-ion batteries. Cobalt miners, some as young as six years old, work in dangerous conditions. In 2019, however, each of these US corporations hid behind a winding supply chain to claim innocence in the maiming of tens of thousands of Congolese children.[10] Dell denied that it ever "knowingly sourced operations using any form of involuntary labor." Apple averred that it "led the industry by establishing the strictest standards for our suppliers." And Google called child labor "unacceptable." The US judge dismissed the case because the companies' actions did not trace directly to the problem. According to the judge's written opinion deciding the case:

> It might be true that if Apple, for example, stopped making products that use cobalt, it would have purchased less of the metal from Umicore, which might have purchased less from Glencore, which might have purchased less from CMKK, which might thus have instructed Ismail to stop purchasing cobalt from child artisanal miners, which might have led some of the plaintiffs to not have been mining when their injuries occurred. But this long chain of contingencies, in all its rippling glory, creates mere speculation, not a traceable harm.[11]

Apple, Dell, Google, Microsoft, and Tesla pointed to model programs they supported to create the public impression that they care more about helping children than making money. Yet together, they knowingly provide the essential cobalt market that indirectly caused the exploitation and deaths of countless children. These corporations used the law itself as protection against legal action. They used the law as their alibi.

The concept of alibi came from my interactions with colleagues before and during a 2022 workshop titled "The Education Alibi: Toward a Critically Reflexive Perspective on the Paradoxes of Schooling in Africa." That workshop examined the promises and pitfalls of school systems designed to equalize opportunities for school graduates. As papers presented at the workshop show, schools' objectives did not always match the social and economic realities of a globalized world where schooling and jobs are not synced.[12] Speaking with colleagues at that workshop helped me realize that the concept of an alibi could also be used broadly to describe the multiple, sometimes conflicting justifications used by US corporations to deflect attention from their destructive practices. Accordingly, I gratefully acknowledge the colleagues who inspired me at that workshop and seek to locate the "education alibi" as part of a broader mosaic of justifications used by US corporations operating in Africa.

In the following chapters, I refer to diversity and race, to Africa as a whole, and to Africa as many different countries, legal regimes, political systems, and ecosystems. Because these terms and categories carry different meanings in different contexts, I explain here how I think about and use these terms, recognizing that language and conceptual frameworks are situational and always changing.

Terms that reference diversity and race, such as *black, indigenous, white,* and *colored* (the latter used in South Africa), follow categories that people with whom I spoke used to describe themselves, me, and one another. I do not mean that I accept the uses of these categories in all situations. I acknowledge the complexity and problematic nature of race and am aware that, despite the occurrence of racialized categories and references to diversity, these categories are constructed, not homogenous, and do not fully represent a person's identity.

I also recognize that the African continent comprises fifty-four sovereign nations (at the time of writing, though this number, too, is contested) with diverse languages, political systems, ecosystems, and trade agreements. My references to Africa as a continent do not indicate that the continent is socially or politically homogeneous or uniform. Instead, I use *Africa* when describing international and multinational corporations and governance regimes that refer to the continent. I do not attempt to represent the entirety of the continent or cover all aspects of its diversity. I use proper names for people, places, and corporations when those names already appear in publicly accessible documents. I use pseudonyms for places and people whose confidentiality I have agreed to respect and protect because they are not already known as public figures.

The eighteenth-century English verse reproduced at the beginning of this preface reminds us that, for centuries, people have fenced off common land for individual use to the detriment of many.[13] English farmers in the Middle Ages raised animals and grew crops on the "commons," collectively managed, common-property land, until the English government ring-fenced the land and built walls to keep the "commoners" out. Thereafter, profits from the enclosed fields went to the aristocracy, and commoners worked for landlords. In my opening remark about the Boston Tea Party, I draw a loose analogy between the English aristocracy and US corporations. To protest the British tax on tea, early American colonists threw chests of tea into Boston Harbor. They objected to British taxation without representation. To protest the English aristocracy's ring-fencing and privatizing of common property, the old English lyric chastises "lords and ladies" who deprive "commoners" of their resources and livelihoods.

The theme of the verse—the enclosure and privatization of the commons—evokes the logic of capital accumulation that traces from the English enclosure movement, which proceeded rapidly between 1750 and 1860, through centuries of Europe's colonization of Africa, to twenty-first-century US corporate land grabs in and extractions from the continent. I include the poem to indicate that the fight for redistributive justice remains a work in progress and requires ongoing political and public action.

Acknowledgments

In writing this book, I have benefited from the generosity of many friends and colleagues. My deepest debts and most profound thanks go to all of those who took me under their wing, patiently answered my questions, showed me what I didn't see, and allowed me to engage in activities that helped me understand US corporate investments from diverse vantages. These include—on both sides of the Atlantic—teachers, parents, farmers, academics, government workers, lawyers, journalists, and businesspeople.

I am especially grateful to "Anathi," "Fortuné," "Amadou," "Kundaeli," "Uduru," "Delgado," "Hennie," "Dr. Urassa," "Lawrence," and all the wise people who taught me more than I thought I could ever know. Some of these people took a professional risk in conveying the details of corporate investments. Although guidelines of confidentiality prevent me from sharing names (hence the pseudonyms, indicated by scare quotes, above), some people I can identify: Yusuf Sayed graciously welcomed me into his research group at the Center for International Teacher Education in South Africa. Discussions with Sarbani Chakraborty, Desiré Christian, Joyce Raanhuis, Melanie Sadeck, and Marcina Singh at Cape Peninsula University of Technology (CPUT) were always enriching. I am particularly grateful to Joseph Pesambili for his professionalism, insights, and friendship, and to Portia Maphuti for her expertise in managing researchers and research teams.

For a careful, expert, and essential reading of this work, I owe a huge intellectual debt to anthropologist Nombulelo Tholithemba Shange. Nombulelo's research on African healing and Khoi struggles for land helped me better understand the many competing interests behind commercializing land and medicines in South Africa. Josh Patzky Miller and Matthew Wingfield also offered incredibly insightful and constructive feedback at a critical time when I was revising this work. Matthew's research on the social and cultural aspects of the climate crisis and Josh's on digital techno-opportunism directly inform my argument about the extractive aspects of corporations and corporate philanthropies.

Aikande Kwayu, a cherished coauthor and colleague of many years, is always on my mind when I write. Aikande and I coauthored much of chapter 1, on hydro-social water systems, and, as I indicate in a footnote at the beginning of that chapter, portions of that chapter appeared in *HAU: Journal of Ethnographic Theory*, volume 11, number 2. I cannot say enough how much I appreciate Aikande's thinking and insights into international politics and diplomacy. I am forever grateful to Aikande and her beautiful, gracious extended family for always welcoming me and inspiring and challenging me to think big, really big. Thank you.

Early research for this work was made possible by generous funding support from the Wenner-Gren Foundation for Anthropological Research, National Geographic, and the Ruth Landes Memorial Research Fund. I am grateful to the National Science Foundation for providing funding under grant number 2211867 to enable me to conduct essential research on global health and human behavior, and to the University of Wisconsin–Madison Office of the Vice Chancellor for Research and Graduate Education for funding a comparative project on human resilience, ritual, and ecosocial change. For processing my research applications over the years and permitting me to conduct research in Tanzania, I am grateful to the Tanzanian Commission for Science and Technology and to Mashuhuri Mushi. I am also grateful to the Rwandan Ministry of Education for the authority to conduct research in Rwanda; to the Republic of Kenya National Commission for Science, Technology, and Innovation for permission to conduct research in Kenya; to the Uganda National Council for

Science and Technology for permission to conduct research in Uganda; and to CPUT's Center for International Teacher Education and the US–South Africa Fulbright Program for permission to conduct research in South Africa.

A big thank-you to Tom Durkin, the University of Wisconsin–Madison's anthropology librarian, who responded so promptly and insightfully to my many requests that soon I wondered if he was AI-generated. He's not. At the University of Wisconsin, I am fortunate to learn from many colleagues and graduate students. Tyler Hook's research on US venture philanthropy in Liberia, Patty Lan's work on international education programs, Shahana Munazir's research on the ethics of care, Leah Entenmann's study of cross-border communities in West Africa, and Ali Baba Sanchi's research on Boko Haram in northern Nigeria have influenced my thinking immeasurably. I owe special thanks to Kevin Wamalwa, whose work on peace and conflict in western Kenya and quiet certainty about life in general are an inspiration.

I had the honor of presenting early versions of this work to audiences at the University of Bayreuth, Simon Fraser University, CPUT, and the Universidade Eduardo Mondlane. These institutions, with their vibrant academic environments and rich intellectual communities, significantly influenced and shaped my research. I am deeply appreciative especially to Erdmute Alber, Liz Cooper, Wandia Njoya, and Ines Macamo Raimundo.

Other friends and colleagues who have enriched my intellectual life, offered support, or given feedback on specific portions of this book include Paul Baker, Janice Burch, Sabyasachi Chattopadhyay, Debbie Durham, Car Eisner, Fleli Hakizamana, Natalie Harris, Avile Hlalukana, Sinoxolo Hlalukana, Denise Lamb, Murthee Maistry, Sujata Majumar, Noviwe Maqungo, Thando Mgwatyu, Mary Mullin, Tere Mullin, Lesley Sharp, Daniel Smith, and Claire Wendland. At the University of California Press, I am highly grateful to Senior Editor Kate Marshall for believing in this book, to Chad Attenborough for careful attention to the transmittal process and artwork, to Emily Park for careful attention to the transmittal process, and to Steven Baker for copyediting.

My father died while I was writing this book, and I want to dedicate this work to him. Although he and I had different thoughts about politics and government, we agreed that corporate takeovers of governments threaten the well-being of people everywhere who want to breathe clean air, live life fully, and steward the earth for future generations. Like me, my father felt that people's sovereignty—not private wealth—was the source of governmental authority in law. He condemned the growing influence of corporations and other special-interest groups in government. He referred to America's billionaires as an "oligarchy"—spot on. He valued debate and believed in the virtues of republicanism and taxpayer-funded public education. This book is my attempt to honor him even as I push the envelope further than he would have gone.

Following my father, I dedicate this work to my husband, Matt Bershady, whose support and love have been my anchor throughout this book's journey. Matt's devotion to me and interest in anthropology, a subject he claims to never tire of, has been a constant source of inspiration. Our son, Isaac Bershady, and his partner, Leslie Huang, bring us immeasurable joy and exemplify commitment and love, hard work, and the importance of taking well-deserved breaks. I cherish every moment spent with them.

Introduction

THE PROBLEM IS NOT THE SOLUTION

Eight-year-old Lily wakes up every morning in Tanzania at dawn. She wipes the soot from her face, blows it out of her nose, and coughs up the dirt and phlegm that accumulated in her throat while she slept. Her mother wipes her face with oil because there's no running water inside their house, and then she says goodbye to Lily, who walks barefoot to the four-room school. There are no doors or windows to keep factory particulates from layering the desks and the children. The pharmaceutical plant up the river opened fifteen years ago. Within that time, healthcare researchers estimate, Tanzanians have experienced a 15 percent increase in deaths from cervical, brain, and esophageal cancers.[1]

Who's polluting the air? A US pharmaceutical company's subsidiary,[2] which is destroying Lily's community while deflecting attention from its catastrophic environmental impact by patching up schools and doling out vaccines. The company's publicity team champions the company's products and promotes community engagement programs designed to improve the lives of workers. This subsidiary and the US parent corporation control their own media stories by creating YouTube channels, designing webpages that glamorize their businesses, and developing "advertainments" that peddle their goods but do not tell Lily's story.

1

US corporations rely on African subsidiaries to negotiate the details of US companies' overseas investments. Subsidiary companies are legally separate from US corporations but are contracted to follow US corporations' directives. US companies benefit from establishing overseas subsidiaries by dissociating the companies' shareholders and directors from overseas problems and leaving the subsidiaries to handle legal issues arising from the parent companies' directives. This separation is possible because US companies' managers can invoke clauses in the company contracts with their subsidiaries to limit US companies' liabilities in foreign countries. US companies can tell their international subsidiaries what to do, but they are not required to take any responsibility for the subsidiaries' actions when things go wrong, even after following corporate instructions.[3]

These arrangements have a significant, real-world impact. I know this not just because I have done extensive scholarly research on the subject but because I have witnessed it. In South Africa, for nearly five years, I daily observed a US corporation indirectly control South African intermediaries who from my perspective manipulated media, rezoned building sites, reinterpreted environmental and cultural heritage laws, and hired undocumented, uninsured day laborers from the Democratic Republic of the Congo, Tanzania, and Zimbabwe. Across the river from where I lived, the building rose, first one story, then two, and eventually, eight stories higher than other nearby structures.

In a farming community in Tanzania where I had lived and worked intermittently across three decades, I observed US global pharmaceutical companies and agribusiness corporations work with subsidiaries to bioprospect, that is, search for plant and animal materials to patent and sell commercially. I saw American investors cordon off fertile river valleys from local communities and set up low-tax zones for export-driven poultry production in Mozambique and Tanzania. I saw rivers drained and water diverted to large foreign-owned sugarcane and corn fields in the name of "mitigating" climate change and "helping" local communities become more socially and economically sustainable.

US corporations' unscrupulous oversight of investments in Africa contributes to worldwide social and economic inequality and environmental destruction.[4] Yet aggressive media propaganda in the United States portrays the presence of US corporations as helpful in reducing poverty and moderating the intensity of economic inequality. Sometimes US media even promote unsettling stereotypes about the need to help save starving Africans or imply that corporations and philanthropies can *reverse* global warming in the immediate term, despite the lack of a credible plan.[5] The Bezos Earth Fund, for example, donated $10 billion to fight climate change, largely by allocating funds to support the development of AI technology.[6] But climate change experts agreed this donation was not the best way for Bezos, CEO of Amazon and one of the wealthiest people in the world, to have a long-term effect on the Earth's climate and weather patterns.[7] He might have divested from fossil fuel industries and cleaned up his megapolluting company, which two years ago emitted two times more hazardous air pollutants than six East African countries combined (Burundi, Rwanda, the Democratic Republic of the Congo, South Sudan, Tanzania, and Uganda).[8]

Publicity stories about billionaires throwing money at catastrophes leave out the gritty day-to-day complexities and heart-wrenching realities with which people in many communities must grapple. They don't tell you about Lily's aunt Gloria, who worked in an agrichemical company, had a miscarriage, and later died of cervical cancer, a disease whose incidence is trending upward in several African countries.[9] Gloria had been working with chlorinated hydrocarbon, a poisonous insecticide, in violation of health and safety laws in the United States but not in Lily's country.

Corporations' defenders might reason that US companies cannot be responsible for other countries' poorly regulated health and safety protocols and are simply doing their job. However, the balance of economic power in these contexts weighs heavily on the side of US corporations, raising a red flag of concern over companies racing to countries where they may take advantage of ill-defined laws or laws not in the best interest of citizens. Power dynamics and inequalities often drive trade deals and labor practices.[10] These disparities can lead corporations to exploit vague laws while claiming to "help poor people" when in fact they are not. US corporations' race to the bottom of the regulatory ladder belies their claim of supporting vulnerable communities. A more accurate and honest assessment may be that they actively seek to invest in places where they are better able to exploit or influence lax environmental, labor, and social regulations.

When I spoke with Gloria in 2018, she said that at the end of her shifts she could taste the poison—*sumu* in Swahili—in her mouth, a comment I heard later from women working in the commercial food industry in South Africa. At first, Gloria only suspected a connection between her work and the miscarriage, so she didn't quit. "I need the money; they say their products are safe."[11] But when I returned five years later, I learned that Gloria had already passed away.

Corporate media don't tell you about the daily life-and-death trade-offs people face: Return to hazardous work, or report chemical manufacturing industries to the government? Sell land to pay for radiation therapy, or die sooner to bequeath land to children? Provide open waterways for people to wash themselves, their clothes, and their housewares, or give those waters to water-polluting industries with the promise of jobs and income? In a more just system of production, labor, and governance, corporations would work with governments to reduce income inequality, inadequate schooling and healthcare, and low and declining standards of living. But these are not issues that US global corporations are going to fix. Why? Because companies' priority is to maximize shareholder wealth. In this sense, corporations are designed to prioritize business practices at odds with a government's economic function of reallocating resources in a pattern different from how they were collected.[12]

THE COSTS

Today, US companies' profit-seeking in Africa significantly contributes to growing socioeconomic inequality and environmental destruction. This was especially the case in the five to ten years before the COVID-19 pandemic when more than half of US foreign direct investment (FDI) in Africa went to the mining sector, one of the continent's largest sources of ecological waste, resource depletion, and social inequality.[13] From 2000 to 2024, the cumulative US foreign direct investment in Africa exceeded $1 trillion.[14] From 2016 to 2020, the cumulative US greenfield investment in Africa reached approximately $23 billion: 37 percent in coal, oil, gas, and renewable energy; 36 percent in software, IT services, communications, business services, transportation, and warehousing; and 27 percent in food and beverages (mainly soft drinks), sugar and confectionary products, grains, oil seeds, and snack foods. The rest went to other sectors.[15] In

2022, the US private sector signed $8.6 billion in key investment deals with African nations and pledged to invest US$44 billion through 2025, focusing largely on the continent's digital industries and energy, health, and agribusiness sectors.[16] These massive investments by US corporations—particularly in the digital computing, health, and agribusiness sectors—are today a chief factor in some of the most serious environmental and social problems plaguing many African nations.

Although China recently surpassed the United States as Africa's top commercial partner, many younger Africans see the United States as the preferred development model for the continent.[17] This perception stems perhaps from the significant US role in shaping global economic rules through institutions like the World Bank and IMF. While Chinese, European Union (EU), and United Kingdom (UK) investments may also arguably be problematic, they generally do not promote the notion that a free market can "save Africa from its own poverty." China positions itself as an investor in infrastructure (roads, ports, energy, airports), promoting its role in terms of diplomacy and friendship. And the EU and UK sometimes frame their investments as reparation for their colonial pasts while presenting markets as neutral means for developing public infrastructure. In comparison, US narratives celebrate "value-neutral, free markets" as a solution to social and economic inequities, portraying American investments as altruistic. Yet, as this book demonstrates, these narratives often obscure detrimental practices, such as resource depletion, pollution, and worker exploitation. Claiming to do good while failing to address these issues lacks integrity and suggests a disregard for accountability.

Of course, there is the fact that many African countries today sit at the bottom of the world's income distribution while the United States and Canada, after China, stand at the very top.[18] Even with almost a billion more people than the United States, Africa, with a total population of around 1.5 billion, emits only 4 percent of the world's total carbon. On the other hand, the United States, whose population is only one-quarter that of the entire African continent, emits 15 percent—nearly four times as much—of the world's carbon.[19] Moreover, if the current trajectory of carbon-fueled climate change continues, millions of farmers in Africa dependent on rainfall will be at risk.[20] Hundreds of thousands already are. To make matters worse, African countries collectively lose

$50 billion annually by not holding multinational companies accountable for paying taxes. Most local judicial authorities do not have the resources needed to effectively challenge multinationals' tax evasion.[21] Corporate-led wealth extraction, facilitated through legal tactics, has effectively shifted governance and regulation in many African countries toward private interests and the market—and is actively contributing to systemic inequalities by reducing investment in public goods and services.

CORPORATE OVERREACH

I began paying more attention to corporate power in Africa a few years back when I was a professor of education in the UK. I had shared a "high table" meal with two corporate guests at my university. A high table is where honored guests sit to eat, a British tradition demarcating status. One of the guests was an investor; the other oversaw product research and development. At the time, I was consulting part-time for their agribusiness corporation, which was expanding into chewing gum and animal feed markets in Africa. Because the companies' raw materials grew in locations subject to drought and erosion, they and other companies competed fiercely for access to limited resources.

To outsmart its competitors, this corporation's research and development (R&D) branch sought to identify places where communities would trust the company to operate ethically. To do this, the R&D office staff wanted to correlate answers to questions such as "Who do you trade with?" and "How far away do your trade partners live?" to create a numeric index of social trust that could help identify precisely where to operate. I found this idea fantastical from the day I began work with the company, in both the "ridiculous" and "interesting" sense of *fantastical*. Still, I was curious to understand how a large US-based, multinational corporation rationalized investments and extraction by reducing complicated social interactions to a single numeric index.

For help in interpreting its index, the R&D office wanted me to give a qualitative answer: "Whom do African farmers *really* trust?"

"Like most people," I explained repeatedly, "people in Africa trust one another, especially if one or the other is related by marriage or birth or if

they went to school together." As I did in most R&D meetings, I emphasized that people rely on kinship, friendship networks, and family ties to
determine who they can trust. To facilitate interaction with its officers, I
met the company partway in talking about "Africa" as a "geography" but
not as an undifferentiated whole. Still, I explained that people in Africa, as
everywhere, consent to authority when they believe the power structures
in the system are legitimate. I gave a short version of the workings of capitalist enterprises in agrarian communities, including those on the African
and North American continents, where noncapitalist forms of exchange
are deeply embedded in social relations. I knew I was making sense and
thought I had begun to spark an interest in anthropology, encouraging
these guests to examine some of their assumptions. But I was mistaken.

Toward the end of the meal, the investor, a fortyish man from Florida
who had flown in on his private jet, turned to me and said, "Someday,
Amy, we won't even need governments; corporations will do everything."

At that very moment, without breaking my gaze, I realized I needed to
end my corporate contract. I was—and still am—not ready to concede governmental power to corporations who serve investors and no one else.
Because investors and others at a high table such as this (I impugn myself,
though I quit that university a few months later) have high status, many
appeal to a time-honored custom of privilege that presumes those with
power have the right to govern the distribution of services and goods.
Popular American sentiment holds that anyone can make it up the ladder
or sit at the high table if they work hard enough.[22] However, research consistently documents that people with disproportionately greater access to
financial wealth and social capital shape and control national and international governance via investment markets.[23] Corporations' claims that by
controlling markets and governing others, they can erase poverty and protect the environment is a bad-faith alibi for the world they help to create.

SMOKESCREENS AND ALIBIS

To win people over to company causes and deflect attention from any
"harms," some companies employ deceptive strategies. They distract
their critics by pointing to their philanthropy. They sabotage legislative

oversight by working through overseas subsidiaries.[24] And they use political influence and wealth to suggest that their own pseudo-independent "watchdog" organizations will monitor corporations' activities. Philanthropy, subsidiaries, and watchdog groups are powerful alibis, or excuses, that divert attention from evidence that may indicate collusion.

Marketing and corporate responsibility departments manipulate public sentiment, using gifts and donations to discourage scrutiny of the harm that corporations may cause.[25] The practice of making a product or a project appear more socially and environmentally friendly than it is (commonly known as greenwashing) can align with a company's effort to enhance its marketability. However, a particular US brand combining a "value-neutral free market" system with eco-friendly charity points to a paradox in the US free market ideology: inequality performs a function. Within a free market system, gifts provide wealthy donors an *alibi* or *a seemingly noble use of charity,* enabling affluent benefactors to amass wealth at the expense of people experiencing poverty and then to gain public approval by aiding the impoverished, all without using force or articulating an explicit political ideology.[26]

More quietly and obliquely, corporate philanthropic gifts are sometimes paid for by the very communities that corporate philanthropies claim to help. Instead of taking a pound of flesh from shareholder bodies, corporate social responsibility efforts sometimes take small change from consumers' pockets. Corporate philanthropic campaigns, such as KFC's "end hunger" program in South Africa, may quietly prey on the sympathies of their own consumers. KFC (formerly Kentucky Fried Chicken) runs an end-hunger program called Add Hope as a part of the US company's corporate social responsibility efforts. Add Hope is funded "by customers rounding up the cost of their meals" in KFC's South African subsidiaries—not by KFC's US parent company, Yum! Brands.[27] Offsetting hunger is laudable. But asking consumers, many of whom are low-wage earners or unemployed, to round up the price of their meal is like asking Peter to rob Paul to make their overlord—here, KFC—look good. Taking money from those in need to fund corporate philanthropy is not laudable when seen for what it is.

By referencing subsidiary clauses and deflecting social responsibility efforts to consumers, US corporations like KFC operate through nested alibis. Americans do not hear about corporate America destroying the land and penny-pinching people overseas because corporations' media report only the parts of the story that support the companies' points of view. They distract attention from the complexity of international relations and financialization by presenting "evidence" of corporations' good deeds. Whether used legally or colloquially, an alibi depends for its plausibility on how well the evidence or reasoning conforms to what people recognize as morally just and acceptable. If the news cycle focused on people's experiences of US corporations' investments—rather than the companies' experiences—Americans might be more motivated to react and act.

Analyzing different plausible alibis—or coincident social codes of morality—reveals the likely tactics that companies employ to evade blame or punishment when their projects encounter difficulties. Typically, senior people or entities higher up on a parent company's organizational hierarchy possess a stronger ability than those in subsidiaries or lower in an organization to deny knowledge of actions committed by others. One of corporations' plausible alibis is that "parent" and "subsidiary" companies operate in different legal domains. If a South African subsidiary violates a US law, the US parent company bears no legal responsibility. If the South African subsidiary violates South African law, the company in the United States, again, can maintain plausible deniability, claiming the parent company was not involved. In this way, US companies can claim to be absent from the "crime." Leveraging different countries' laws and working with subsidiaries across international borders can plausibly remove US corporations from litigation and rebuke.

A version of this legal maneuvering was evident in 1987 when KFC in the United States had to divest from South Africa because the US Congress imposed economic sanctions on the racist South African apartheid regime in 1986. KFC divested the sixty outlets it then had in the country to a South African company called Devoco (yet continued to receive administrative fees). When the US Congress lifted sanctions about five years later, the number of KFC restaurants in South Africa had grown to three hundred. The US "parent" company reacquired its assets from Devoco and began profiting again from the KFCs in place. The company had grown fivefold, but technically, the US company had been absent from the scene.

By temporarily divesting, KFC in the United States could secure its investments until the political climate changed.[28]

Using third-party contractors to monitor environmental and labor violations can aid deniability. Prescribing nongovernmental remedies for corporate violations, US corporations set up their own advisory boards and teams of investigators to monitor injustices and oppression. As discussed in the preface, when a class action suit charged Apple, Dell, Google, Microsoft, and Tesla in 2019 for violating child labor laws in the Democratic Republic of the Congo (DRC), where the companies source cobalt to manufacture lithium-ion batteries, Dell turned the case over to a four hundred–member corporate nongovernmental organization, Responsible Minerals Initiative (RMI) to monitor.[29] All five corporations belong to RMI. RMI is their corporate auditor. But the corporation-backed organization procures information from third-party sources whose teams spend a day or week in the field interviewing owners, managers, and workers. Transmitting information across multiple years and parties evokes a whisper down the lane or telephone game. Information exchanged sequentially becomes highly modified.

Auditors possess deep knowledge about labor practices and irregularities in mineral mines that have been linked to US corporations. Likewise, the people who actually work in dangerous sites know what happens there. When those workers tried to bring a lawsuit against the companies, a US judge refused to hear their case, in effect deferring to the companies' independent authority to investigate their business practices. Taking justice into their own hands, US corporations employ teams of investigators to check supply chains on which corporations rely to create their products. Asking a company to monitor itself is like asking a villain to police its own villainy.[30]

Philanthropies, subsidiaries, and in-house watchdog groups are powerful alibis that operate in tandem. Corporate philanthropies use gifts to enhance the company's public image and increase customer loyalty. Subsidiaries delay decisions and divert blame from the corporate "sovereign." Corporate auditors promote fairness and equity without passing judgment on members' programs. Like governments, corporations build institutions and international networks that maintain order and create agreement. Yet their hegemony is not total. Like governments that corporations at times co-opt, corporations are also vulnerable to rules, decisions, and other forces emerging from the larger world that surrounds them.

Corporations and their investors can make rules and persuade or coerce compliance, but they are also immersed in a larger social matrix that affects them. Sometimes people within local communities and state governments embrace and invite corporations to do business there.[31] Other times, corporate investors and leaders exercise their own volition and economic power to invade social domains. Thus, realities underlying corporate investments in other countries are far more complex than viewing Africa as completely under the control of western firms, with relatively powerless participants in those countries unable to affect the terms or outcomes of investments. US corporations are not all-powerful, but the balance of economic and political power strongly favors them.

LIKE DAVID AND GOLIATH

When I started working on this project, I knew I needed to consider the impact of US investment on local communities and how local communities can influence corporate actions. Rather than focusing on one sector in one community, I wanted to understand how various sectors, such as energy, utilities, real estate, health, and education, are integrated. The aim was to comprehend how US companies operate remotely and how subsidiaries and local communities manage or alter investors' projects.

To better understand global inequalities and connections, I found older literature to be crucially helpful, particularly the works of Sidney Mintz, June Nash, Nancy Scheper-Hughes, Sol Tax, and Michel-Rolph Trouillot. Mintz's book *Worker in the Cane* tells the story of a sugarcane farmer named Don Taso while highlighting the rapidly changing patterns of rural life in Puerto Rico. Mintz wrote this work to focus on people rather than abstract models of culture. However, after completing it, he realized he needed to examine the broader, global system of sugar production to understand the challenges that Don Taso and other farmers faced. This was his purpose in writing *Sweetness and Power*.

Mintz's insights laid the groundwork for anthropologists to explore the intricate relationships between local communities and the international economy. Anthropologists who wanted to understand the complicated connections among people, commodities, ideas, and money began to focus on encounters between local communities and international corporations. In her powerful book *We Eat the Mines and the Mines Eat Us*, June Nash analyzed individual perspectives in an international commercial system. Building on Nash's work, Mintz, in *Sweetness and Power* (1984), examined the history of sugar plantations in terms of core and peripheral countries. The core countries were primarily colonizers and former colonizers, and the peripheral countries were largely colonies and nations that had been colonized and exploited by the core countries.

As a result of Nash's and Mintz's research, anthropologists began to shift from studying localized ethnographic cases to analyzing regions' uneven economic integration into a capitalist world economy. However, in looking at the bigger picture, Mintz and others, in my view, went too far in looking for global patterns and neglected to consider individual experiences. I am committed to keeping sight of individuals *and* revealing a largely hidden system integrated across many sites.

Today, it is commonly observed that the world operates as a global system, stitched together by far-reaching trade protocols, governance covenants, and communication networks. A now older literature celebrated the unprecedented mobility of populations, financial capital, and ideas in the age of globalization, a period that included significant events such as the dissolution of authoritarian states beginning with the fall of the Berlin Wall, the reconstitution of the former Soviet Union, and new digital communication technologies.[32] However, some critics argued that globalization undermines democracy, weakens the authority of states to create and enforce laws, and diminishes cultural diversity.[33] They contended that "globalization" has become a form of "corporate hype" that distracts from a more nuanced understanding of how people across vast distances connect.

In light of critiques characterizing globalization as a superficial manifestation of corporate interests, anthropologists have increasingly sought to engage with the complexities of social issues by studying the world system as individuals and communities make and are made by it. This engagement particularly emphasizes understanding perspectives that emerge from the "edges" of society, a concept articulated by Michel-Rolph

Trouillot, a student of Sidney Mintz.[34] Trouillot urged anthropologists to scrutinize the framework of wealth and labor that underpins and legitimizes Eurocentric visions of world power.

Building on Trouillot's framework, I argue that while the global economy is embedded in the legacies of colonialism, it is not wholly dictated by them. Drawing on Nancy Scheper-Hughes's and Sol Tax's concepts of forceful and action-oriented anthropology, and David Graeber's *Direct Action: An Ethnography*, I adopt an "engaged" approach in taking the position that US corporations wield disproportionate power on the world stage.[35] However, in contrast to the older literature that described globalization as all-encompassing, I emphasize that corporations are not without their Achilles heels and not without constructively critical change agents.

Corporations are *not* the unitary bodies their marketing departments make them to be, but are complex, changing, contradictory assemblages of people and positions, sometimes working at cross-purposes. US corporations, backed by laws, are the Goliaths on the world's stage, I argue, while laborers, consumers, activists, and environmentalists are the Davids who, as underdogs, may yet surprise us and win. The world system is not inevitable, and David and Goliath are not always adversaries.

To analyze the complexities and contradictions within corporations, I draw on Bakhtin's concepts of simultaneity and heteroglossia, and I use anthropologists' concept of mobilizing myths. For Bakhtin, simultaneity is "a real co-presence of contrasting elements in tension" and "not a mere wavering between two mutually exclusive possibilities."[36] The concept of simultaneity allows that people can hold logically, factually, or ontologically discrepant views at the same time (such as I love you but don't love you, or Africa is not a laboratory for testing unproven technology but we are testing unproven technology in Africa).[37]

Bakhtin's notion of heteroglossia, or double-voiced-ness, indexes the multiplicity of socio-ideological discourses, languages, and speech genres that penetrate and are performed through action and the media. For instance, in advertising or imagery, the meaning of KFC's icon, Colonel Sanders, is shaped primarily by context rather than history. The contextual high status of fast-food convenience elides a history of southern white colonels from Kentucky.[38] Identifying this hierarchy and elision draws attention to the need to theorize coherence in the presence of persistent differences, allowing for a more nuanced understanding of the interplay between corporate power and public reception to corporate messages or offerings. While Bakhtin developed the concepts of simultaneity and heteroglossia to theorize coherence when differences persist, I use them to collapse the binary between seeing corporations as powerful and people as not, and vice versa. In other words, heteroglossia and simultaneity are useful for understanding the contextualized—and contextualizing—discursive-justificatory aspects of alibis.

Redirecting an anthropological lens to understand how anthropologists generate knowledge about globalization, some scholars have identified differing approaches to the topic, paradoxically reinforcing binaries in their analyses. Some researchers concentrate on the challenges posed by globalization, while others focus on how people thrive and flourish despite challenges and disparities. For example, Sherry Ortner suggests that many anthropologists have centered their attention increasingly on the problems associated with neoliberalism as both a financial and a governmental formation. Ortner contends that this emphasis has led to what she calls "dark anthropology," ethnographic meditations on the "harsh dimensions of social life."[39] As Ortner describes it, "dark anthropology" examines people's subjective experiences of domination and oppression under neoliberal and immoral conditions.

Ortner contrasts dark anthropology with what Joel Robbins has called an "anthropology of the good." Robbins argues that observers must analyze communities' cultural visions and strategies for promoting health, well-being, morality, and happiness to appreciate the worlds that people in those communities create.[40] Robbins pressed anthropologists to move beyond depicting human suffering and focus instead on "the good," or what Tanya Luhrman calls "moral possibility," as distinguished from "moral doom."[41] I am not comfortable with the colorism implied by the term "dark anthropology" and even less so with the binary of dark versus good anthropology. Instead, I wish to emphasize across this book that doom versus happiness, harness versus possibility are, again per Bakhtin, entwined.

All this is to say that, yes, an alibi may provide a compelling explanation for not doing something or being someplace else as, for example, when it is in fact the case that a US corporation's lawyers are not themselves versed in another country's laws. Thus, to apprehend or defend an alibi requires analyzing it, comparing social actualities and moralized claims to understand concurrent possibilities and logics embedded in interactions and events.

Corporations' alibis rest on the rationale that commercialization, privatization, and profit maximization help an impoverished African continent by addressing societal imbalances using the tools of economic efficiency. As the work of anthropologist Gillian Tett has shown, those "rationales" are corporations' *mobilizing myths*.[42] Mobilizing myths of market efficiency and of the "law" of supply and demand disguise the realities of market volatility. Myths integrate social experiences with a broader set of assumptions about how the world is or ought to operate. Myths arrange and represent aspects of social life in more accessible, concrete forms than complicated analyses of history. Unpacking corporations' myths facilitates the analysis of corporations' hegemony: their abilities as powerful entities to create consent within a population without the use or threat of force.

However, other myths that corporations embrace—such as the myths that introducing new, advanced ideas and technologies will uplift impoverished communities and that strategic international investments in infrastructure and key industries will alleviate entrenched international economic inequality—sound suspiciously like the mobilizing myths underwriting Europe's "civilizing mission" and colonization of African people and territories. In the colonial era, trading enterprises like the Dutch East India Company, the German East Africa Company, the British East India Company, and the New York ivory traders in East Africa sent their representatives to African harbors to extract payloads of raw materials and commodities for external markets. A hundred years later, the operations of multinational private companies on the continent—and the trade delegations they send from the United States—are in their effects a lot like those revenue-producing cargo ships. How can anthropologists be both realistic about today's global realities but optimistic about the possibility of change?[43] My solution, similar to that of Andrea Welker, is to denaturalize "the company" and engage directly with its contradictions.[44]

US INVESTORS' PROMISES

While Lily sat in school, breathing pollutants, nineteen US-based companies visited Tanzania to identify investment opportunities. One was Abbott Laboratories, a pharmaceutical manufacturer. Another was Alliance One Tobacco, based in North Carolina. With a combined market worth of over $1.6 trillion, those nineteen firms were ten times richer than the government of Tanzania. They came to the country to persuade Tanzanians that they could help by providing jobs, generating revenue for the country, and even building new schools and health clinics. What attracts these companies to Tanzania and other countries? Lower environmental and labor protections than in the United States, for one thing. Getting government approvals from the Tanzanian government to build manufacturing plants there is sometimes easier than in America. Plus, US companies threaten *not* to invest if overseas countries raise their standards.

In fact, 2022 wasn't the first time corporate America showed up in Lily's community to persuade people to hand over land, water, air, and cheap labor—and it won't be the last. In December 2021, two hundred miles north of Lily's home, the Coca-Cola Foundation, the beverage company, arrived in Nairobi, Kenya, to contribute $512,000 toward national drought interventions, a drop in the bucket compared to what the company is worth and what the Kenyan government needs. That donation also did not stop Coca-Cola from continuing its massive use of water in Kenya—even amid a drought. Instead, it almost certainly helped deflect scrutiny from that ongoing exploitation. But for every liter of sweet sugary beverage the Coca-Cola Company concocts, the company takes two liters of fresh, potable water from Kenyans, diverting the water from Kenyan lands to private enterprise.[45] Taking this water negatively affects Kenyans' health and communities: Kenya is experiencing its most severe drought on record, threatening millions of people with starvation.[46] Water availability has decreased by 50 percent over the past five years, and more than 23 million people in the region face daily household water insecurity.[47] In western and eastern Africa, Coca-Cola is choking waterways. Plastic waste and grayish water have prompted some Tanzanians to call the Mlalakua River by a different name: the Coca-Cola River.[48] On the one hand, Tanzanians, like many in Africa, consume and enjoy Coke regularly. Sara Byala's insightful book tells "how Coca-Cola became African." On the other hand, reframing destruction as something good adds up to an alibi. It diverts scrutiny from the detrimental effects of toxic water on African communities.

US corporations also consistently disguise their extraction of natural resources by highlighting their "sustainability" efforts. Examples abound. In 2009, the chocolate candy company Mars Inc., which sources cacao from Côte d'Ivoire, promised to harvest cacao sustainably but ended up destroying thousands of acres of rainforest and driving people further into poverty.[49] In 2018, six people in Ghana died from a collapsed mining tunnel operated by the US-based gold mining firm Newmont, which strip-mines and thereby devastates indigenous lands. Yet Newmont's webpage trumpets that their systems "ensure effective health, safety, community relations, and environmental protection processes" and "advocate for excellence in engagement with Indigenous Peoples."[50] Corporations' self-representations in public relations discourses, in label disclosures of their products and charitable donations in opposition to their actual footprint on water, land, energy, health, education, and other public resources underline their diversionary tactics or double-voiced-ness by reframing social disruption and environmental degradation as an economic opportunity for impoverished communities.

I find corporate philanthropic practices deceptive and dodgy, and I strongly object to the idea that Africa should become an investment gold mine for US corporations. Even if giving money to offset a national drought or an underfunded healthcare or environmental protection system does help some people in some communities, it would simply hide the more significant damage companies cause through their deals with governments and their operational practices. It would not contribute to solving the larger problem of global climate change. In fact, throwing small money at countering climate change and community destruction caused by big money is like putting a Band-Aid on a hemorrhaging body. It does not address the root cause. Big Pharma's public relations documents imply that their purpose is to make people like Lily healthier and happier. Yet that is how corporate America wants you to see their work: saving Lily from her own poverty when in fact corporate America contributes to it.[51]

Corporations exist to make money and to reinvest at least some of that money into expanding their businesses. Governments' job is to protect citizens and ensure that their living standards continue without using up the resources needed in the future. If a government halfway around the world is held hostage to a US corporation using precious water during a severe drought, or to a US fossil fuel industry pumping particulates and carcinogens into the air, will those governments' citizens have sufficient clean water and air to survive and thrive? Will overseas governments protect their resources for the benefit of African communities? Or will US corporations commodify water, land, air, and the world in its entirety to match investors' expectations? Anyone in North America, or elsewhere for that matter, should recognize the interconnection of our planet: The water here, the air quality there—the planet knows no nation-state boundaries.

FIELDWORK AND SETTINGS

This book focuses on Tanzania and South Africa, as well as Kenya, Mozambique, Rwanda, and Uganda. It builds especially on ethnographic research I conducted through extended and short-term fieldwork in Tanzania between 2010 and 2023 and South Africa between 2019 and 2023.[52] It also draws on a brief 2022 visit to Mozambique and, more generally, on research I conducted in Kenya, Rwanda, and Uganda. At all times and in all locations, I trained my attention on international networks that linked local dynamics to the world beyond.

Between 2010 and 2016, I conducted field research in Tanzania with my colleague Aikande Kwayu for about one month every year during my summer break from university teaching. This fieldwork was built on research I began in 1990, among ethnic Chagga in the Kilimanjaro Region, on gendered and generational changes in sending girls to secondary school. In 2010, with a Firebird Foundation grant to cover transportation and research permits, Aikande and I began to collect oral histories from senior Chagga people who could tell us about educational and environmental changes. One of their primary concerns was water depletion and the loss of wildlife, mainly elephants and primates that used to traverse and thrive on the mountain. Climate change and the rivers' desiccation also negatively affected farmers' crops and coffee yields; the latter provided needed income to pay for school fees and sundry items such as sugar, tea, clothes, and bus fare.

A grant from the National Geographic Society enabled us to investigate coffee farmers' lifestyle changes relating to their water use and management. Our selection of farmers followed a snowball sampling method and drew on our network of friends and (for Aikande) family to identify people willing to share their stories. People we interviewed helped us understand the effects of water privatization on the Chagga indigenous water management system. Building on this fieldwork, in chapters 1 and 2 I discuss corporate water privatization and agribusiness investments in eastern and southern Africa.

Between 2019 and 2022, I conducted field research in South Africa for about six months every year. I had visited the country briefly in 1998, 2008, and 2010 to attend weeklong conferences. In 2019, I lived in South Africa from June to December; I then applied for and received a grant from the US Fulbright program to study water conservation efforts in South Africa. A major drought over five years (risking "Day Zero" in one major city, when no water would remain) galvanized public awareness about climate change and compelled the government to deprivatize commercial wine farmers' water reservoirs. The global COVID pandemic delayed that research, but as I was already living in South Africa, I spent late 2020 and 2021 watching Amazon build its new continental headquarters on a parcel of land with precarious water supplies and bearing cultural significance to indigenous Khoi and San peoples. I also observed overloaded trucks carrying migrant workers from Malawi, Zimbabwe, and elsewhere—rarely wearing masks or maintaining social distance, despite the health advisories at the time—arriving at the site daily to work under dangerous conditions. I discuss the Amazon project in chapter 3.

In 2022, the Fulbright project began, so I traveled with South African colleagues to schools in the Western Cape Province winelands, and for much of the next eighteen months, I spoke with farm laborers, teachers, parents, and business leaders about farmers' water conservation plans and their donor involvement in community development and school financing. I also observed communities' healthcare experiences during the COVID pandemic, including their concerns about attempts by US pharmaceutical companies and the Gates Foundation to keep US-patented technologies out of the hands of African doctors and scientists. I discuss health and education in chapters 4 and 5, respectively.

I wanted to account for similarities and differences across Africa's today fifty-four sovereign countries. Highlighting connections demonstrates that although the continent consists of independent nation-states, corporate investors and philanthropists often portray the continent as a generic whole. In a sense, they are correct. "Africa is a country" in that it is one landmass, a distinct part of the world. However, when referring to a sovereign state, "country" lacks specificity.

Americans who travel abroad sometimes say "I'm going to Africa" instead of "I'm traveling to Uganda" or "to Kenya" or "to Malawi" or the like.[53] On one hand, this formulation may suggest the speaker recognizes that Africa "existed" before European countries carved Africa into colonies. But more likely "Africa is a country" reflects a stereotype that Africa is one big undifferentiated whole.

If I dig deep enough, I, too, treat particular places as indicative of a larger whole. I see London as "England" and "England" as "Great Britain." But there are so many ways of connecting while differentiating these locations. When it came to "Africa," I spent the first two decades of my life knowing little to nothing about the continent, which is why I wanted to live "there" to make up for my embarrassingly provincial, white suburban education. Then, when I spent years working and living in Tanzania, I began to formulate a sense of the continent based on facets that I assumed would be comparable in other locations. In Tanzania, I was politely bossed around. I was told, directly, to do this and that. And I loved it. I became accustomed to taking orders from people I lived and worked with. I was supposed to have been teaching English to secondary school students during my early research, and I did, but more than that, I learned how to subject myself to body-straining social situations and gentle orders from my elders. People taught me how to be a person as they taught one another.

Then, several years later, I traveled to South Africa, and I bridled against the social setting. The legacies of apartheid racism were so palpable that I sometimes simply wanted to be invisible. Black South Africans called me "Madam" and sometimes stepped aside as I approached. Social microexpressions of deference made me feel uncomfortable. I realized that a kindness underlay these gestures, but I also sensed an ingrained fear that if I or others moved out of our "lane," a fragile, varnished social order would be broken.

Although this book addresses problems common throughout much of Africa and the world, it focuses especially on areas of northern Tanzania and Western Cape Province in South Africa where I engaged in fieldwork. These places could not be more different, yet they share some important features.

AFRICA IS NOT ONE COUNTRY

The world's highest equatorial mountain, Mount Kilimanjaro, stands more than 17,000 feet above the surrounding plains in Kilimanjaro Region, in northern Tanzania. The mountain provides spiritual and material sustenance for ethnic Chagga people who live below its snowy dome. Before Europeans arrived in the mid-nineteenth century, Chagga people traded with merchants from Arabia and India, who sent enslaved Africans, ivory, and hides to their home countries. By the early 1890s, German and British missionaries introduced coffee to Chagga farmers, who embraced this cash crop wholeheartedly, united by a strong sense of community and self-sufficiency. By the 1920s, albeit under colonial rule, Chagga people ran their own coffee cooperatives and used the proceeds to build health clinics and schools. Upon independence in 1961, the new government under President Julius Nyerere pursued a socialist path for development. When the government nationalized coffee production and centralized state ownership of farms and factories, Chagga communities, by and large, disapproved of the state's elimination of their cooperatives and coffee companies. Many preferred to manage commerce privately and through local leaders.

Many Chagga people also strove to get the best education for their children by pooling resources to enroll their children in higher education. Several cohorts of Chagga men (women rarely attended school beyond the seventh grade) studied at Makerere University College in Uganda and then moved on to senior national and international positions. One such person, Edwin Mtei, made it all the way from "herding goats" as a child, as he wrote in his autobiography, to working as a senior economist with International Monetary Fund in Washington, DC.[54]

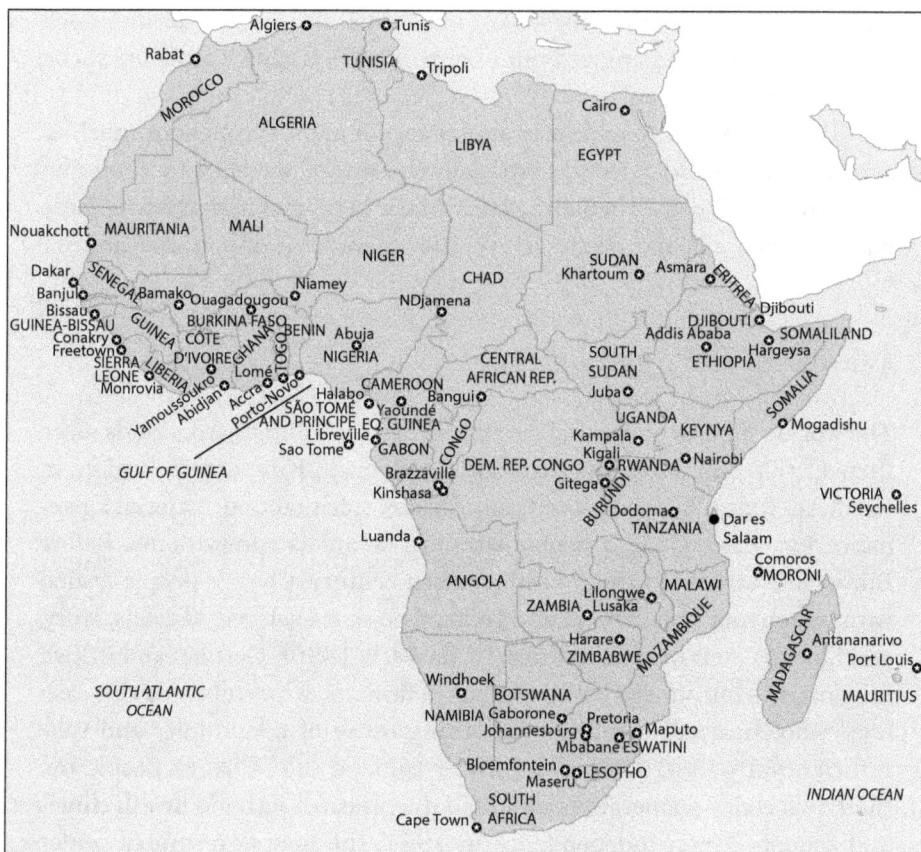

Map 1. Map of Africa.

In the 1980s, Edwin Mtei advocated economic decentralization and the privatization of industries and services. Many Chagga farmers were pleased with the prospect of a market-driven economy until they realized that international conglomerates, not their own communities' cooperatives, would be the new owners of coffee companies. In the late 1990s and early 2000s, climate change and irregular rainfall (drier periods followed by excessive rains) cut into crop yields and profits. Today, small coffee farmers and massive international conglomerates compete to access Kilimanjaro's waters. Chief among the international conglomerates is the

Coca-Cola Company, which works with WaterAid, a US-based nongovernmental organization, to expand clean water access to rural communities. While some Chagga farmers approve of this venture, others do not want foreign donors to control the national water infrastructure. (I discuss WaterAid and Coca-Cola in chapter 1.)

The other location discussed in this book, the Western Cape Province in South Africa, is quite different. The area is larger than the Kilimanjaro Region and is home to a larger number of ethnicities. Most people live in the city of Cape Town and the surrounding townships. Population groups in the Western Cape include Khoi and San indigenous people, groups from Western Europe, South and Southeast Asia (because of the European trade in enslaved people from Southern Asia), and Nguni-speaking peoples in southern and eastern South Africa.

Before the arrival of Europeans to what later became South Africa in the late fifteenth century, Khoi and San inhabitants raised sheep, goats, and cattle in and around today's Table Mountain, where rains make the area suitable for agriculture. By the sixteenth century, Khoi-speaking indigenous people traded with Dutch settlers, the latter reaping a material advantage through the exchange. The two groups fought violently for access to land and freshwater. Four hundred years later, some of the Dutch settlers' ancestors formed the National Party, led by white supremacists who rewrote the law to segregate the city and country in a system called *apartheid*, meaning "separate" in the Dutch-derived Afrikaans language. Under apartheid, the National Party expelled Black Africans from Cape Town and forced "mixed colored populations" to live in segregated neighborhoods.

By the early twenty-first century, Cape Town remained a city sharply divided by race and class, despite the end of apartheid and the government's commitment to achieving socioeconomic equality. While living there between 2019 and 2023, when I would travel from one side of the city to the other, I was usually the only white person on the bus. The bus terminus at Top Deck Market was a stone's throw from a four-star tourist hotel and a KFC, but many white South Africans never knew that Top Deck Market existed. Today, US companies including Amazon, McDonald's, IBM, Google, Microsoft, PepsiCo, and KFC vie for scarce real estate in "white," and wealthy communities in and near downtown. While many Cape Town residents take pride in these companies, others regard them as evidence of South Africa's "recolonization"—not by white European settlers but by US corporations.

By looking at key examples in South Africa, Tanzania, and other countries, this book tells the story of how US corporations rely on a series of alibis—misleading public claims about the benefits their businesses offer, plus legal and political maneuverings—to carry on what are sometimes ecologically and socially destructive practices. Deploying alibis aids corporations in exploiting workers and extracting wealth for foreign shareholders in a manner that resembles the history of colonial extraction and subjugation in the countries where they operate.

THE JOURNEY

My research in Tanzania and South Africa across five sectors of water, land, farming, health, and education combined ethnographic and news media sources with a comparative methodology that examined Kilimanjaro and Cape Town in relation to each other and to the United States. I collected accounts of teachers, parents, construction workers, traditional and biomedical health practitioners, small-business people, entrepreneurs, farmers, and municipal service providers in both locations. In addition, I gathered insights from lawyers and investment advisers in the United States. In Tanzania, I interacted with people using a combination of Kiswahili and English. In South Africa, except for occasionally greeting people in the Xhosa language, I interacted with people entirely in English.[55] I visited families in homes located in both posh and impoverished neighborhoods. I followed media stories of foreign investments in the water, agricultural, real estate, health, and education sectors and asked the people I interviewed to interpret these media reports. I approached participants' narratives the same way I analyzed media accounts: I stayed attuned to the moralities of exchange and legitimacy, as well as the organizing tropes and repertoires used to convey ideas about social justice, financial transparency, and adherence to the rule of law.

To avoid an overdetermined narrative that depicts corporations solely as villains and people only as victims, I highlight points of social tension that sometimes lead to new ways of thinking and interacting, depending on the perspectives of those with whom I spoke. But because my ethno-graphic focus centers largely on people whose lifeways are reconstructed by more powerful economic and political forces, this book emphasizes the effects of external investors on the well-being of the people they claim to help.

One lesson I learned from the people I have lived and interacted with is that information about economic change gathers slowly. People are often only vaguely aware of the implications of new investments for their lives. Investors' proposals promise particular outcomes, but trade terms can change in the boardrooms and behind the scenes before they are imple-mented, and initial events or activities can result in consequences that local communities did not anticipate. For that matter, even when com-munities anticipate negative consequences, investors' agents typically sideline antagonists' concerns, using their political and economic capital to influence government policies, regulations, and the political climate.[56]

This book unpacks how this kind of corporate strong-arming takes place. It documents the long-term impact of some foreign investors' projects on the lives of real people and real communities. It introduces individuals like Anathi, a thirty-year-old Xhosa farmer in South Africa's Eastern Cape, and Kundaeli, Uduru, and Bibi Alilya—farmers in Kilimanjaro Region, Tanzania—who all must contend with crushing intel-lectual property rules and depleted resources that foreign corporations have found ways to control through negotiations with governments. Small-holding farmers have seen how some investors manage a water system with which those farmers irrigate their commercial orchards and vegetable gar-dens. This management system undermines and pollutes local ecosystems, though investors sometimes claim that their practices are sustainable.

The book also highlights people like Tauriq Jenkins, high commis-sioner of the Goringhaicona Khoi Khoin Indigenous Traditional Council in Cape Town, who fought with others in the Khoi community to prevent Amazon from building its South African headquarters on sacred Khoi land. It shares the accounts of Lawrence, a South African police officer, and Dr. Urassa, a physician in the Tanzanian Health Ministry, who express their frustration with foreign pharmaceutical companies and philan-thropic organizations treating them "like guinea pigs" and exploiting patient data, thus depriving a national health system of essential health statistics about its own population. Each of these individuals' stories, like others in this book, vividly depicts an economic and political system in which foreign companies can run roughshod over local governments, ecosystems, and communities while extracting wealth for foreign shareholders. The urgency of addressing the issues raised in this book cannot be overstated.

I have written this book because I believe that if more people realized the extent to which US corporations exploit land and people in Africa and elsewhere in the world and then hide behind US law to avoid responsibility, they would be less likely to take corporate press releases at face value and more likely to demand scrutiny of corporate claims. Many US corporations' words do not meet their actions. Instead of cleaning up water and improving agriculture, or supporting civil society and the common good, corporate America and its philanthropies are destroying habitats, exploiting labor, extracting wealth, and undermining governments. It is an economic, social, and environmental crisis that we are all implicated in, and one that we all need to pay attention to.

1 Water Rites and Wrongs

In the United States, as elsewhere in the world, people tend to pay attention to the amount of water they use, monitoring and regulating this use through utility bills, fixing dripping faucets and leaky pipes, and buying low-water-use appliances. Giulio Boccaletti writes eloquently about the laws and policies that national governments, including that of the United States, have implemented to support water conservation.[1] Many other scholars have observed that measuring water by cubic meters and rates of flow with smart water meters and other technology allows water to be used more sustainably.

Despite all this precise measuring in the name of sustainability, the notion of sustainability is more complex than it seems. A decade ago, governments and international organizations adopted sustainability as a major policy commitment, as did many corporations and educational institutions. Agencies did so in response to climate emergencies, water-related epidemics, and stresses on livelihoods in already impoverished communities. Unfortunately, powerful conglomerates have found ways to

Sections of this chapter related to Kilimanjaro were coauthored with Aikande Clement Kwayu. See Amy E. Stambach and Aikande Clement Kwayu, "Witness to a Passing," *Hau: The Journal of Ethnographic Theory* 11, no. 2 (Autumn 2021): 412–27.

get around the underlying objectives of these sustainability initiatives, frequently employing the buzzwords "sustainability" and "corporate responsibility" in ways that allow them to continue to prioritize their short-term economic growth over the long-term sustainability of environments and communities. By promoting practices as sustainable—even when minimal scrutiny shows they are not—they have found ways to position themselves as "for the people" instead of "for their shareholders."

One of the ways they have found is to tout their contributions to public water protection initiatives. In the early 2000s, governments and private stakeholders across much of Africa began to manage water distribution systems jointly. Many governments claimed this was a way to secure funding for developing new distribution systems. Companies could also benefit from the appearance of supporting a public service that would aid local communities and small-holding farmers, rather than just industrial agriculture businesses.

These public-private partnerships, however, have not necessarily led to sustainable water extraction processes. Instead, because an essential role of private investment in public water systems is to provide up-front capital to governments, corporations can use the offer of these investments to influence how governments manage their water distribution plans, thereby protecting company interests.[2] However, the corporate influence on national governments can have disastrous results for local communities and small-holding farmers. Indeed, since large corporations can all too easily overwhelm local community interests, they can quickly drain aquifers and watersheds unless their practices are restricted. At the same time, these private-public partnerships—effectively corporations' capture of governments by creating arrangements in which their interests heavily influence public policy—might even be a screen or alibi whereby publicizing investors' "charitable gifts" divert attention from corporations' unsustainable, extractive water use.

When I began investigating how US corporations take and use water in Africa, I wanted to find out how small-holding farmers understood and practiced sustainability and how what they did compared with corporations' practices. I was not at all sure that everyone's definitions would include the replacement rate of water use or the costs versus benefits of conservation, and, indeed, farmers I spoke with approached the idea of tracking water consumption very differently than companies did.

In Kilimanjaro Region, when I asked what people did to ensure they had enough water when they needed it, farmers rarely spoke about water directly in terms of costs or measures, mainly because most did not track how much water they used. Although some local officials kept accounts of water drawn from the community water pump, such quantification generally was not part of farmers' practices. Instead, when I persisted in asking farmers to estimate how much they withdrew and used from springs and rivers, most focused on the culturally significant, socially meaningful ways people engage with one another over water.[3] Most did not give a number but described water distribution as a leveling mechanism that brought people together to sustain social solidarity.

One man, who tended more than twenty coffee trees, told me after a studied silence, "Water comes from the mountain. We don't measure it; we share it among ourselves." Another person, a mother of seven, echoed a sentiment I heard from others: *Mvua mfalme; humnyeshea tajiri na maskini* ("The rain is king; it falls on rich and poor"), making her point that the supreme source of life, rain, falls on everyone and levels social inequalities. Along similar lines of seeing water as connecting people yet highlighting farmers' water use planning, I heard the phrase *lima chini ya fereji*, or "plow downhill from the water furrow," because that is where wealth collects.[4] This saying evinces Karl August Wittfogel's classic concept of hydrosocial processes: Human systems of politics and power shape, and are shaped by, the circulation of water.[5] In Kilimanjaro, the farmers' emphasis of the connection between water uses and social equality highlights how their understanding of the local social order intricately connects with water management and distribution. When companies intervene in this connection, they undercut how people sustain their relationships with one another through their use and distribution of water.

This idea that water distribution is intricately connected to people's sense of social connectedness and day-to-day well-being was also reflected in how some Western Cape Province residents understood their water consumption. One day, a few years after a severe drought that took millions of people to the brink of Day Zero (no water left), I asked Bulelwa, a black ethnic Xhosa woman who lived in iPhilippi Township, South Africa, how many house-holds shared a single outdoor water tap. I had seen different numbers, depending on whether I visited the municipal, provincial, or national gov-ernment websites or one of the many nongovernmental organizations involved in water-related programs. I found that although most township residents did not count the number of houses assigned to their tap, many did make a mental note of how long a person was at the tap or how much water people used. Bulelwa, whom I knew well through mutual friends, was direct: "My neighbor's daughter just lets it gush! When she washes her feet, she lets the water run!" "What else could she do?" I asked. The woman responded, "Fill a bucket, take it home, then pour dirty water down the outside drain." She herself had had a private drain installed in the ecologically fragile sands behind what she called her shack. She paid a "shark," an unlicensed plumber, to dig a hole, line it with PVC, then put a plastic milk crate over it.

When I asked if pouring dirty water into the sands was environmen-tally responsible, Bulelwa retorted, "Environmental!? Amy, look at where we live! We live in squalor, that's not environmental!" Her point was apt, and although I felt chastened when I realized I had projected a version of a "responsibilized" citizen into my question, I also understood that her comment highlighted how water inequities in the province reflected the segregationist legacies of the apartheid-era government.[6]

Living on the "other side of the tracks" from iPhilippi, a forty-year-old Afrikaans-speaking white woman, Sheila, dealt with the city's multiyear drought by digging her own private well, outfitted with a pump to bring water to the surface. Like her neighbors, she had a swimming pool tucked into her walled-off compound. She drained and refilled the pool every other week. When I asked her what would happen if everyone did the same, she responded, "I don't care—the government is not going to take care of us." For her, sustainability meant holding on to her comfortable standard of living.

For many people, whether wealthy or impoverished, knowledge of water infrastructure and technology has become necessary, yet with a difference. People living in iPhilippi, for example, clearly understood the fragility of the water infrastructure because it barely existed in their neighborhood. In contrast, most middle-class people like Sheila realized infrastructural pre-carity only on the verge of Day Zero.[7] Yet, on both sides of the class divide, people did not use absolute measures of water as a primary means of indexing "sustainability." Instead, different ideologies—I call them *common pool* and *privatized*, recognizing that they connect—framed how people thought about water use and distribution.

WATER GRABBING

In water-poor landscapes, people have vied and died over water for millennia. Archaeological evidence from Olduvai Gorge in Tanzania shows that up to 1.8 million years ago, early humans lived and thrived around precious water sources. On Table Mountain, South Africa, indigenous Khoi and San people competed to access freshwater. When the Portuguese circumnavigated the continent in the fifteenth century, they relied on indigenous communities to provide food and water. Later, when Dutch, French, and English settlers landed, they dammed the rivers, built reservoirs, and used water mills to tap aquifers. European settlers drove off wildlife, cleared the land, redirected streams, and established commercial agricultural estates: coffee plantations in Kilimanjaro and wheat, tobacco, and wine grape farms in South Africa. Settlers justified their increasing use of water through European property law, which holds that ownership stems from investing labor into the land to produce benefits for stockholders. And according to property law, the person who owns the land also owns the water underneath and flowing across it.[8]

Recognizing that European settlers had imposed a legal framework and a growth-oriented economic system that expropriated natural resources from African communities, many African nations by the mid-twentieth century began to fight for independence from European rule. African leaders redeployed a property rights framework to press for national sovereignty, and as they established independent governments, they reformed laws to integrate common pool and private property regimes. Notably, newly independent governments in Ethiopia, Kenya, Mali, Mozambique, Tanzania, and Zambia worked in collaboration with local communities to develop state-sponsored water infrastructure, highlighting the participatory nature of the process.[9]

By the late 1960s, countries including Ghana, Guinea, Senegal, and Tanzania shifted from a growth-oriented capitalist market economy to a common property system that reframed customary practices to align with socialism. Pressed to generate electricity and build infrastructure, governments impounded and used water to develop state-owned farms, hydroelectric power plants, and industries.

Two decades later, many of these countries faced stagnating economies, civil disquiet, and growing national debt, and governments began looking for international loans to help them invest in national development, specifically from the World Bank and the International Monetary Fund (IMF). In the late twentieth century, many governments, including Tanzania's, obtained development loans from these institutions, but on condition that they semi-privatize public utilities. Some influential leaders, particularly those with capital to invest, favored privatization. In exchange for agreeing to semi-privatize public assets, these individuals sought a percentage of ownership, received shares in private companies, and partnered with multinational corporations. However, many low-income countries lacked a strong financial class or industries for building infrastructure. As a result, most contracts were awarded through wealthy leaders' political connections to companies based outside the continent.[10]

As new investment opportunities emerged, foreign direct investors rushed to purchase lands with valuable resources, including freshwater, earth minerals, oil, and hydropower, that could yield significant financial returns. They worked with leaders in the international economic development system to actively promote legal and regulatory frameworks aimed at attracting FDI. What began with European settlers' takeover of indigenous communities' access to water became an increasingly enclosed system of development assistance, managed through the World Bank and the IMF, establishing investment treaties, offering tax incentives, and ensuring the protection of foreign investors' rights while also enriching a small group of people in Africa. Despite this enclosure and privatization of common pool resources, indigenous communities showed remarkable resilience. Some Tanzanians called this legalized system of privatization "corruption," while others, more prosaically, called it a system run by "blood-sucking ticks."[11]

This history of the transition from a common property to a private property regime benefiting investors occurred in a similar manner across different eras in various regions settled by Europeans, including Argentina, Australia, Canada, Chile, New Zealand, the United States, and many countries in Africa, including Botswana, Namibia, Kenya, Zambia, and Zimbabwe.[12] Privatization also occurred in South Africa but with a notable difference. In 1994, the first freely elected, post-apartheid South African government, headed by the African National Congress (ANC) party under the leadership of Nelson Mandela, came into power, promising to balance business interests with economic redistribution. The white-dominated, segregationist Nationalist Party had supported a growth-oriented private property system; that system had materially dispossessed the majority-Black population by forcing the majority to live on reserves called Bantustans.

While other African countries were shifting from a common property to privatization to meet the requirements of external lenders and donors, the South African government, eager to avoid further undermining its common property system, instead developed expansionist economic policies. This approach encouraged South African businesses to establish and invest in companies outside the country, with the idea that returns on this investment would help South Africa grow its national economy. South African companies, predominantly white owned (relevant, given the history of European colonialism), began operating in other African countries, including Tanzania. South African businesses invested there in water, electricity, and air travel infrastructure. More recently, they have invested in the agrichemical and pharmaceutical industries. Although Tanzanians had supported Mandela during the ANC's liberation struggle, many were not pleased with the influx of South African investment capital, because most of it came from wealthy white South Africans whom Tanzanians had not envisioned as their new trading partners. One Tanzanian woman, an independent business owner in the banking industry, joked half-heartedly as we shared a ride to town in her pickup truck, "Whites from South Africa are now our new colonizers." I later came across this phrase in South Africa in reference to American investors.

For the three decades after 1994, the South African government struggled to balance its own majority's interests in keeping investment capital in the country with the minority's interests in finding profitable foreign investments. Capital flight reduced tax coffers, resulting in less funding for public infrastructure projects that could benefit the majority of the population. At the same time, significant wealth inequality that continued to parallel racial segregation plagued the country, leading some people to advocate for more government intervention, including provision of a basic income to everyone.[13] Advocates eager to find a way to improve the situation for the Black majority suggested redistributing land, which appealed to a majority but raised the possibility that investors would take their money out of the country and invest it elsewhere.

The South African government responded to the debate over redistribution versus privatization by enacting the Broad-Based Black Economic Empowerment (BEE) Act in 2003.[14] This act aimed to enhance the economic status of the nonwhite majority by providing access to business development loans and mandating that Black people own a significant percentage of South African industries. Organizations monitored and promoted the BEE process, yet no consensus emerged about its impact in reducing overall economic inequality. Some critics argued that the program primarily enriched a small percentage of wealthy Black South Africans while allowing most major companies to remain under white control.

To appease voters worried about privatization's effects on communities and local livelihoods, the South African government encouraged national and international investors to develop "corporate social responsibility" programs—an approach that appeared on paper to incentivize corporations in assisting the country in supporting its impoverished populations and limiting environmentally damaging industrial practices.[15]

The turn toward corporate sustainability initiatives coincided with a remarkable shift in how corporations, multilateral agencies, and government agencies discussed addressing environmental devastation: now as an investment opportunity doubling as a global civic duty. In South Africa's Vaal River valley and Durban industrial basin, the mining industry released industrial solvents into rivers and aquifers for decades.[16] Then, in March 2024, international agencies and corporations began promoting polluted water as an investment opportunity. In an article, "Is Wastewater the New Black Gold?" the United Nations asserted, "Wastewater is a valuable resource in a world where water is finite and demand is growing."[17] The article linked pollution to an opportunity to recover phosphorous and nitrates from sewage and sludge and sell it as fertilizer: "Everyone can do their bit to achieve the Sustainable Development Goal target to halve the proportion of untreated wastewater and increase safe water reuse by 2030." Reformulating industrial wastewater as an investment opportunity classifies a common pool resource as a commodity and pollution as desirable. Wastewater investors' sustainability campaigns attempt to give water-polluting industries "green" legitimacy. It's crucial to reassess and change this perspective so as to prioritize genuine environmental responsibility over mere economic gain.

Three types of sustainability—economic, social, and environmental—are intricately entwined in this complex combination of corporate investment, international lending, citizens' calls for social and economic fairness, and the semi-privatization of government programs. On one hand, capital growth requires investments that generate profit to keep companies sustainable and in business. "Sustainability" in this big-firm sense refers to capital growth; it prioritizes safeguarding investors and beneficiaries, employees, consumers, and the planet. On the other hand, sustainability implies conservation and maintaining the status quo.

Social sustainability is multifaceted: people hold different views about what is good and essential to sustain. Maintaining healthy communities and ensuring secure livelihoods means that communities must have access to the resources required to sustain human life, clean (not only partly reclaimed waste) water being chief among them. "Environmental sustainability" refers to maintaining the ecological balance necessary to support current and future life. It occurs when humanity's rate of habitat destruction is within nature's restoration rate.

Because "sustainability" refers, paradoxically, to both conservation and change, various groups, perhaps tactically, use "sustainability" to reference different, sometimes incompatible needs and ends.[18] Such different hydro-social deployments of sustainability are highly fluid and culturally contextual. Accordingly, in the following section I examine water distribution, first from the perspectives of Kilimanjaro small-holding farmers, and then from those of some Cape Town township residents. Unpacking multiple perspectives offers a more nuanced understanding of what is truly sustainable in our world and what is not.

KILIMANJARO'S WATERWORKS

Central to an indigenous understanding in Kilimanjaro Region of how to distribute water sustainably is whether a person contributes their time and labor to maintaining and digging new furrows or sends a representative on their behalf. Yohane, an active contributor to maintaining the furrow system, claimed to speak for others when he said, "If a person doesn't show up on Monday to redirect the channels, that person will not have water for the week."[19] Bibi Alilya, Yohane's neighbor, agreed: "Your neighbors are your family. If you don't help them, they won't help you." Yohane's job was to allocate water to farmers every Monday morning. Bibi Alilya's daily work involved drawing water from a river near a spring for washing, cooking, drinking, and bathing. Water was for her a powerful symbol of life and spirituality. Yohane's management style and Bibi Alilya's water stories reveal what I call an *ethnic Chagga water regime* that exists concurrently with a private-public water system that measures and quantifies water use.

Water Spirits

Born in 1919 into the Lema clan, Bibi Alilya was one of the oldest women in Nshara Village when she passed away in 2012. Bibi taught me the names in Kichagga of plants, animals, seasons, and medicines and reminded me that the annual calendar started in what she called the "Missionaries' June." She named the springs from which she collected water as a child and the furrows that began as seepages in her father's upper yards. Her memory was sharp, her heart full of passion, and her generosity ever flowing.

One evening as we sat outside under the stars with several of her grandchildren gathered around her, Bibi recalled, "The mountain was so beautiful [and] full of snow when I was a child living at my father's house." Higher up the mountain, ice "fell like water." Lower mountain rivers would become full between March and August.

"It is not like that anymore," Bibi said. "The mountain has changed. The snow is shrinking. You would never see stones and rocks in the rivers in the past."[20] But today the low river water exposes the rocks.

Bibi remembered the springs, *kishokhu,* and named them individually: Kimukyo, Mulotu, Mwanga, Kwara, Kiringao, Samanga, Mugha wa Ng'ombe. Some of them were named for places, others for people or qualities of light and water. The names of these springs, like those of furrows, sometimes change from generation to generation.

"Mugha wa Ng'ombe means 'cattle's water,'" she explained, because if diseased cattle with rinderpest or hoof-and-mouth disease drank the water, they were healed. "Even people could be healed by that spring. But they needed to drink it before dawn."

One of the oldest springs, now dry, was located just below what is today a primary school. Called *kimangele* for the small (*ki*) tinkling sound it made (*ngele*), the spring was "where people used to pray before the missionaries came and offered other ideas of where to pray." Over time, collective Christian baptisms overlay the cool, clear springs as a mode of healing. People would pray to the upper god, Iruwa, and the lower gods or spirits of more recently deceased family members. The upper god was like the sun. The lower gods were living souls, spirits, who were buried first inside their own house and later exhumed and reburied on nearby patrilineal property. "Which is why we'd never pour hot water on the ground," Bibi said. "We didn't want to burn them."

One of Bibi's favorite stories to tell—and one many old people in Kilimanjaro narrated—was how the Chagga people came to settle this part of Kilimanjaro. Invariably, the story began with a family fight that exemplifies lineage fissure and segmentation and links water to territorial politics. Two brothers from the Usambara Mountains—Nyari and Nghwa—stopped at a cool spot where two rivers met. They disagreed and fought, then went their separate ways.

One of the brothers, Nyari, traveled up-mountain along the Kikafu River to a place called Ngira, located between the Namwi and Marire rivers. The other brother migrated west across the plain and settled on Mount Meru. Others soon came to join him, and in time, the people of Mount Meru would become rivals to those people who joined Nyari in Ngira.

Nyari, in Kilimanjaro, moved into a large cave called Sienyi, located inside a rock between the waters. He and his wife had a son, Mashami, who fathered Uroki. Uroki had three sons—Mushi, Nkya, and Lema—all of whom migrated upriver. Mushi, the first-born son, chose a place now called Foo for his land. Nkya, the second-born, settled in Kyaalia, then moved all around the area; and Lema, the third-born, chose Nronga, near the Masama River. These three sons are the founding ancestors of today's three maximal lineages (or clans, *ukoo*), still found in the Kikafu River basin: Mushi, Lema, and Nkya.

Each of these clans engineered furrows, called *mifungo*, that ran for miles from streams and springs to their gardens. First, people dug furrows in the highest habitable zone, then, as communities expanded and people moved downhill, they grafted higher furrows onto others. All of these gravity-fed lines moved the water to their desired places. In Foo, a man named Ngalata, who belonged to the Nkya clan, dug what is today known as the Wangalata furrow, sourcing Mwanga River. Likewise, in Nshara, where Bibi Alilya moved when she was married, the uppermost subvillage, Marukeni, comprised six original furrows: Moghee, Ushafu, Makando, Kiwali, Kishenge, and the main furrow, Nshara. The other six subvillages in Nshara had the same names as their furrows, each after the person who had first engineered them, though later generations sometimes changed the names, perhaps to blur responsibilities for managing the water furrows.

Water Rights

I recount the foregoing story in detail because it is a mobilizing myth that integrates social history with the physical environment, providing a *charter* or authorization for people's mountain occupancy. Like stories about a nation's founding, the narrative affords Nyari's descendants the right to use and control the water.

I also tell this story because many of the very oldest people on the mountain take it to be a self-evident truth or an orthodoxy. Bibi's charter for land occupancy rests on relationships of descent and affinity. Her origin story integrates personal histories of individuals with a wider set of assumptions about the way water rights and distribution must operate. But even Bibi conceded some authority to the regime of title-deed property rights. Her son-in-law was a real estate lawyer, and she also supported the revenue-generating partnership between the local council (whose leaders descended from Nyari) and the short-term leasing of lands to private small-business owners.

"So long as no one is buried on a plot of land," Bibi stipulated, noting she did not condone disturbing burial sites, "I am OK with leasing land to make money." Bibi was unfazed by new small businesses operating on ancient graves; her social action charter focused on members who had recently passed away.

In other words, Bibi's story, along with her own biography, demonstrates the changing social context in which charters for controlling land and water are embedded. To believe in the Nyari myth, one needs to accept a transcendent justification for the ranking of clans. To justify new arrangements, made when the government reprivatized formerly socialized lands, one needs to renarrate the geographic scope of ancestral lands and accept the new charter of property deeds. In brief, Bibi's story illustrates a customary *common property* system transitioning to a *private property* regime.

Water Management

Like Bibi Alilya, Yohane descends from a distinct lineage whose members migrated to the fertile slopes of Kilimanjaro more than three hundred years ago. In his early eighties when I spoke with him, Yohane still showed up every Monday just after dawn at the big tree that people call the public square to allocate river water to his neighbors. He evaluated who needed what, whose farms were exceptionally dry, and who was away and did not need water that week. The water travels through ancient irrigation channels that his ancestors engineered. Yohane's job was to maintain the waterways. The following field note describes what he did on a typical Monday:

> 6:40 am, Monday. January 2018. Yohane is already present at the public square. It had rained for several days, so only forty people gathered, thirty-seven men and three women. Yohane kept an eye on who came at what time. He looked at the clock on his phone and asked,
> "What time is it on yours?"
> "One minute to seven," someone replied.
> Within a minute, Yohane began allocating the water. He told the people which households would receive water on which day, and he continued to schedule through the following week. Farmers listened, no one questioned, and when Yohane said, "Okay, thank you, have a good week, you may go," they dispersed and began redirecting water to one another's coffee and banana gardens.

Once a year, at the beginning of the farming season, Yohane slept along the river at the mouth of the furrow before he announced the annual work party at the start of the farming year in March. He called the opening "the mouth of my mother," and the furrow channel the birth canal. He propitiated water spirits who guard river sources and who permit waters to flow. After opening the furrow for the season, Yohane directed the water to his father's grave, located on the boundary between the households of his fathers' two wives and shaded by banana thatch. "I sometimes sleep on his grave," he explained, "praying and talking with my father." The irrigation network that Yohane managed symbolically mirrored the Chagga social body and helped to illuminate ideological elements of sustainability that differed from the quantified measures of sustainability embedded in policy-specified water regimes. Usually in December, at the end of the season, Yohane met with other leaders to discuss what crops to plant, such as beans, tomatoes, cabbage, and onions; when and how to organize initiation ceremonies; and, more often these days, how to engage with foreign investors who covet Kilimanjaro's waters.

Water Conglomerates

In the early 2000s, seeing fissures between the multimodal customary and the national water systems, international investors began to move into Tanzania to reengineer Kilimanjaro's waterworks. In 2013, the government of Tanzania enacted the National Irrigation Act, which gave international investors priority over small-holding farmers.[21] A water management program pitched to farmers as designed to help them ended up bypassing subsistence cultivators. In 2019, the Confederation of Tanzania Industries (CTI) supported the private sector water program because large international investors were draining these domestic companies' water sources and depleting the country's aquifers. Many small enterprises located in urban areas, such as hair salons, roadside restaurants, small bed and breakfasts, and car repair garages, were unable to access sufficient water to meet their operational needs. This shortage forced a few to drill their own wells and many others to purchase water delivered in trucks by private companies to supplement municipal supplies.[22]

Seeking to turn down the firehose of water gushing into conglomerate industries, CTI drafted a code of ethics to cover water use in industry but, at the same time, appears to have severely restricted roles for small farmers and customary water managers. Consequently, today, the vast majority of customary water furrows that once flowed down the slopes of Kilimanjaro are now literally cemented into a privatized water system that diverts water away from ethnic Chagga lands and into the reservoirs of foreign-owned companies. The furrows Yohane was involved with were exceptions.

In the century-long transition of common pool to private market water use, beginning in Bibi Aliya's birth year 1919 to the present, the beneficiaries of privatized water have not been small-holding farmers in Africa, as corporate publicity offices promised, but multinational corporations—including Coca-Cola, holding $100 billion in assets at the time of this writing.

DIVERTED MONEY, DIVERTED WATER

The Coca-Cola Company owns no land in Tanzania, but its Kilimanjaro-based bottling company, Bonite Bottlers Limited (BBL), sources water from Kilimanjaro's aquifers. Among the world's most highly prized water sources are the aquifers, snows, ice, and rivers of Mount Kilimanjaro. Headquartered near Moshi, BBL bottles and distributes twelve Coca-Cola drink brands, including the bottled water Kilimanjaro Drinking Water, popular among tourists.[23] Not only are sugary beverages like Coca-Cola's products contributing to an obesity epidemic and public health calamity in Tanzania, but the corporate branding of fresh drinking water commodifies a common pool resource, water, here as "Coca-Cola's."[24] As Sara Byala put it, Coca-Cola "bottled" the continent.[25] Nerve!

An extensive body of scholarship focuses on transnational organizing against Coca-Cola and the impact of corporate concessions on local communities.[26] In Tanzania, when small-business owners in the region joined forces with CTI to curtail Coca-Cola's extreme water use and water branding, Coca-Cola's representatives resisted, not because the US company could not afford alternatives but apparently because it wanted to continue using water in large quantities at low cost, without stringent regulations imposed by the Tanzanian government.

Owned by Berkshire Hathaway and the Vanguard Group and headquartered in the United States, the Coca-Cola Company boasted a net income in 2023 of $10.6 billion.[27] The company markets itself as *environmentally sustainable* and as "water balanced and return[ing] 100%+ of the water used in our drinks,"[28] which seems impossible. But, on scrutiny, the company's fine print clarifies that it will build, upgrade, or privatize an existing public wastewater treatment station to the degree that, after additional treatment, dirty water will be suitable for new use, though not necessarily suitable for people to drink.[29]

Regenerative water treatment means cleaning water used to wash the bottles to the degree that it can be used to wash more bottles. (Or, when plastic bottles are used, it means cleaning the water used to clean bottling equipment.) *It does not mean returning any of the freshwater to the Kilimanjaro aquifer.* In some of the sites around the world where Coca-Cola extracts water for its products, the company puts water back into the aquifers. However, these waters used to recharge aquifers often carry chemical and microbial contaminates, and water treated through reverse osmosis and advanced systems can activate contaminants already present in the aquifer, causing them to enter the water supply.[30] The notion that it is possible directly to recharge an aquifer to its previous, pre-extraction state is entirely a myth.[31]

Recognizing that the company's franchise takes precious freshwater from communities, the Coca-Cola Company has undertaken corporate social responsibility programs, including a $1 million charitable intervention to "improve water access for 70,000 Tanzanians." Like many other US corporations operating internationally, Coca-Cola has pursued charitable programs not by partnering with the host government where it operates or with local communities, but in a two-step process. First, US corporations establish charitable foundations as separate, tax-exempt legal entities in the United States that they register under IRS code 501(c)(3). The Coca-Cola Company and the Coca-Cola Foundation are thus separate but connected entities. The company donates a percentage of its annual income to a trust, which invests that income and uses the untaxed income generated by those investments to fund the Coca-Cola Foundation's chosen charities.

In the second step, corporate foundations join with other US donors, nongovernmental organizations, and the US government. In the case of Coca-Cola's project to improve water access for 70,000 Tanzanians, the

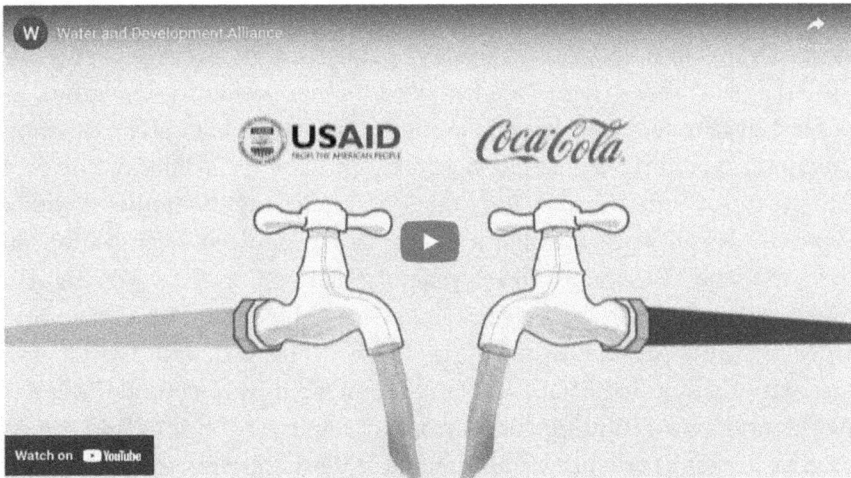

Fig. 1. USAID and Coca-Cola: a partnership.
Source: Globawaters.org/wada, accessed June 8, 2024.

Coca-Cola Foundation partnered with the United States Agency for International Development (USAID) to raise funds aimed at improving water security in drought-prone areas (figure 1).[32] However, Tanzanians were not directly involved in distributing the foundation's contributions, despite the potential for their involvement.

Engaging local communities is essential for developing effective long-term strategies to address water security, as they possess a deep understanding of their specific water needs and the challenges people face. Communities' participation ensures that funds are utilized appropriately and reach those in need, promoting accountability in the distribution process.

Before its defunding in 2025, USAID adapted its approach to enhance transparency and build local capacity. However, even then, it courted corporate-led foreign assistance proposals primarily benefiting corporations, including Coca-Cola.[33]

Coca-Cola's provision of funds to a US governmental agency enhanced the company's image as an environmental steward and community service provider. Yet such a public-facing image diverted attention from the firm's extractive resource use and its influence in shaping US trade and foreign assistance policy; it functioned as an alibi.

In addition to boosting its public service image by funding government aid programs like USAID—which also helped it gain leverage over water resource programs—Coca-Cola has used its foundation to strengthen its public image in regions where it maintains unsustainable water extraction practices, including Tanzania. Because the Coca-Cola Foundation is a US-registered philanthropy, it cannot operate legally in another country. However, it can work through a Tanzanian-recognized organization, in this case, the Water and Development Alliance (WADA). WADA is a research consortium led by scientists from Ohio State University and other US and African institutions. In turn, USAID and WorldServe International, another 501(c)(3), tax-exempt organization, fund WADA.[34] WorldServe's own funding comes from private contributions and grants from faith groups and other foundations.[35] WorldServe's board includes a Pennsylvania-born US citizen who is also the founder of the largest private water-drilling company in Tanzania (suggesting to me a conflict of interest since the US private business investor would have a significant commercial interest in influencing how funds are spent in Tanzania[36]); a former CEO of AG Financial Solutions; and two American sports celebrities (possibly lending their names for a cause that was more complicated than they realized). As these funding routes and circuitous networks suggest, relations between corporate America and water extraction in Tanzania appear to be entangled.

Although USAID and the Coca-Cola Foundation portrayed their relationship as equal, jointly pouring water *into* Africa (see the adjacent figure), the money trail suggests instead that water flows out of Africa as money flows into US-based private, for-profit and nonprofit entities. To follow the circuit, consider how the water project for Tanzanians was funded, and then where the money went.

FUNDS RAISED

To help fund its charitable intervention, the Coca-Cola Foundation partnered with USAID to provide matching funds to WADA, a recognized US nongovernmental organization in Tanzania. Government funds added to private "corporate giving" burnish the corporation's public service image and potentially enhance any leverage the company might have over how the funds are spent.[37] To further augment their combined funds, the Coca-Cola Foundation and USAID courted another party, Waterboys. Waterboys is a US-registered nonprofit founded by another sports celebrity. It is also circuitously funded by WorldServe *and* the Coca-Cola Foundation *and* USAID.[38] Text buried in a USAID news release announcing a donation made with the Coca-Cola Foundation to WADA for Tanzania reports: "Together, WorldServe International and Waterboys, an American charity founded by US National Football League (NFL) athlete Chris Long, are contributing $1 Million in co-financing to scale project activities" associated with the Coca-Cola Foundation–USAID water development plan.[39]

Coca-Cola's effort to unite these many donors into a charitable-giving arrangement appears to be a stroke of marketing genius. It not only allows Coca-Cola to boost its "corporate responsibility" reputation but could also place the locus of power in this putative water access intervention within the Coca-Cola Foundation. Overall, the project brought together two governments, three nongovernmental organizations, and at least three American sports star donors into a corporate-led pseudo-multilateralism that highly favors Coca-Cola and, it appears, a US-owned private water-drilling firm in Tanzania. Such a model, I contend, advances US corporations' and private donors' investment interests, not those of Tanzanians. Diverting attention from how funds are raised and from the programs they support represents a serious and unethical corporate takeover of bilateral foreign assistance programs in the United States.

MONEY SPENT

So, where does the Coca-Cola Foundation's "charitable giving" go? In the case of the portion of money underwriting water to 70,000 Tanzanians in thirty-six villages, the money flowed first to various US organizations, including the Water and Development Alliance, located in Columbus, Ohio, where funds supported investigators' supplies and travel, and then it trickled back to Tanzania-based WorldServe International, which divided it again into smaller channels. In Tanzania, some funds went to WorldServe's rent and salaries, and other amounts ended up with the University of Dodoma, where cholera threatened to spread through dirty water.[40] The Coca-Cola Foundation did not ensure the provision of clean water for university students or the 70,000 residents but did provided valuable technical training and useful community service projects for students. However, a more equitable corporate tax system might better fund a student tuition waiver and improve water infrastructure.

The Coca-Cola Foundation-USAID partnership also paid to send US students to Africa to test new solar-heating equipment under the guise of student exchange and research collaborations, and to US university engineers to install solar-powered well pumping systems and train Tanzanians in their use.[41] In the end, the Coca-Cola Foundation–USAID project ended up digging deeper, more rapidly depletable wells, serving not 70,000 but 25,000 Tanzanians in thirteen (not thirty-six) villages.[42]

Projecting costs is difficult, and delivering on only one-third of a project's promised goals is understandable. However, even allowing for cost miscalculations and applauding the training of Tanzanian engineers, the project raises questions. It focuses on humanitarian aid, yet it appears to help private companies extract more profit from the solar-powered well-drilling enterprise. It depletes rather than conserves aquifers (aquifer depletion is a serious problem in many parts of the world[43]) and it shifts a sizeable portion of the donation to non-Tanzanian institutions and agencies. From Coca-Cola to solar water pumps, the WADA charitable project diverts funds and scrutiny.

CORPORATE ENCLOSURE

The program funded and carried out by the Coca-Cola Company, its foundation, and USAID is but one example of what many researchers have called a corporate-state-philanthropic "constellation" that dominates virtually every dimension of contemporary life in many places around the world.[44] With environmental tipping points in sight, obesity surging, and small farmers being driven off their family lands, the case for taxing corporate water monopolies grows stronger every day. As I see it, among the many unethical practices in the USAID–Coca-Cola case in Kilimanjaro is the duplicity of the Coca-Cola Foundation (not of USAID) in invoking local sustainability as a reason to contribute a (mere) US$1 million to improve water access for Tanzanians—particularly given that Kilimanjaro farmers' lifestyles create a nearly zero-waste water footprint. Kilimanjaro farmers reuse, recycle, and repurpose water, consume little, and live mainly off the public infrastructure grid.

This is not to romanticize the farmers' lifestyle or say that they see their lifeways as desirable. In fact, many would like to enclose freshwater further so they can continue managing it by mobilizing extended-family networks. But Coca-Cola superimposed a commercial water regime designed to produce sugary drinks for consumers whose fresh waters it was diverting. It contorted the concept of "sustainability" to prioritize the economic stability of corporations and their shareholders. Corporate-led water extraction practices disrupt people's access to water and local control and stage easily manipulated campaigns of sustainability that frequently do not match the needs or social logics of people living in regions where extractive industries operate.[45]

"The changes taking place around Mount Kilimanjaro are not caused by activities of communities around it," said Jacob Nkya Kungayi, a mountain farmer and neighbor to Yohane.[46] Yet it is precisely these communities that bear the repercussions.

DONORS' WATERWHEELS

Coca-Cola's water resource monopolization model is a circular race to the bottom of the water pool and the top of the capital wealth chain. The corporation's actions justify protections for water-thirsty businesses through a string of nested alibis. Using precious freshwater to produce sugary drinks like sodas diverts scrutiny from the greater need for freshwater to sustain human—and all organic—life. Establishing philanthropic organizations to provide citizens with access to water looks good for corporations but weakens citizens' confidence in governments. Yohane, for example, did not trust the Tanzanian government to protect his family's ancestral water system, believing instead that the government prioritized foreign investors' interests in controlling Kilimanjaro's waterways.

Yet Coca-Cola's corporate philanthropic model is not the only architectural waterwheel recirculating water into donors' hands. Before I close this chapter with a brief comparative look at water privatization in South Africa in the wine and tourist industries, consider one more way corporate America controls Tanzanian water through private philanthropies.

Late in 2022, billionaire MacKenzie Scott, former wife of Jeff Bezos, the billionaire CEO of the US corporate behemoth Amazon, Inc., donated $15 million to the 501(c)(3) US organization Water for People so that it could supply drinkable water to people in rural parts of low-income countries, including Tanzania. Water for People works in nine Latin American, Asian, and African countries.[47] Its corporate funders include Kimberly-Clark, Caterpillar Foundation, and Colgate-Palmolive.

Several months after she donated millions to Water for People, Scott contributed an additional $7 million in Africa to the Village Enterprise, another 501(c)(3) organization, with the gift explicitly directed to vulnerable women in Tanzania. Village Enterprise's news release quoted the organization's CEO, Dianne Calvi: "As East Africa is going through its worst drought in four decades, [Scott's gift] is crucial for ensuring long-term prosperity for the most vulnerable households."[48] Village Enterprise's supporters include Google, Facebook, USAID, the Hilton Hotels Foundation, and Starbucks.[49]

US media championed Scott's method of donating, which did not require recipients to account, through annual reports, to the donor for how the moneys were spent. But her method scarcely constituted the progressive kind of bilateral relations needed: It did not empower Tanzanian farmers, it did not empower the country's government, and it empowered Tanzanian women only to the extent that the US-based Water for People and Village Enterprise enabled and brought Tanzanian women into the partnership. Had Scott asked me what she might do to foster greater water security in Tanzania, I'd have advised her to give directly to Tanzanian entities. Of course, if she had done that, her charitable organization could not write off her donation as a US charitable tax deduction. But so be it. She does not need the tax breaks.

Whether followed by corporate philanthropies like the Coca-Cola Foundation or private donors like Scott, the current mode of US corporations investing in Africa, then "donating" moneys to make investment projects look good, generates wealth for investors but weakens governments, both when organizations get tax breaks and when donors use money to influence policies. Weakened governments cede power to corporations, contributing to the downward spiral of state power and upward spiral of corporate power that further marginalizes people. The way global water monopolies subsume the voices of citizens and governments illustrates that corporations' influence is powerful and growing but, as I show in later chapters, is not inevitable or total.

WINE ESTATES IN SOUTH AFRICA

In South Africa, commercial vineyards guzzle water that could otherwise flow to everyone. Cape Peninsula Wine Estate (a pseudonym) is a boutique wine farm at the top of the mountain overlooking "Our Effort," an informal housing settlement where Pumla lives. Pumla is a Xhosa-speaking South African single mother who lives with her two daughters. Our Effort is so named because people living there work hard and put a lot of effort into getting by. There is no plumbing; thirty people share one outhouse and draw water from a shared outside tap. Every morning, Pumla fills a bucket, takes it to her house, made out of a metal cargo container that came in on a freight ship, and washes her children's faces. She then rinses breakfast dishes in the water—she connected an electrical line to a township streetlight to boil water for tea and oatmeal—before pouring it onto two plants outside. If anyone uses water frugally, it's Pumla.

The owners of Cape Peninsula Wine Estate, "Gordon and Cynthia Nolan," are white and live uphill from Pumla's township. They dealt with the city's water shortage by digging a private well outfitted with a pump to bring water to the surface and to irrigate their wine estate. The Nolans hire workers from Our Effort Township to plant, prune, and tend grapevines on some of the steepest slopes in the region. Pumla cooks the meals for these vineyard workers.

Capitalizing on a disastrous fire in 2000, likely made worse by climate change that destroyed indigenous fynbos and forests, Gordon and Cynthia decided to expand the wine farm. They directed workers to clear and terrace an additional ten hectares of land. Fifteen years later, they added a wine bar, hired a former America's Test Kitchen chef (once highly rated by Frommer's Travel Guide) and opened a large deck for al fresco dining, and began advertising on international tourist sites. By 2025, Cape Peninsula Wine Estates was drawing thousands of customers each season from South Africa and elsewhere in the world.

According to the Water Footprint Network, 29 gallons of water are needed to make a single glass of wine, and about 145 gallons to make a five-glass bottle.[50] Cape Peninsula Wine Estates indicates that it produces about 9,000 bottles annually. In water footprint terms, that would mean the estate used 76 million gallons of water over ten years. Although droughts occur regularly in the Cape Town region, the area's mountains and forests enjoy moderate rainfall, creating microclimates suitable for agriculture on the slopes. Nonetheless, outside interests that have built and expanded in the area have heavily challenged the city's water supply. Whereas most Cape Town residents do not have showers, much less household running water, estate owners like the Nolans and hotel suites on the estates possess state-of-the-art showers, tubs, and appliances. Like Pumla, many residents rely on communal outhouses and taps. Considering the region's shortage of water, the wine industry's water use seems frivolous and irresponsible.

When a US-based investment fund, Eileses Capital, purchased wine estates in South Africa in 2018, wine estate owners and restauranteurs like the Nolans had mixed reactions.[51] On one hand, skeptics worried this was the end of South African ownership. On the other, many thought that US investors' infusion of capital might help grow the export market. In 2019, the United States accounted for 4 percent, or about 43 million liters, of South African wine exports; industry leaders expected that percentage to grow. Although South African exports to the United States are duty-free under the Africa Growth Opportunity Act (AGOA), some in Africa perceive AGOA as a twenty-first-century version of colonialism because AGOA is about lowering the cost of African imports to the United States, not supporting any nation's sovereignty.[52]

When a California-based investor established a new export vineyard north of Cape Town, one reason South Africans gave for welcoming this sale to an American was that the new owner might provide "sustainable employment." Yet sustainability was a portmanteau word behind which gathered many interests. As it happened, the grape farm laborers who lived in Pumla's township, south of this new vineyard, had no long-term guarantee of employment, even if they had worked harvesting grapes and trimming vines for years. Developing a water-thirsty export wine industry to employ part-time laborers by turning rare fynbos lands into terraced vineyards rested on contradictory interpretations of "sustainability." Not only were environmental and economic sustainability at odds with each other, but the community of Our Effort was forced to deal with polluted water running down from the vineyard.

At the lower end of Our Effort settlement, open sewer water ran into the ocean. Community members organized for change but were undercut by foreign donors who promised to provide infrastructure to help the underbudgeted municipal and national governments.

Today, powerful organizations such as the Coca-Cola Foundation seem to hold more influence than individual citizens or indigenous communities when it comes to national and international policy efforts to allocate water. Such foundations appear to proffer drinking water and sanitation facilities as alibis to divert attention from their intensified water use. Sustainability discourses circulating in globalized media about water management and conservation emphasize the power of individuals to make or break the planet. But, with more than 70 percent of the world's freshwater used by global agricultural and manufacturing industries, providing infrastructure to underresourced communities in order to legitimize a corporation's enclosure of water may be a stratagem and an alibi—a diversionary tactic to redirect attention from corporations' water-guzzling practices.

Although the United Nations has warned of a global water crisis, some say water is a limitless resource, that it ends only if the Earth ends, because we have multiple ways to clean dirty water.[53] But treating wastewater relies on other energy sources—pulse-light UV radiation, chlorination, fossil fuel or solar energy—all of which require additional inputs from functioning, well-maintained infrastructure. Water intersects with human social systems. It's used in industry, in commercial agriculture, in mining systems. Corporate leaders may contend that multinational corporations like Coca-Cola are reducing their water footprints in Africa. But that glosses over the fact that the *overall* industrial water use by major multinational corporations like Coca-Cola is *increasing* and that wastewater treatment creates its own unsafe water.

Lack of clean water is a global problem. Are corporate leaders from the United States—or from China or the European Union—doing anyone any favors in Africa by polluting, capturing, and using for profit the freshwater resources the continent has held for centuries?

REPRISE

Analyzing corporate-led water management schemes using the concept of alibi reveals that private interests in water management reflect a broader history of resource dispossession in which corporate entities extract resources and then return "gifts" to the end of deepening corporate power at the expense of rural communities. While some agencies and investors may clearly want to support farmers and communities like those of which Yohane, Bulelwa, and Pumla are a part, many often ignore the adverse effects of company actions on already self-sufficient farmers or people impoverished through resource dispossession. Recognizing that businesses seek to "do good" in order to maximize shareholder value can inform policy decisions related to water security and drought mitigation by promoting more open and frank discussion about the societal implications of corporate philanthropic investments.

The provision and denial of water clearly reveal what is and is not regarded as important to those laying claim to managing it. But water is not the only sector in which the corporate capture of common pool resources operates. Public-private partnerships function across multiple domains. While many popular and scholarly accounts of these partnerships examine primarily one industry or one case, this book develops an integrated approach to investors' operations.

Having traced in this chapter transformations in the social organization of water systems and how these transformations have impacted some people in Tanzania and South Africa, I turn in the following chapters to examining how corporate-led "sustainability" campaigns play out to corporations' benefit in the areas of agribusiness, real estate development, global health, and education technology. Analyzing the cross-sectoral integration of corporations' alibis is crucial for scholars, policy makers, organizations, and individuals interested in environmental and social sustainability because no one sector, resource, or community operates in isolation; the challenge is to understand how corporations' operations and alibis link these sectors, resources, and communities and to redirect and redesign the interconnected tributaries of resource governance.

2 The Corporate Capture of Agriculture

Tanzanians plant banana trees to shield their coffee crops from the intense sun in the tiny backyard farms circling Mount Kilimanjaro. Alongside the vegetables they grow for sustenance, the coffee benefits from the area's high altitude and volcanic soil—a product of the ideal agricultural conditions and shrewd farming. The people of the Chagga tribe have worked on this land for hundreds of years, passing it down from one generation to the next. As a gateway to Kilimanjaro, the Chagga villages mark a complex area, creating an exceptionally desirable coffee-growing climate. These characteristics shine in the cup, with elegant jasmine and citrus notes balanced by warm, brown spices.

—Promotional copy on Starbucks package

I took the adjacent photograph (figure 2) at a Kilimanjaro farm in 2023. The photo captures a water furrow that runs through the farm. The water that once regularly filled this furrow is now absent, as is the farm's age-old centerpiece, which the furrow once irrigated—coffee.

"The last time you were here was five years ago," said Kundaeli, a thirty-five-year-old farmer who lives a half day's walk from Yohane's home. "At that time, we were attempting to restore our coffee groves; we sprayed our trees, watered them, and cared for them as if they were our children." However, about four years ago, two things began to change, and these changes led Kundaeli to abandon coffee cultivation. The first was that foreign-owned coffee estates began undercutting small-scale farmers' prices; the second was that a drought that had begun in 2021 persisted.

Fig. 2. A dry water furrow, Kilimanjaro Region, Tanzania. Photo by author.

"The rains have almost disappeared, and we no longer have clearly defined wet and dry seasons," he added, echoing what I heard from other farmers.

Kundaeli and other Kilimanjaro farmers formerly made a living from growing and selling coffee. As early as 2020, however, farmers began clear-cutting their coffee trees or letting them die. Many discovered that growing coffee was no longer profitable, indicating that the entire coffee value chain, including labor and production costs, needed to be addressed. In the late 2010s, companies like Starbucks bought Kundaeli's coffee (see figure 3), describing it as full of "shine in the cup, with elegant jasmine and citrus notes balanced by warm, brown spices." A few years later, international buyers abandoned Kundaeli and other Kilimanjaro farmers for two reasons. First, the global buyers began to insist on a purchasing model that left the farmers with almost no profit. The proposed direct-purchase model saved international conglomerates money by circumventing cooperatives that farmers relied on to help them negotiate prices that ensured them a profit. The companies' proposed contracts required farmers to sell to them directly at multiyear fixed prices with predetermined but minuscule profits. Farmers such as Kundaeli felt these deals would leave them without enough to make ends meet and did not want to accept "forced trade" agreements.[1]

Second, companies took advantage of conditions created by the COVID-19 pandemic by purchasing their own coffee farms.[2] Although corporations had already begun this strategy, their purchases during the pandemic took it to another level. Previously, global coffee companies sent teams of inspectors and tasters to farmers' groves to check for quality. But during the pandemic, international companies cited social distancing as a reason to avoid visiting and renewing growers' contracts. Multinational corporations instead began to purchase and consolidate large tracts of land, and on these plantation-sized estates, they produced their own coffee as a monocrop. This new production and sourcing model helped companies reduce input and labor costs. However, large-scale monocropping of coffee depletes the soil, threatens plant and pollinator diversity, and requires vast amounts of water that will monopolize water resources in the area.[3] As a result, this new production and purchasing model left small-scale farmers not only without their former customers but also with reduced resources to run their farms. In this way, monocropping and monopolies reinforced each other in centralizing global corporations' control over coffee production and distribution.

Seeing the ruinous effects of the coffee industry's consolidation on Kundaeli's farm, I remembered the many other farmers in eastern and southern Africa I knew who also defined their present conditions and future goals as uncertain due to climate change and multinational corporations' agricultural intensification.

Another of these farmers in Kilimanjaro was Uduru, a friend of Kundaeli. When he opened the door to greet me, he seemed in good health—hearty and full of fight. I met him at his home, a comfortable four-room domicile overlooking his orchard and vegetable farm. Twenty years my senior, he fit the mold of a contented gentleman farmer. It turned out, however, that things were more difficult than they seemed. The room where we chatted was piled high in the corners with his notebooks. An open door in his sitting room revealed a view of the cattle shed and chicken coop outside.

Uduru handed me a soda—a Coke, of course—that he'd purchased earlier at the market. He and his wife cultivated papaya, bananas, oranges, cabbage, tomatoes, beans, "you name it," he said in English. They sold the best produce to tourist hotels and restaurants forty miles away in Arusha and the rest at the biweekly Machame farmers' market. Their business was doing well.

For the first hour or so, our conversation seemed to confirm that "hard work brings wealth," a notion I wrote about in *Lessons from Mount Kilimanjaro* (2000). Kilimanjaro's farmers have visibly been reaping the benefits of commercial farming for the better part of a hundred years. Although their fields are small—less than an acre in Uduru's case—the soil is sufficiently rich for 70 percent of farmers to have maintained a high standard of living, until recently. Indeed, Kilimanjaro Region, where Uduru lives, has a higher standard of living than most Tanzanian rural communities. Children wear shoes and jackets, and the bars and kiosks along the road indicate that people can spend money on pleasures. Machame has a hospital; a large, expensive tourist hotel; a dairy factory that makes yogurt; several churches and mosques; and—at the time of my visit—a Farmers' Cooperative Union building. The main road is paved, which is unusual in rural Tanzania.

Uduru seemed pleased with the agricultural boom. However, as the day wore on, his story shifted. He mentioned that his widowed neighbor could no longer make ends meet by selling coffee and bananas from her farm. He also observed that the local agricultural cooperative seemed more like a bank than a community-run social and economic support system. Then he brought up NPK, the nitrogen, phosphorous, and potassium fertilizer he and all farmers used in their small farms or gardens (*mashamba*). Uduru noted that the fertilizer had become expensive and seemed ineffective. In small quantities, NPK is nontoxic; farmers have been using it along with cow manure for much of the past century. But now, some thought they needed to increase the amount of fertilizer to increase yields. Yet doing so was costly, risked toxicity if overused, and created dependency on the fertilizer to maintain the higher production levels. As he spoke, I began to sense he felt something was wrong with the way things were going. So I asked him.

But he shook his head and said he wasn't sure. Then he said the birds were missing, and the streams were drying. I had noticed this, too. Was it because someone had logged and exported so many rainforest trees? He said that might be a problem. But even if we both knew this problem might be attributable to the Tanzanian exporters, I also knew he wouldn't blame them and felt that they, like anyone else, only needed money. And the farmers? I asked. Are they suffering from inflation—their costs have gone up, while their returns have gone down? "Yes," he said, though he also pointed out that this squeeze happens all the time but that, typically, farmers' incomes bounce back. This time, he said, was different.

Then he spoke cryptically: "When famine sets in, tie your child's leg."

I must have had a worried expression on my face since he then explained what he meant. "I am not saying maim or harm your children," Uduru clarified. "I simply mean that if you need to do something unpleasant short-term for a longer-term advantage, do so." Uduru spoke about moral calculations, not the quantified balance of losses and profits. In this case, Uduru used the saying to suggest that there was no easy option for the farmers in the region and that they would have to find a way to accommodate, without colluding with, corporate industrial agriculture.

Farmers like Uduru cautiously work with foreign investors because they believe these companies will bring prosperity to the region—not immediate wealth and riches but longer-term advantages. Investors sell their projects on the promise that, in the short term, they will provide jobs for people in local communities and that, in the longer term, they will teach and integrate farmers and their children into a thriving capital-market economy. But experienced farmers like Uduru are cautious because they've heard these promises before. "Fast talk, slow action," is how Uduru described foreign investors.

The challenges that farmers like Uduru and Kundaeli are facing are not just problems in Tanzania. In many households in the Eastern Cape and KwaZulu-Natal provinces of South Africa, for example, farmers—mainly women because men work in cities—face similar situations. In conversations with me about their struggles to deal with global corporations investing in their local natural resources, many people in these South African provinces, like Uduru, use metaphors and imagery such as that of a broken body to communicate their challenges. Many also, if more quietly, voice concerns about land dispossession and environmental hazards related to intensive commercial agriculture, using the language of politics, environmental justice, and economic inequality. For many farmers, these global corporations operating in their regions have become a source of frustration, and the farmers often feel powerless and vulnerable as they attempt to cope with difficult situations.

LEGACIES OF COLONIALISM

As in the United States, where the government uses eminent domain to expropriate property for public use and then contracts with developers to build on it, governments in Africa invoke the power of the state to acquire and transfer property from one use to another. In Tanzania and many other African countries, governments have used the power of eminent domain to redistribute land to people dispossessed of lands during colonialism. In the past ten years, however, multinational corporations have increasingly challenged governments for supremacy in the global economy, and, as this has happened, US corporations have pressured African governments to work in the interests of corporate leaders, not African citizens. This trend, however, is worrying for many reasons, not least because it feels reminiscent of problematic projects undertaken in Africa by foreign powers in the past.

In recent years, "racial capitalism" has emerged as a conceptual framework to comprehend, on a global scale, "the mutually constitutive elements of racialization and capitalist exploitation."[4] Racialized social hierarchies are "'deep structures' of Eurocentric development" that originated in and reproduced white colonial-settler conceptions of "non-European/indigenous inferiority to justify material (dis)advantage."[5] Structural and systemic legacies of colonial-era resource extraction—linked to the duplicity of an ideological nineteenth-century European "civilizing mission" to develop indigenous economies without actually distributing material resources—increase people's estrangement from systems dominated by foreign owners controlling resources for financial gain.

Aware of this history, many South Africans today are politically attuned to and outspoken against the explicitly racist pre-1994 apartheid laws and legacies that led to racialized social class and market-driven economic inequalities. Thus, for many people in South Africa and elsewhere, racial capitalism serves as both an implicit conceptual framework for critiquing injustice and an unjust reality that reinforces power dynamics along racial and class lines. This includes international agribusinesses operating in Africa today.

In both South Africa and Tanzania, beginning shortly after the 2008 global financial crisis and gaining momentum during the COVID-19 pandemic, many small-holding farmers consolidated their family farms and leased them out to international conglomerates. In exchange, farmers received compensation from international companies but not enough to make ends meet and certainly not enough to replace a way of life that integrated sustainable gardening and small-scale commercial farming.

While taking a long trip one day in 2022 through the Overberg, South Africa's agro-industrial heartland some 2,000 miles southwest of Uduru's and Kundaeli's farms in Kilimanjaro Region, I could see out the car window hundreds of acres of commercially cultivated wheat and corn undulating in the breeze. One didn't need to make complicated inquiries to find out that many of these farms contracted with foreign companies. Some fields displayed the names of seed brands planted in a given year: Cargill, Pioneer, Pannar, DeKalb, and Bayer Monsanto. The signs, prominently displayed on the edges of the fields, were another stark reminder of the way US and European corporations now control what is planted on some of the richest farmland in Africa. In South Africa, however, where the wounds of apartheid are still very recent, these signs also point to something more than just foreign control of agriculture: they also point to a deeper history of social and economic exploitation by foreign powers.

Anathi, the thirty-year-old Xhosa woman living in the Eastern Cape, raised goats, pigs, chickens, and geese and sold eggs, meat, corn, and tomatoes from her two-acre hillside farm. When I spoke with her over a meal, Anathi described facing problems similar to those that Uduru and other farmers were facing in Kilimanjaro, and explained how she, too, was trying to make the best of a bad situation. However, some of the specifics are different; for one thing, whereas Kilimanjaro's farmers have dealt with drought, South African farmers have had *too much* rain. In April of that year, a torrential storm—more damaging than Anathi's seventy-year-old mother said she had ever experienced—ripped away the family farm and washed animals into the river. A year's worth of rain fell on the day Anathi's piglets were washed away.[6] She responded by corralling rather than free-ranging her animals, a decision requiring her to buy commercially processed animal feed and veterinary products because infections are more common when livestock live in close quarters. "Now I need to pay for the pigs' food and healthcare instead of just letting them free-range," Anathi reported.

Climate change skeptics may say that corporate America is not responsible for the destructive rainfall on Anathi's farm any more than it is responsible for the drought in Tanzania. But science does not support that argument. In fact, scientific evidence suggests the contrary. US food and beverage companies are major emitters of greenhouse gases across their global operations, generating more than 600 million metric tons of greenhouse gases annually.[7] Greenhouse gases spread around the world and cause climate change by trapping heat. They contribute to respiratory diseases from smog and air pollution and factor into extreme weather, wildfires, flash flooding, drought, and the interruption of supply chains.[8] US food and beverage companies' greenhouse gases thus contributed to the extreme rains in South Africa, one of the deadliest disasters of the century.[9]

Yet even before a year's worth of rain in one day washed away her pigs, Anathi's life was entangled with the US global food and livestock industry. Because of US corporations' stranglehold on global patenting biology (calling it intellectual property), Anathi and other livestock owners face severe legal limitations in their options for replenishing their farm animals. Since small-scale pig breeders like Anathi often purchase animals from industrial South African piggeries that source pig genetics from American companies headquartered in Tennessee, they are not able to breed animals on their farms. This is because under US property law, the South African pig subsidiaries can sell her only spayed or neutered pigs because the Tennessee corporations *own* the pig DNA. The South African industrial piggery is beholden to the Tennessee company not to sell reproductive-eligible animals to Anathi. Unfortunately, purchasing new piglets from the piggery is expensive for farmers like Anathi, and they often cannot afford new ones, particularly if they've just suffered significant losses after a torrential rainstorm. Whether they like it or not, South African farmers' lives are inextricably linked to biotechnology firms in the United States.

Considering the lack of power that small-scale farmers like Anathi have in a market dominated by the US global food and livestock industry, it is unsurprising that they feel caught in an unjust system. But for South African farmers, the struggle to remain independent and viable is also connected to a larger history. Sixty years ago, during apartheid, Anathi's grandfather envisioned that land forcibly taken by white South Africans would eventually be returned to Xhosa and other Black and indigenous South Africans. "When we have land," was her grandfather's refrain, Anathi's mother told me. His dream, she said, was that someday he would own land himself and then pass it on as farms to each of his children and grandchildren. But when apartheid ended and South Africa democratized in 1994, this redistribution did not happen. At that time, 87 percent of arable land was in the hands of white South African farmers (less than 5 percent was held by white farmers in Tanzania at that time and at the time of Tanzanian independence in 1961), and the government made only limited efforts to give back land to Black farmers.[10] While the South African government has made some (if still minimal) progress in distributing additional land to Black people, ethnic Xhosa farmers like Anathi and her family, who were denied good farming land and other market resources during apartheid, must compete with commercial white farmers who can draw on national and international commercial networks and capital advantages accrued from the apartheid system.

As a result, the significant disparity in wealth and income that the racial apartheid system created persists to this day. This situation has helped create the conditions for the way foreign corporations today exploit natural resources in these regions—including their use of patents that force African farmers to do business on their terms.

Because of their lack of power in this international corporate market, Kundaeli, Uduru, Anathi, and other small-holding farmers and livestock owners in rural Africa will continue to face extraordinary and unjust challenges in the future, especially as long as US companies hold patents over farmers' crops and animals. Biotechnology firms' climate change narratives—which influence government policy in ways that often do not consider small-scale farmers' practices—will also impact this power imbalance. But small-holding farmers can be potent antagonists to large agribusinesses. Many people who study the growth of foreign-owned corporate agribusiness are pessimistic that the situation will change for small-scale farmers in these regions. But this defeatism is unhelpful, and many farmers are fighting to hold onto their land. It's essential to bring attention to this struggle.

For Kilimanjaro and South African farmers, family farms are their communities' ancestral backbones. Farmers fight for their ancestral lands. Generation after generation has tilled the soil. Quite literally, deceased ancestors rest and reside there. In Kundaeli's orchard, he and I walked across his grandfather's grave. Although I wanted to circumnavigate it to show respect, Kundaeli was nonchalant, remarking, "It's okay; this is my grandfather." On Anathi's farm, her grandfather's resting place, topped with a marble cross and surrounded by flowers, faced north, toward the river. Given the importance of land to farmers, it is no wonder that they want to fight for it.

For several reasons. people around the world should be concerned about the struggle that small-scale farmers face as they fight to survive and thrive in the future. Not only are farms culturally meaningful to many farmers, but small farmers contribute significantly to global food security. Farmers cultivating less than two hectares of land produce 28 to 31 percent of all crops worldwide and deliver 30 to 34 percent of the world's food supply.[11] Most cannot afford precision farming, nor do their small family plots allow it. However, small-holding farmers' techniques are often climate friendly and ecologically sustainable. Customary livestock and crop management practices allow for high species diversity. Closed cycles of production and waste minimize the careless loss and destruction of limited material inputs. And the interdependencies of animal and human energy not only maximize resource efficiency but create "affective intimacies" between people and livestock that contribute to ecosystem sustainability.[12]

In contrast, industrial agriculture favors monocropping rather than synergistic mixing of plants. It separates crop and livestock production systems rather than minimizing wastage by combining farming with animal husbandry. Instead of diffusing crop species to allow adaptation and promote conservation, which in turn contributes to the integration of social, environmental, and economic aspects of sustainability,[13] corporate agriculture relies on chemical fertilizers, patented hybrid and genetically modified seeds, and the use of digital and remote surveillance technologies to plant, monitor, dose, and harvest fields. Genetic patents and seed monopolies deprive farmers and local communities of the ability to produce healthy foods through ecologically and socially sustainable methods; meanwhile, the manufacture and use of synthetic chemicals damage the environment, threaten human health and safety, and undercut small-holding farmers' traditional crop management practices.[14]

To divert scrutiny from their damages, US agricultural corporations work through subsidiaries, change their names, and provide social services and gifts to communities, local schools, and governments—all practices analogous to providing an alibi.

One example of the multinational shell game of name changing and obscuring damages by giving gifts is the nexus of activity surrounding maize production in South Africa. Working under the "enclaving" conditions by which corporate officers' actions and decisions are legally separated from the national or local economy,[15] intensive agro-industrial maize production on the fragile Mistbelt grassland of KwaZulu-Natal Province has controversial implications for workers' health and their ability to litigate against extractive farm industries.

In 2012 Iowa-based DuPont Pioneer acquired Pannar Seeds and, five years later, merged with Dow AgroSciences to form DowDuPont. Two years later, the agricultural division of DowDuPont renamed itself Corteva, and Corteva then separated from DowDuPont (which was dissolved).[16] In South Africa, Indiana-headquartered Corteva Agriscience began to partner with Pannar Seed (formerly Pioneer Hi-Bred International), in the early 2020s. Due to intensive large-scale agricultural land use, South African grasslands planted with bioengineered seeds are highly fragmented, leaving small-holding farmers isolated on insufficient and infertile lands.[17]

To lend a "helping hand and spread hope for subsistence farmers" who are not licensed to use bioengineered seeds, most often because they lack capital and land, Corteva supports small-holding farmers who plant potatoes and preserve their produce for winter use.[18] For laborers exposed to hazardous substances when working on plantation-scale farms, the South African Occupational Health and Safety Act No. 85 requires workers to use protective clothing. However, when that clothing is damaged, workers, not employers, are responsible for replacing it.[19] This creates problems for low-paid farmworkers who need to use wages for necessities such as food and shelter.

Litigating against employers backed by corporate agribusiness disclaimers on product use and safety is next to impossible for farm laborers.[20] Yet, anyone who looks at Corteva's online "community commitments" pages will read that corporate outreach is "fighting malnutrition in Africa" by developing bioengineered sorghum and training scientists from Africa "at the Pioneer Hi-Bred headquarters in Iowa."[21] But this development does not help improve the wages or labor conditions of farmworkers. The company claims to address the problem of inequality by providing communities with its corporate products. However, this again does not improve wages or labor conditions. A lack of understanding and interest in the lives and well-being of small-holding farmers and workers will only lead to more harm for them in the regions where the companies operate.

Patience Mususa, an environmental anthropologist who has studied copper mining in Zambia, argues that people are "immanent in the environment and, in turn, the environment is immanent in them."[22] Mususa's insight is particularly illuminating when contemplating the experiences of small-holding farmers in South Africa and Tanzania. The easily contorted language of "sustainability" and the environmental framing used by agro-industrialism today often separate people from nature. In her work, Mususa challenges this kind of anthropocentric view of the environment as distinct from humans. Focusing on the interdependence of people and the environment, she acknowledges the vulnerability shared by people and other components of an ecosystem. Specifically, Mususa complicates the distinction between people and ecosystems by considering how people intersect with the environment in instances of extraction, climate change, and food production. Mususa's study of the copper mines in Zambia highlights the need to recognize the distributed agency between people and ecosystems in addressing environmental risks. Similarly, the challenges faced by small-scale farmers in Tanzania and South Africa today demand that we acknowledge the interdependence of people and the environment.

People and the environment are mutually constitutive: they are not separate, as the corporate agriculture model of human mastery over nature so often suggests.

DIGITAL TECHNOLOGIES, SAFETY DISCLAIMERS, AND MOVABLE ASSETS

The human and environmental impact of corporate agribusiness in Tanzania and South Africa touches on nearly every aspect of people's lives in the communities where those corporations operate, including water resources, the legal system in which small-scale farmers work, the economy and culture, and people's physical and mental health. Understanding the extent of this influence requires understanding both the scale of the companies' footprint in these regions and the nature of their business there—including the technologies they employ to maintain their market control.

In Pietermaritzburg, the regional capital city of KwaZulu-Natal Province—1,800 miles southwest of Kundaeli's and Uduru's farms and 400 miles northeast of Anathi's—I met two Slovenians at the annual South African Royal Agricultural Exhibition. At first, I did not understand why Slovenians were participating in this South Africa show until I later learned that their eastern European government had launched a new digital technologies industry, promoting trade and investment in block chain and artificial intelligence products. These Slovenians were marketing precision farm equipment: digital technology for collecting satellite weather data and tracking soil humidity and crop growth.

Precision farming enables engineers at a remote distance to monitor production and make trigger decisions to buy or sell a particular crop, even to buy farmers' land. "We're just beginning to expand our market," one of the merchants said, "but if you want to see drone technology used on a large scale, go to Greytown," a 9,000-person sugarcane-producing community situated on the banks of a tributary of the Umvoti River ("the place to vote," in the Zulu language). The next day I traveled an hour north to the area.

Two hundred years ago, Greytown was in the territorial heartland of Shaka-Zulu, one of the most powerful chiefs on the continent. Shaka's army conquered lands as far away as Tanzania. In 1913, the South African Dominion of the British Empire segregated Zulu people from white colonizers, and settlers planted sugarcane and required Zulu people to work on settlers' farms. Today, in Shaka's ancestral territory, two large agrichemical seed companies drive the economy: US-based Corteva Agriscience and Pannar Seed. Corteva Agriscience opened its Centre for Seed Applied Technologies (CSAT) in Greytown in 2022. Even before I went to Greytown, it was clear how much Corteva had worked to build its reputation there. A school agriculture teacher whom I met at the show told me about the donations her students received from Corteva for their school farm. She even displayed a banner recognizing and thanking Corteva for their sponsorship. I had also seen the company celebrated on the South African national news (CNBC Africa) and heard stories from colleagues and friends about the vast sugarcane plantations the company supplied in Greytown.

As I arrived on Greytown's outskirts, I saw the sugarcane fields along the road. Track irrigation sprayers were rolling down the fields at the edges of which perched dozens of tiny white houses for workers and several large storage depots. Two drones buzzed in and around the edges of some other fields. I continued down the road until I approached Corteva's colossal new building, surrounded by an electric fence and guarded by two security officers. After I parked the car and walked toward the entrance, one guard came over to me, asked for my documentation, then summoned a Corteva company scientist. I introduced myself and asked about a public showroom I had heard about demonstrating Corteva's and Pannar's activities (Pannar shares Corteva's offices). But the Corteva scientist said there was no showroom because "Corteva is new and under American ownership, and we're just beginning to work things out." But, like the pharmaceutical companies whose shell games I discuss in chapter 4, the company was new primarily in name.

Today, Corteva Agriscience, created two years after the US-based companies Dow AgroSciences and Pioneer High-Bred International merged, operates in thirteen countries, including Kenya, Tanzania, and South Africa. In these countries, Corteva's products and services produce fungicides and insecticides, peddle digital technologies, and provide remote digital management of vast monocropped estates.[23] Corteva operates alongside Illinois-based John Deere and, until two years ago, collaborated with StollerUSA in more than seventy countries as Grupo Stoller, the "largest biostimulant and plant health company in the world."[24] Corteva also collaborates with consultancy businesses, such as AgriAfrica, a South African private agency whose leadership team claims roots in Western Cape Province's wine-producing farm community.

In their overlapping continental African operations, Stoller, Corteva, and AgriAfrica pool their areas of business expertise to cultivate separate but complementary customer bases. Stoller and Corteva pair the latter's biotechnology with the former's chemical compounds designed to kill forms of plant and animal life considered damaging to crops. Stoller manufactures products such as Mover, Co-Mo, and Sugar Mover that, like all chemical pesticides, need to be handled properly because they are potentially toxic to both their targeted organisms and humans.[25] Stoller disclaims responsibility for any health-related harms its products may cause. Its safety data sheet identifies Mover as dangerous if inhaled, notes that Mover "may damage fertility or the unborn child," and is "harmful to aquatic life."[26] An established body of evidence confirms that the heavy use of insecticides and herbicides disrupts human and animal endocrine systems, and studies have shown that cancer has risen in the years since these chemicals were introduced in sub-Saharan Africa.[27]

Two of other Stoller products, Co-Mo and Sugar Mover, include additional disclaimers. "Stoller does not guarantee" the "accuracy or completeness" of "the information contained in this Safety Data Sheet," and "the information contained herein is furnished without warranty of any kind." Nevertheless, because the compounds are dangerous, the company requires users, many of whom have no training in biochemistry or in reading product labels, to find out more, on their own, about the product's safety. "Users should consider these data only as a supplement to other information *gathered by them*," reads the label, which adds that Stoller "assumes no responsibility for results obtained or for incidental or consequential damages arising from the use of [its] goods and data." Such labeling in effect blames farmers and farmworkers, not companies, for causing pesticide poisoning and environmental contamination.[28]

Blaming end users, and offloading responsibility for researching safety information onto them, protects companies from liability, not workers' health, and may lead users to underreport accidents. In South Africa, for example, where cases of acute poisoning are frequently overlooked, finding a public health inspector to prosecute violations may be difficult. Inspectors may not wish to jeopardize multinational investments in the country or risk public health professionals' access to workers living on commercial farms.[29] Moreover, companies do not test the effects of their chemicals on people in South Africa, where health status is widely variable, nor do they consider whether South African farmworkers are literate in the language of product labels. To be sure, the entry of international corporations into the chemical industry on the African continent presents an opportunity to improve health and safety practices by providing greater guidance to workers about safe handling. However, regulatory frameworks are often not well coordinated, legacies of abusive farm labor systems persist, and pesticides banned or tightly restricted in the United States remain widely available in agricultural markets across Africa.

As a result, among sugarcane plantation workers, hazardous exposure is so normalized that workers say they no longer think—or want to think—about health and safety. For example, a woman I met at a Greytown *spaza* shop (a roadside stand selling processed foods and sundries where people often sit on stoops and chairs to hang out and chat) told me that although she wore protective clothing when she worked on the farm, at the end of her shift, she—like Gloria in Tanzania, discussed in the introduction—could smell and taste the pesticides. Nonetheless, she would return to work the next day, trying not to think about the pesticides.

To help companies reduce legally actionable incidents and deflect attention from their operations, agribusiness consulting companies like AgriAfrica recommend investors buy "movable assets" and promote non-profit initiatives that provide gifts to local people.[30] For example, AgriAfrica recognizes that foreign investors' land acquisitions may be subject to community objections that the companies are killing the land and taking it from indigenous people, which they are. Many small-holding farmers, like Anathi and Kundaeli, hold highly affective attachments to the land and often realize only when it is too late that the terms of investors' contracts and pesticide uses do not favor them. AgriAfrica instructs investors to buy only movable assets such as tools, machinery, fertilizer contracts, and distribution and sales contracts, rather than the land itself, in order to protect their financial interests. Under these arrangements, land remains the government's property from which lessees rent for a given time.

AgriAfrica's business brochure states, "If the political climate were to change, then the investors' assets can be loaded on trucks and removed to a more stable site where work can progress again."[31] AgriAfrica's carefully worked-out action plan appears to minimize legal issues and maximize investors' financial security. It can potentially leave local communities in difficult situations, with chemically treated monocropped fields that pose risks to people's health, and leave small-holding farmers like Anathi and Kundaeli without the means to harvest, process, or store agricultural products. Investing in movable assets is not illegal, but it disadvantages the communities involved.

INITIATIVES TARGETING AFRICAN WOMEN PROVIDE COVER

Seemingly to divert public censure with manufactured accolades, AgriAfrica offers short-term, low-wage employment to farmers whose lands investors use. Indeed, one of AgriAfrica's economic development mantras is that employment enhances the quality of life of workers, especially for women,

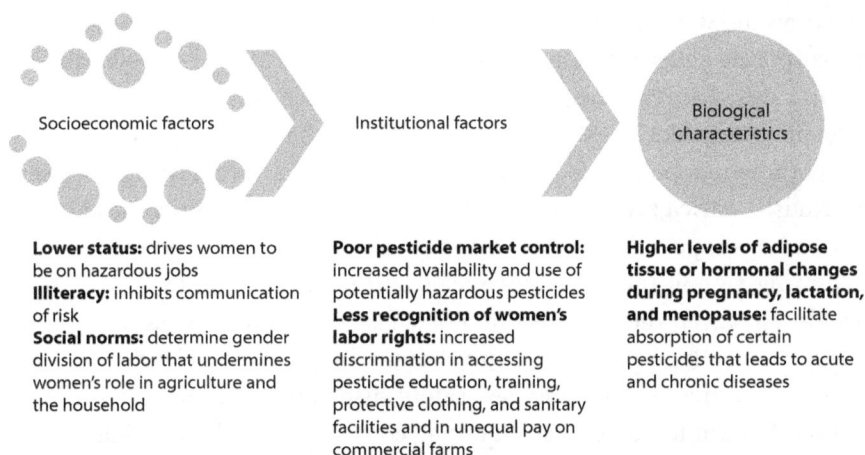

Socioeconomic factors   Institutional factors   Biological characteristics

Lower status: drives women to be on hazardous jobs
Illiteracy: inhibits communication of risk
Social norms: determine gender division of labor that undermines women's role in agriculture and the household

Poor pesticide market control: increased availability and use of potentially hazardous pesticides
Less recognition of women's labor rights: increased discrimination in accessing pesticide education, training, protective clothing, and sanitary facilities and in unequal pay on commercial farms

Higher levels of adipose tissue or hormonal changes during pregnancy, lactation, and menopause: facilitate absorption of certain pesticides that leads to acute and chronic diseases

Fig. 3. Factors that make women workers more vulnerable to exposure to pesticides, leading to potential health risks. Source: Atinkut, Freyer, and Bingen, "Women in Agriculture."

even though health researchers have documented for decades adverse reproductive health effects for women working with industrial-strength pesticides (figure 3).[32]

According to my resource network in Tanzania,[33] women working on large, chemically treated foreign-leased plantations have a higher incidence of miscarriage and reproductive health problems than other women in their communities who are not employed on these farms. As in South Africa, these women and their families hesitate to demand a comprehensive investigation into chemical poisoning for fear that investors will cancel their contracts and cease their leases payments, a portion of which goes to communities.

Perhaps recognizing that reproductive-age women bear the greater burden of pesticide-related health difficulties, investment firms such as AgriAfrica frequently sponsor community programs intended to address "women's issues." Often these programs reinforce historical white Western gendered and racialized stereotypes that portray Black women as cooks and household providers. For example, AgriAfrica's public relations initiative, Kulisha Africa (*kulisha*, meaning "to feed" in the Kiswahili language), features a woman holding a hand hoe in a field, wearing a bright patterned fabric, and smiling at the camera. The race- and gender-stereotyped picture portrays the woman farmer as capable but weak, able to be saved or aided by corporate generosity—an image reminiscent of colonial-era educational efforts aimed at rescuing perceived vulnerable Africans. Not only do donation programs like Kulisha Africa demonstrate that hunger persists despite corporate monopolies' pledges to end it,[34] but philanthropic programs such as Kulisha Africa provide charitable alibis for industrial agricultural investors who support highly mechanized, intensive crop production often requiring significant use of chemicals and infrastructure to achieve high yields. However, these yields often decrease over time, necessitating even more chemicals and infrastructure to maintain production levels.

Like the digital technologies, safety disclaimer sheets, and movable assets that hinder farmers from taking control of their lands while corporations erode the farmers' livelihoods, nonprofit initiatives for women provide a cover for corporations to avert blame should their products prove pathogenic. Covering up environmental and social destruction with modest donations intended for women draws attention away from the principal concern: the destruction of biodiversity and the socioeconomic costs that corporate agribusiness investments impose on small farmers.

CORPORATE IMPERIALISM AND THE DESTRUCTION OF LOCAL FOODWAYS

Scholars in eastern and southern Africa have given researchers across the globe sharp analytic tools for thinking about land and farmers' deep dissatisfaction with corporations' wide-ranging political and economic powers. Before Naomi Klein popularized the notion of "disaster capitalism" among American readers,[35] Africanist scholars wrote about how the environment intersects with other power systems to create uneven land access and susceptibility to environmental disasters. I am thinking of the works of Francis Nyamnjoh at the University of Cape Town, Chachage Seithy L. Chachage and Issa G. Shivji at the University of Dar es Salaam, Layla El Awad Simsa'a at the University of Khartoum, and many others who document how the benefits of global economic development are unevenly distributed.[36] Racial, economic, gendered, and ethnic disparities in wealth and environmental vulnerability are interconnected.

Histories of violent land expropriations in South Africa, Zimbabwe, Kenya, and many other places, including the New World and Caribbean, favored European colonial settlers who often put Black and Brown people into their service as laborers. Postcolonial and postapartheid policies have striven for land redistribution, but individual titling regimes sometimes unexpectedly worsen inequalities by "making a market out of land"—land that is imbued with cultural, political-economic, and family values.[37] Today, contract farming runs parallel and connects with the operation of large estates and can give small-holding farmers a degree of bargaining power if they collectivize and receive credit from contractors. But dependency emerges from these same advantages: small-holding farmers accrue debt to agribusinesses because they must buy the companies' fertilizers and seeds.[38]

A notable example of how global agribusinesses leverage patent laws to boost corporate profits is the extensive production of genetically modified maize, commonly referred to as corn in the United States. The widespread adoption of genetically modified corn has had a negative impact on food sovereignty and traditional farming in Africa.

Corn has many uses: as a food, an investment commodity, a plastics substitute, and ethanol-fueled energy. Engineered varieties contain high protein and vitamin A concentrations to enrich nutrient-poor human and animal diets. Because it lasts long in storage, investors can hold on to it until its market price rises high enough to return a profit. Converted into a resin or used to make ethanol mixed with gasoline, corn can help reduce greenhouse gas emissions (even though, when fertilizer and land use are taken into account, corn bioplastics and ethanol biomass production create more carbon emissions per unit of energy than regular plastic or gasoline).[39] Companies invest in corn because it is malleable; it can be shaped into many different commodities—including financial ones.

Because the soil and climate in South Africa and Tanzania are conducive to growing corn, that crop today is deeply embedded in the wheel of plantation-scale agricultural industry in these areas. In the KwaZulu-Natal South Africa region, for example, this wheel—with corn as its central connection—involves several specific actors (figure 4). One spoke on this wheel is agricultural seed companies and investors. When companies such as Corteva, Pannar, and Bayer Monsanto create products that cut

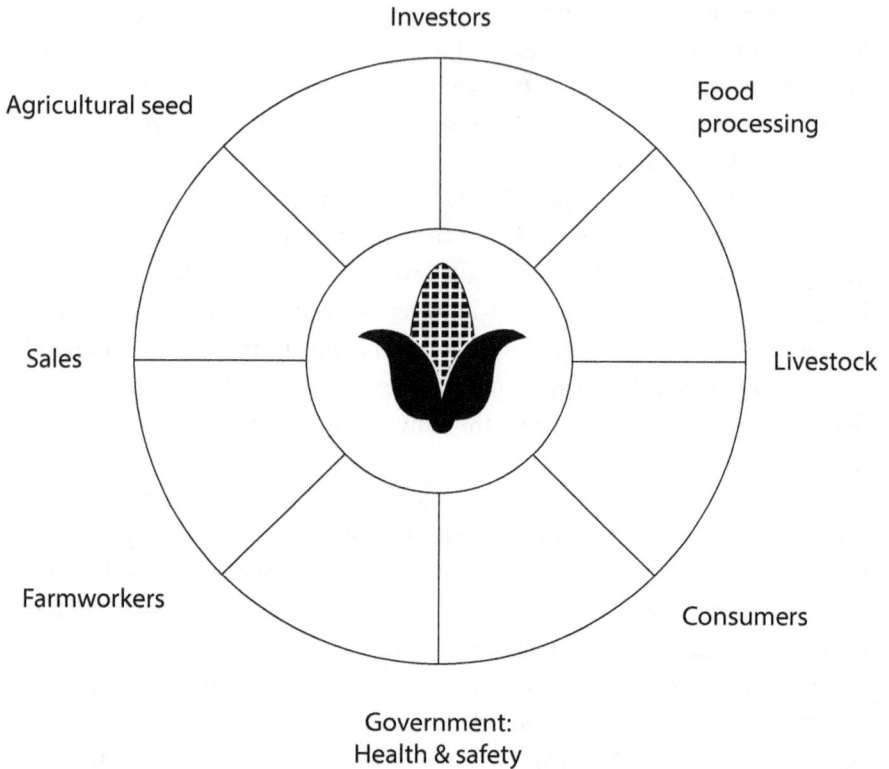

Investors

Food processing

Agricultural seed

Livestock

Sales

Farmworkers

Consumers

Government:
Health & safety

Fig. 4. Spokes on the wheel of the large-scale corn industry. Drawing by author.

costs and scale production, consulting companies such as AgriAfrica pass on advantages to investors. Another spoke on the wheel connects corn as food with consumers and livestock uses. Food-processing industries supply companies' technologies internationally. Another connects corn to food-processing industries that ship fresh or processed products across national borders.[40] Two more spokes—farmworkers and sales reps— supply the physical human labor needed to convert the raw product into a consumable that keeps the wheel of the industry moving. A final spoke, perennially underfunded, are government-issued health and safety regulations for labor and manufacturing. This wheel metaphor approximates how people treat corn like a currency or a tender connecting labor, trade, law, health and safety, and finance.

But corn's exponential increase in value occurs in the financial market, not on farms. Farm industry investors drive Kundaeli's, Uduru's, and Anathi's land dispossession, and investors know corn is a reliable futures commodity, even if it "goes bad" in any given year. If farmers want the fixed prices that buyers guarantee, they must buy and use companies' genetically modified organisms (GMOs) and pesticides; those GMOs and pesticides harm the land, water, and people. Farmers receive only the lowest estimated costs because consolidators can store the corn and sell it for different uses, and they fix prices low enough to make a profit. Agribusinesses move to other places when farmers' land is no longer fertile or the political-economic situation no longer favors investors. Agribusiness economically sustains investors, not farmers. Farmers, at best, break even while investors deplete soils. At the same time, products like DroughtGard (a biotechnology trait for corn that enables it to grow with very little water) and Roundup Ready (a biotechnology trait, that prevents crops from being killed by glyphosate and other herbicides) may slowly consume annual yields.[41]

The companies' patented products also create serious health risks from which the companies appear to divert attention. Plant-killing chemicals, including not only glyphosate but MCPA and dicamba, found in Roundup-branded products, drive up the risk of non-Hodgkin's lymphoma and other cancers for people heavily exposed to the products.[42] At the same time, Bayer Monsanto, operating through Bayer Fund global philanthropy,[43] claims to improve the quality of life for people worldwide. Even though some of the company's Roundup brands poison helpful micro-organisms in soils and cause cancer among regular users, Bayer claims its programs are "combatting malnutrition and food insecurity; enhancing STEM education; and providing support services for patients and families managing cardiovascular disease and cancer."[44] But creating a problem and then claiming to solve a different one diverts attention and shows extreme audacity.

Working in different settings, anthropologists studying agribusiness philanthropy have offered ethnographic evidence to show that agribusiness programs, on the whole, do not help those in need. In the United States, agribusiness lenders that forward-book farmers on annual yields push them to overuse water and chemical inputs and push many into bankruptcy; programs designed to reduce farmers' credit burden hurt them.[45] Corporate animal farms in Anathi's, Uduru's, and Kundaeli's regions of Africa and in the Dakotas, Illinois, Iowa, Kansas, and Missouri in the United States spread antibiotic resistance and airborne illnesses, even though companies' charitable philanthropies support animal and community health clinics. Agribusiness websites visually convey a commitment to employee and animal well-being in the US Midwest and South, but the companies' headlong plunge into contract farming "impose[s] needless harm on animals, land, workers and communities."[46] In Tanzania and South Africa, where there are even fewer legal or economic protections for independent farmers, small-scale farmers are particularly vulnerable to this kind of abusive system.

Corporations also threaten extreme fines and prison for farmers in order to lock them into this system. In Tanzania, farmers were initially prohibited by Tanzanian law from sharing seeds and could face a twelve-year minimum prison sentence, a fine of more than US$100,000, or both for violating the ban. The amount of the fine is something that, the head of Sustainable Agriculture Tanzania has noted, "a Tanzanian farmer cannot even start to imagine. The average wage is still less than 2 US dollars a day."[47] Yet today, per Pannar Seed's terms, Uduru and his neighbors must never sell seeds to one another, or they will be considered criminals. Although information about the number of Tanzanian citations the company has issued in defending this patent law is not available, public records on hundreds of such cases in the United States, where farmers' hands are also tied, document that farmers sometimes resow their previous years' seeds.[48] Although statistics for this practice in Tanzania and South Africa are difficult to identify, the situation there is likely to be much worse.

Despite the de jure end of colonialism, economic relations in the current world system are still structured to facilitate high-income countries extracting resources from low- and middle-income countries. On top of this extraction, the increasing heat and drought due to climate change diminishes agricultural production and output in the latter countries. Contract farming is a form of corporate colonization, forcing children of farmers to move to cities and older farmers to become sharecroppers.

In eastern and southern Africa, industrial farming has reshaped rural areas, led to environmental devastation, and changed the lives and practices of people in local communities. Similar changes have occurred in many other regions of the world.[49] Real estate developers, foreign investors, and agribusinesses have transformed rural landscapes and encouraged upwardly aspiring contract farmers to protect their interests through the same legal property regimes that dispossess them of their family lands.[50] For example, in Kilimanjaro, property investors dangle money to farmers like Kundaeli and Uduru whose vegetable gardens and coffee farms are dry and dysfunctional. If it weren't for the fact that ancestral graves lie on these farmers' lands and that people feel a connection to one another, surely many more people would sell, leave the mountain, and move to cities. Hoping to access the profits generated from these land sales, secondary school graduates aspire to study "real estate law."[51] The region's land is fertile. Although, as I noted, rivers are disappearing, freshwater continues to stream down the mountain, making the area rich for agricultural investors to move in and dispossess small farmers of their lands.

Given the negative impact of this kind of large-scale industrial agriculture centered on corporate property law in these areas, it is worth asking, How is it that the companies managed to move into small-holding farmers' lands and fragile ecosystems in the first place? Why do people, such as the students studying real estate law, come to cooperate with technological responses that obscure the more significant problem that methane, carbon, and nitrous oxide associated with plantation-scale industrial farming and agrichemical manufacturing trap heat and warm the planet? Although a desire to have a higher standard of living by making more money through this kind of farming is likely and understandably part of the appeal, much of the displacement is enabled through greenwashing, a marketing tactic used to diminish resistance to foreign corporate investments by highlighting only the benefits of large-scale industrial farming for local communities. As this book highlights, this tactic has been a successful tool for companies eager to reap profits from Africa's labor and natural resources.

GREENWASHING: AN ALIBI IN AGRIBUSINESS MARKETING

One of the most effective strategies companies have used to convince people in South Africa and Tanzania to accept the large-scale degradation of natural resources and the loss of control over their homelands has been to tell people that the companies will do something that sounds good but that obscures its negative impact. This tactic involves not outright lying but, instead, what the scholar Emiko Ohnuki-Tierney has called "communicative opacity."[52] Names, terms, and symbols have many contextualized meanings, and different people can draw many different meanings from the same term or name depending on the context and because of the lack of mutual understanding. International agribusiness corporations know this and have used it with great success.

Writers and word spinners at public relations and ad agencies masterfully deploy communicative opacity. They bank on the ambivalence of key symbols and phrases—such as "guarding against drought and climate change"—to manipulate the meanings of these ideas for specific purposes. For example, Bayer's Monsanto product DroughtGard, whose name suggests it helps protect against drought, does not actually prevent droughts. Instead, it contributes to the very problem the name implies it addresses. The company markets the product as a technological response to climate change but endorses industrial practices that exacerbate the problem.

Similarly, about two decades ago, agribusiness marketeers presented genetically modified vegetable crops to the public as a significant tool in combatting hunger. But this portrayal was misleading. It obscured the fact that genetically modified crops narrow the basis of food security by replacing healthy food grains with monocultures of rice, wheat, and corn.[53] Environmentalists refer to this kind of communicative opacity as *green-washing*—a kind of alibi for environmentally and socially destructive practices that gives the impression that corporations care about the environment while, in fact, they do not.[54]

Greenwashing promotes the notion that improvements in how businesses produce their products protect or improve the environment. For example, the solar-powered "climate-smart" technology that the two Slovenian vendors marketed at the Royal Agricultural Exhibition in KwaZulu-Natal Province focused on increasing investors' financial yields rather than redressing climate change. The vendors' kiosk banner flatly said that "climate-smart" technology would pay for itself within one year by allowing absentee landlords to control irrigation remotely via "fertigation," and even that it could control the "climate."[55] Similarly, Microsoft's digital technology marketing in Africa declares of its rare earth mineral technologies that "this is how the future will look," forwarding in this phrase an illocutionary speech act strategy by which a powerful actor operates to make its statements true, such as "We declare you guilty" by a jury or "This is the future" by a Microsoft billionaire.[56] Such marketing fails to account for the rare earth minerals needed for the company's technologies, the lives risked mining or farming, the petrol needed to process or transport the technologies, the greenhouse gases created in production processes, and the growing human-social insecurity and resource expenditures involved in nuclear-powering AI technologies.[57] Instead, these advertisers promulgate a faulty logic that "if we adapt" by using digital and remote technologies, "we will mitigate climate change."

Certainly, addressing climate challenges with technology is not inherently bad. However, the way the technology's advertising unfolds— namely through a mode and manner that operates tactically through a communicative-semiotic technique of *opacity*—perpetuates dispossession by diverting consumers' attention from the causes and consequences of climate change. In referencing "climate-smart technologies," companies make sustainability look like a "civilizing mission" to "save" poor Africans from disaster. The duplicity of promising change without actually redistributing wealth reinforces African communities' alienation from agricultural investment systems in which foreign owners control wealth for their own profit. Despite this doublespeak, greenwashing has provided a potent tool with which corporations create an alibi for socially, economically, and environmentally destructive business practices. By simultaneously integrating their corporate giving into local communities and creating dependencies among African farmers, this alibi has allowed them to enhance both their reputations and their exploitation of the fertile agricultural lands in Tanzania and South Africa.

REPRISE

The significance of the issues highlighted in this chapter lies in the alarming impact of corporate control of agriculture, mainly as it affects small-scale farmers in regions such as Kilimanjaro and the Eastern Cape and KwaZulu-Natal provinces. It also resides in the rapid expansion of corporate globalization into production across the integrated sectors and industries of food processing, health and safety, and old and new biotechnologies. The scope and rapidity of corporate globalization has created an imbalance of power, favoring corporate interests, undercutting farmers' markets, and perpetuating economic inequality. Historical inequities introduced in the colonial era have contributed to the undervaluation and exploitation of indigenous and Black farmers. Historic inequities have also led to a power dynamic whereby corporations today dictate terms to farmers like Kundaeli, Uduru, and Anathi, thereby undermining their autonomy and bargaining power and raising concerns about global food security, environmental sustainability, and economic justice.

The theoretical value of identifying corporations' alibis is to trace their presence and variation in agriculture and other sectors of production. Large-scale farming and patenting of biotechnologies represent different forms of enclosing the commons, with the former based on the idea of operating more efficiently on a larger scale and the latter on the belief that privatizing nature is a reasonable form of regulation. To downplay their involvement, US agricultural corporations divert scrutiny from the damages they cause by changing their names, operating through subsidiary companies, and offering social services and gifts to communities, schools, and governments, in addition to engaging in greenwashing. Examining these intricate tactics raises questions about the intentions behind their actions, suggesting that what often appears to be a cohesive tapestry conceals a tangled web of deception and self-interest.

3 Amazon in Africa

Corporate investors often use tactics such as greenwashing in agribusiness to justify environmentally harmful practices. However, agribusiness is not the only industry that employs diversionary tactics to pursue environmentally destructive activities; the e-commerce and artificial intelligence (AI) sectors also do this. Many people do not typically associate e-commerce and AI companies with concealing exploitative resource extraction behind misleading justifications. Nonetheless, that is exactly what Amazon Web Services (AWS) did when it expanded its cloud computing headquarters in Cape Town, South Africa.

Amazon's multimillion-dollar investment project created thousands of jobs, but most of these positions did not pay well, and the project came with a significant downside: the property was located on a floodplain and held sacred significance for the Khoi and San peoples, the descendants of the first inhabitants of the southernmost area of Africa.

After the project was publicly announced but before construction began, the City of Cape Town rezoned the parcel for new use. It granted the developer permission to construct a nine-story complex featuring 70,000 square meters of office space for Amazon Inc., the US digital technology giant. Paramount Chief Aran of the Goringhaicona,[1] a Khoi leader in charge of one of the twelve Khoi traditional houses, argued against the project, explaining, "Our heritage will be completely destroyed. This place has great spiritual significance for us."[2]

The land where Amazon wanted to build its headquarters was in the western part of Cape Town. The area remained largely undeveloped despite its location in an urban area. The site included numerous waterways and harbored endangered and protected wildlife. In addition to the Goringhaicona, residents of a densely populated small neighborhood, Observatory, located west of the floodplain, were also against Amazon building its headquarters on the site, concerned about its environmental impact. When Amazon announced its plans to build there, representatives of the Goringhaicona along with the Observatory Civic Association (OCA), established by Observatory neighborhood residents, sent a letter to Amazon's developer, Liesbeek Leisure Property Trust (LLPT), announcing they planned to go to court to stop the development project. Leslie London, head of the OCA and professor of public health at the University of Cape Town, said that opponents questioned the project's zoning, environmental, and heritage approvals.[3]

The parcel in question was not only susceptible to flooding but was also situated in an environmentally sensitive and protected area that contained a variety of natural habitats, including wetlands, grasslands, and rare plant species. The city assessed the risk of flooding as "minimal," claiming the proposed construction would not harm protected wildlife such as sacred ibises, Egyptian geese, and the endangered western leopard toad. However, to build on the floodplain, Amazon's developer had to convert one of the rivers into a vegetated swamp, an activity at odds with managing runoff. "Treating a river like a stormwater ditch is inconsistent with any climate change mitigation strategy," London stated, emphasizing the importance of preserving open land and waterways to help mitigate flooding and recharge groundwater and aquifers through natural percolation.

Urging Amazon to withdraw from the project, London and the OCA sent Amazon's CEO, Jeff Bezos, then the wealthiest person in the world, a registered letter articulating in bold text: *"We believe your investment will forever associate Amazon with everything you would not wish to stand for: environmental destruction, greed over protection of heritage and the environment and a complete abdication of any commitment to addressing climate change."*

Receiving no response from Bezos, the OCA sent a letter to MacKenzie Scott, Bezos' former wife, hoping to appeal to her more public-minded philanthropic perspective. "But Scott also never responded," London said, "and Bezos's agent in South Africa referred us to their own subsidiary's spokesperson, Jody Aufrichtig." South African–born Aufrichtig defended the Amazon project down to the detail and provided a backstop for Amazon Inc. "There is no groundswell of unhappiness," Aufrichtig emphasized to international media, only a "few vocal objectors" who did not like the outcome of the approval procedures.[4]

But events inside South Africa suggested a very different story.

When Amazon publicly announced its involvement in the project, aware it would lead to significant public concern, the company relied on its developer to both assuage and undermine that criticism. One of the ways the developer sought to lure opponents to its side was through largesse—offering assistance to the Khoi and San communities and promising them jobs. In an effort to release Amazon from future fault or blame for violating cultural rights, Amazon's developer promised to build a First Nations cultural center as part of the site. Then, attempting to level the tidal wave of 50,000 objections against the project (which was more than a "few vocal objectors"), Amazon's developer and the newly formed First Nations Collective staged an on-site jobs campaign targeted at youth. But many Khoi and environmentalists continued questioning the developer's motives, pointing out the obvious fact that Amazon's headquarters could easily be built elsewhere in the city on one of many many less culturally significant or ecologically fragile parcels.[5]

Over the next four years, pro-development factions tried to make the most of an opportunity as the Amazon project became yet another case of what opponents charged was a large American corporation driving a wedge between already diverse indigenous and environmentalist communities and running roughshod over land and people.[6]

One of the most publicly vocal opponents of Amazon's project was and remains Tauriq Jenkins, chair of the A/Xarra Restorative Justice Forum at the Center for African Studies at the University of Cape Town. An Observatory resident, he is also high commissioner of the Goringhaicona Khoi Khoin Indigenous Traditional Council.[7]

One late afternoon—shortly after the City of Cape Town approved the Amazon project but still before any significant construction had begun—

Jenkins and I were surveying the construction spot. "We want this area declared a national heritage site and preserved as an ecologically sensitive area," he said. "Building on someone's sacred territory using the excuse of creating jobs is fraudulent. It's like paying someone to dig up their ancestors' graves. Who in their right mind would do that?"[8]

During the controversy leading up to the project's approval, the Khoi First Nations Collective, a group of First Nations people favoring the development, emerged. Although this group hardly represented the entire Khoi people, Amazon's developer claimed its opinion, rather than other First Nations groups and representatives like Jenkins, reflected the Khoi communities' wishes. Discounting one group while supporting another, the developer capitalized on division to further the site's development.

The developer provided Amazon Inc. with the perfect excuse, an alibi, for not being present when claims of illegality or immorality arose: Amazon could claim to be absent from the scene when, for example, the developer, it appears, hired undocumented workers, when protesters in South Africa demonstrated, or when courts closed and then reopened the contested area for construction. Similarly, Amazon could claim not to be responsible when the developer worked to marginalize the Khoi people and environmentalists fighting the project or when, as eventually happened, 150,000 tons of concrete pounded into the wetland drove off wildlife.

At the time, most international media reports focused on what constitutes cultural heritage and how such heritage should be factored into economic development decisions.[9] However, that media discussion did not shift the balance of power in the debate, and Amazon's developer ultimately advanced its objectives. In the end, the developer's actions highlighted a dodgy "cat and mouse" tactic of overcoming opposition by making promises to some local groups, dividing the opposition, using contractors to call ecologically fragile and culturally sacred land "degraded," then converting sacred land into an asset for its shareholders. The case of Amazon in Cape Town resembles the extractive practices of the agribusinesses discussed in the previous chapter. It is part of a more extensive transnational and historical story of foreign ecological and cultural exploitation in Africa in which profit consolidation through land capitalization is rooted in the global expansion of investment capital.

Looking at how this land development in South Africa helped Amazon extract wealth for its foreign investors raises another issue. Amazon is the world's largest e-commerce company and one of the global leaders in the AI industry. Amazon Web Service's larger project, beyond building Amazon's headquarters on the parcel in Cape Town, was to turn this land into real estate for its cloud computing services in South Africa. In addition to disrupting the surrounding ecology and destroying the cultural heritage of communities for whom the land is sacred, the installation of Amazon's cloud computing headquarters adds a dramatic element to the travesty. Industry economists refer to the ability of companies like to AWS to digitally mine users' web browsing as the fourth industrial revolution, Industry 4.0, referring to rapid societal change due to increasing interconnectivity and digital and AI technology. For Amazon and its developer, desecrating and building on this land in Cape Town provided only insignificant returns in the short term. The true profit from this project would come in the long term, as it would provide a major site in Africa for reaping digital data from new users and businesses in the region—a richer and deeper and longer-lasting gold mine. Although long-term profits may be assured for Amazon from building its headquarters here, the longer-term impact on South Africa is much less clear.

Amazon's development in Cape Town, like the foreign investments discussed in previous chapters, underscores how economic sustainability in a short-term investment market is generally incompatible with environmental and social sustainability. Financial investments in these projects cross national borders and legal jurisdictions in ways that create knotty chains of command and ambiguous lines of authority regarding labor and environmental protection laws. The different or "deterritorialized" legal protocols and governmental jurisdictions that these international investments traverse create opportunities for companies to explicitly contest and obliquely change rules and regulations for implementing land tenure and land use management.[10] Exploiting ambiguities in laws and rules by expanding into deterritorialized markets regardless of longer-term environmental and social sustainability issues is part of a savvy, sustainable, and profit-generating business model. As a result, companies that seek to expand in this way will often see their investment and stock value increase, thus generating private wealth. Amazon's use of chains of intermediaries to turn physical land in the city of Cape Town into a commodity and then transform that real estate into investment capital for Amazon's cloud computing business on the African continent generates wealth for investors but impoverishes the region's ecology and splinters indigenous communities.

To consumers, cloud technology like the one Amazon uses, which sails across continents, can appear to operate without anyone driving it—as if it does not even have a real estate component at all, let alone one with significant ecological and social impact. This "now you see it, now you don't" aspect of the company's investment has consequences for the rest of the world. To understand the role that developers and investors' subsidiaries play in turning land into commodities for investors' expansion into digital data mining and to reflect on what appears to be the inhumanity of a corporation and its CEO not acknowledging community concerns, it is helpful to contrast Amazon's corporate investment policies with what actually happened on the ground in Cape Town.

FOREIGN INVESTMENT AND A HISTORY OF LAND THEFT IN SOUTH AFRICA

"Over there," Tauriq Jenkins said, pointing to Amazon's development site just as the sun began to set behind Table Mountain. "Right where they're building—that's where the first land displacement occurred. That's ground zero for property theft from indigenous and First Nations South Africans."

Although Jenkins was pointing at Amazon's current development on this sacred parcel of land, with "ground zero" he was referring to a displacement that occurred there hundreds of years ago when seventeenth-century Dutch colonists under Jan van Riebeeck's command forced Khoi and San from the riverbanks and pushed them to the stark, sandy interior. That displacement signaled the beginning of the transatlantic trade in enslaved Africans and the centuries-long subjugation that would follow.

"Van Riebeeck planted a hedge, a row of shrubs to separate white European farms from indigenous lands. That was the start of apartheid. It happened at this location," Jenkins explained. As with the national discourse in the United States about European settlers displacing Native

Americans, for South Africans, this history of the Dutch supplanting indigenous communities in the region was virtually axiomatic, shared by everyone.

"We've had a long and violent history," Jenkins continued. "The Khoi and San were the first to live in these lands." For more than three hundred years after Van Riebeeck's arrival there, colonizers from the Netherlands, Germany, Britain, Portugal, and other European countries violently upended Koi and San communities and dispossessed them of their lands.[11] For this reason, the thirty seven–acre site on which the Amazon building stands embodies for Khoi and San descendants' centuries of struggle against conquest and oppression.

The earliest written records of the land that the Amazon headquarters now occupy show that, in the mid-seventeenth century, three traditional houses of Khoena (plural of Khoi) lived in the region—Goringhaiqua, Gorachouqua, and Goringhaicona. San moved to the area seasonally, and Khoi and San intermixed, often trading and socializing around the springs and rivers where they watered livestock.[12] Indeed, Dutch chroniclers referred to Khoi communities as Camissa or Watermen. "The Watermen live in this Table Valley and behind the Lion and Table Mountains," van Riebeeck wrote in his journal.[13] The creolized form of ||khamis sa,[14] meaning "sweet water for all" in the Khoi language, became the name for the Camissa River.

In 1652, Dutch soldiers seized the Camissa River Khoi settlement. "We had to tell them that their land had fallen to us by the sword," van Riebeeck wrote in a passage many human rights activists today take as apt evidence of a violent crime against humanity.[15] For many present-day Capetonians, 1652 marks the beginning of the end of indigenous land possession. Over the coming centuries, European settlers diverted and engineered the Camissa River and its tributaries to flow beneath the city. Control of indigenous trade ended. In the early 1800s, following a war between Boers or Afrikaners (descendants of the original Dutch colonizers) and the British, the City of Cape Town became a British territory. Railways expanded, diamond and gold rushes followed in the colony's interior, and the Second Anglo-Boer War ensued (1899–1902). Britain declared victory and made Cape Town the territorial capital in 1910. Britain made no significant changes to the long-standing suppression of indigenous rights in South

Africa, and the concentration of wealth and power among the white population remained firmly intact—a concentration that continues today.[16]

This ongoing suppression of the rights of indigenous populations in South Africa was codified anew when, in 1950, two years after its election to government, the white National Party instituted the Group Areas Act, which authorized the government to identify people by race and residentially separate them. The seat of white nationalist power was Stellenbosch, a wealthy town in the grape-growing region northeast of Cape Town. People today still remember having to submit to a test to determine their race. "The measure of whether you were Black or Colored," said Amandla, a retired schoolteacher who grew up in the years following the Group Areas Act, was taken as follows: "If a white official put a pencil in your hair and it stayed there, then you were Black. If it didn't, you weren't." Typically, the apartheid government classified the Khoi and San as Black or Colored, depending on their family histories.[17] Although apartheid officially ended in the early 1990s, Cape Town remains de facto highly segregated, and descendants of the European settler population continue to own the greater amount of valuable land and hold the lion's share of wealth.[18] Today, this concentration of wealth and landownership has direct repercussions on the ability of the Khoi and other indigenous populations to develop and maintain the political and financial power needed to decide the fate of lands connected to their heritage.

By the early 2000s, the democratically elected government of South Africa began to lease and then sell government lands to private parties. Although South Africa never fell prey to IMF and World Bank requirements to privatize public infrastructure, the country nonetheless adopted IMF-type programs. It privatized public land, including the parcel on which Amazon's Africa headquarters now sits. But the sale to Amazon was not the first time this land was used in ways that went against Khoi people's wishes and from which they were excluded. Under apartheid, for example, a recreational area for white railway workers was built on the site and later a golf course. However, the scale of the destruction proposed under Amazon's watch was on an entirely new level.

In 2015, Liesbeek Leisure Property (LLP) bought the land and the infrastructure on it, including buildings, water and electrical supply, access roads, and drainage system, for R12 million (US$950,000).[19]

Almost immediately—*without a sale*—LLP transferred the property to Liesbeek Leisure Property Trust, an entity LLP created three months before it bought the property.[20]

By making this transfer to the trust, LLP enabled the LLPT to develop the plot. Yet LLPT had to secure two approvals, one to rezone (a city decision) and the other an environmental approval (a province decision). In addition, the National Environmental Management Act, in tandem with the National Heritage Resources Act, obligated the developer to undertake a heritage impact assessment and submit it to Heritage Western Cape (HWC). Heritage Western Cape rejected the developer's impact assessment in February 2020. But the developer found a workaround. As Leslie London, head of the Observatory Civic Association, put it, the developer "did some fancy paper trail footwork to provide the fig leaf they needed to bypass the heritage approval."[21]

In 2020, HWC let its objection to the proposal expire. For the city—which was pro-development and eventually approved the trust's rezoning request—and for the developer, this expiration appeared to overcome the heritage assessment hurdle and give the developer a green light to repurpose the land. The municipal government publicly applauded the plan, enabling the R4.5 billion development project to move forward, with the developer's principal investor, Rand Merchant Bank, to earn R400 million annually—a 9 percent return on an initial investment of R12 million (US$950,000).

Then, beginning March 26, 2020, the COVID-19 virus arrived, which halted the project. The government issued alerts—popularly known as lockdowns—ranging from "Every person is confined to [their] place of residence" to "Any operator of an outdoor facility where gatherings are held must possess a certificate" limiting the number of participants allowed. The lockdown made it impossible for the developer to begin work at the site. In September 2020, the city's planning tribunal—eager to get the project going despite the pandemic—trumpeted Amazon as the anchor tenant in the local economy, which was being battered by the pandemic lockdowns. In April of the following year, the mayor of Cape Town, Dan Plato, reiterated the go-ahead for clearing the land and preparing the site. Echoing the developer, Plato called the project and Amazon's involvement a much-needed boost to the city's pandemic-affected economy.

At this point, Amazon's developer went into high gear.

Practically overnight, the LLPT's contractors erected a chain-link fence along the site's perimeter, surveyors set boundary corners, and truckloads of men appeared each morning at the gate. Many were from other countries, including Zimbabwe, Malawi, Tanzania, and the Democratic Republic of the Congo (DRC), countries where undocumented migrants often came from, searching for work in South Africa.[22] In my conversations with many of these workers, few knew anything about Khoi and San heritage or the David-versus-Goliath debate between the local community and Amazon Inc.; they had other important matters on their minds, like working, making money, and sending some of it home to their families.

For and against the project, community activists also moved into a state of high action. A battle of words and images played out in South African media, on the streets, and eventually in the courts. Marinus Fredericks, paramount chief of the Aman (Nama) Traditional Council, promised to mobilize all Khoi and San to stop the development.[23]

"This area has a unique spirit of place," Goringhaicona paramount chief Aran asserted. The development would destroy "sacred ancestral burial grounds," he continued, and subject the space to "tons of toxic concrete bulk" beneath the surface. Many Khoi and San regard the land as a "mass grave where their ancestors' bodies lie."[24] The Amazon project threatened their spiritual desires to connect with the land and their ancestors. It also threatened to become one more example of the way foreign investors disregarded indigenous people's land and culture, part of a history of violence dating back hundreds of years and a long battle the Khoi and San people find themselves still fighting.

BATTLES ON THE STREETS

Walking down the street in the Observatory neighborhood, I noticed a message spray-painted on the north wall of the local community center: *Fuck off Amazon,* in one red cursive stroke. A few days later, walking on the other side of the street, I pitched my orange peels into a trash can and looked down to see *Get the fuck out of our neighbourhood Amazon* stickers pasted on the cans (figure 5). By this time, the spray-painted message on

Fig. 5. Sticker on the side of a trash bin located on a street in
Cape Town, South Africa. Photo by author.

the building had already disappeared under a layer of white paint, but the
trashcan stickers remained for several months.

A few weeks after seeing those messages, I noticed another, more
thought-provoking one. It was hidden from view from the street and visible only if you walked down to the river: a four-foot high, boldly stenciled

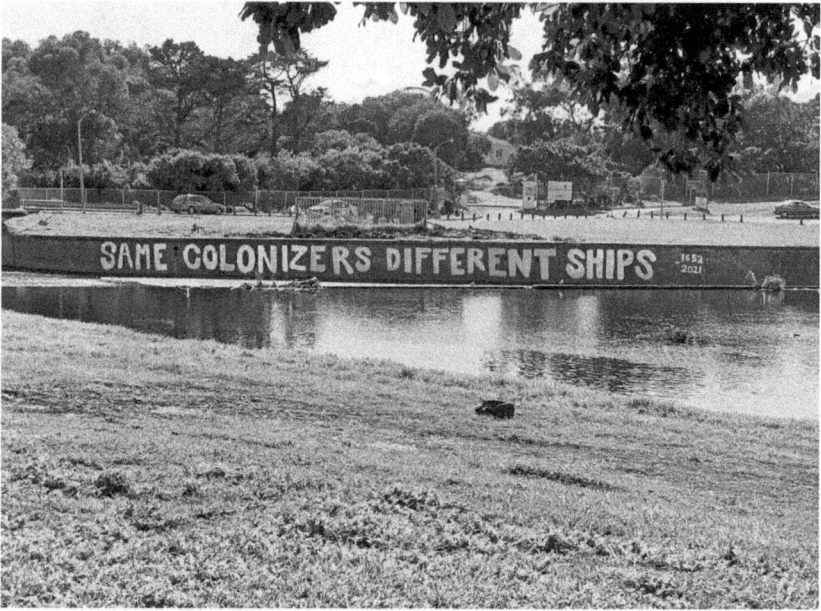

Fig. 6. Wall art message, Cape Town, South Africa. Photo by author.

street art message featuring water and shipping imagery. SAME COLONIZ-ERS DIFFERENT SHIP 1652–2021, read the provocation painted on the wall channeling the Liesbeek River (figure 6). The message equated the 1652 establishment of the Dutch Cape Colony with the city's final 2021 approval of the Amazon complex. It compared corporations to colonizers: both set up shops on other people's lands, extracted resources using underpaid workers, and then created commodities that earned their shareholders untold wealth while leaving occupied territories economi-cally impoverished and environmentally degraded. Within a few weeks, the graffiti was painted over, but the project's opponents remained.

That was May and June. For the next several weeks, the *New York Times* and other US media picked up the Amazon development controversy but did not report the feeling on the streets.[25] No one contested that the area was the site of the first resistance to European settlement or that the land and water were sacred to Khoi. Nor did anyone with whom I spoke doubt that developing the site would irreversibly change the landscape.[26]

Instead, many worried about how to protect cultural heritage by defining it. Is heritage merely the artifacts and heirlooms passed down through generations, or does it also encompass a collective identity connected to the land? Ultimately, the discussion focused on whether heritage is tangible or intangible, and whether it can exist only in material form or in an ephemeral state. The answer would determine whether the developer could continue building.

In response to the South African requirement for the developer to conduct a heritage impact assessment of the site, the developer hired a consulting archaeologist. This consultant reported that heritage can indeed be intangible. However, the developer did not accept this report and instead commissioned a second heritage impact assessment.

The second assessor concluded that the site's cultural heritage significance was "notional"—not worth considering—because the area contained "no tangible form" of heritage. The developer accepted this latter report. Using visual criteria as the sole indicator of heritage excluding "places to which oral traditions are attached"—as stipulated by South African law (section 3(2)b of the NHRA) and UN conventions[27]—the developer dismissed arguments that the site is sacred to Khoi people. With the second heritage consultant's report in hand, LLPT began to dispute Goringhaicona claims that the site was protected or protectable.

Next, the developer articulated a modified indigenous narrative amenable both to the company and the newly organized First Nations Collective. Although the First Nations Collective (FNC) did not speak collectively for the entirety of the Khoi people, the heritage assessment author, Rudewaan Arendse, suggested it did—apparently referencing comments from the First Nations Collective themselves. He described the collective as having made "it clear that they, and only they [meaning the FNC, and no other Khoi groups], own the indigenous narrative." Arendse proposed supporting specific heritage themes, as by "naming internal roads inspired by people or symbols central to the First Nations narrative," building an "eco corridor gateway featuring eland horns" made of concrete, and "establishing a heritage-eco trail that goes around the site." He questioned the credibility of the Paramount Chief Aran, suggesting Aran was impaired by alcohol and citing a four-hundred-year-old diary entry by Jan van Riebeeck to describe the Goringhaicona as "made up of drifters and outcasts."[28] This name-calling was unacceptable to many people, and in March, the matter went to a South African court.

According to international convention, heritage can be intangible: language, songs, dances, and rituals.[29] These practices happen in the moment, often without being concretely memorialized in landmarks or physical objects. But the developer's definition of heritage impact, which the assessor was successful in arguing, was that if one did not see heritage, physically—that is, if there was no material icon or visible marker in the land—no heritage exists, a position best summed up in LLPT's statement that *"the sense we have of this site in this landscape is of scruffiness and un-used-ness"* and that *"the great historical significance of this site and its context are not visible at all and have left very little obvious impact on the landscape."*[30]

"Scruffiness" and "un-used-ness" fanned the flames of community opposition, with hundreds of people appearing at the construction site to once again protest the development. Earlier, as noted, the opposition had gathered 50,000 signatures in less than two weeks against the project (this number tripled and then quadrupled within the year). As the project got under way, the opposition used a crowdfunding site to raise R95,000 (US$6,500) for a lawsuit, which it won in March 2022 when the court issued an injunction ordering Amazon's developer to halt construction. But the opposition lost on appeal six months later. As the court cases played out, a propaganda war in the media, along with anonymous email and social media attacks, peppered the community activists and indigenous opponents with strong denunciations.[31]

In the meantime, the construction continued, even during the months the court injunction was in effect. In fact, the court cases seemed to light a fire under the construction work. Pile drivers arrived; cement trucks and multistory cranes drove onto the site. I witnessed construction continuing well after sundown, even though the developer's contractor promised Observatory residents that work would conclude promptly at sunset.[32]

With all the pounding and banging, the ground shook and undulated like a massive earthquake during the early months of the project. It was as if Amazon's developer wanted to get as much hardware into the ground so development would be as far along as possible, as quickly as possible, so that the area would be damaged to such a degree that any future efforts at restoration of its original state would be untenable. Indeed, the project's opponents recognized that construction was likely to be at such an advanced stage by the time the court cases concluded that even if the court agreed that the development approvals were illegal (which in the end, it did not), it was very likely that demolition of the construction would not occur. "An outcome in which we would be told we were right but that nothing would be done to correct it was a very real possibility," the OCA reported to its constituents.[33]

Fostering a public belief that, once started, the project had to continue appears to have been another of the developer's tactics designed to serve the interests of its future tenant, Amazon. Promising jobs and claiming "eventually" to restore degraded land kicked the can of responsibility further down the road. Amazon's developer deployed time as an agent. In forward-booking deliverables, the developer depended on time to divert public scrutiny from the developer's twists in securing the site for Amazon.[34]

DANGEROUS JOBS

Interested to know who worked on the site, I occasionally stopped to talk or walk with day laborers who sometimes left the site for a break. Joshua, 24, was from Zimbabwe. Pangani, 34, came from Tanzania. Fortuné, 37, and Amadou, 28, were from the Democratic Republic of the Congo. These men came to South Africa to earn money to send home to their families. Pangani said the "sharks," unlicensed taxi drivers, picked them up at 6 a.m. from the informal migrant area of Kaya Township,[35] where they had no running water or electricity, and returned them after the workday ended. Other workers, all South African, arrived on flatbed trucks, traveling to the Amazon site without safety belts much less seats to sit on, in violation of South African national health and safety laws (figure 7).

Employers paid day laborers a few hundred Rands, or about US$10, a day, depending on what the workers did and how long they worked. There were no paid sick days, pensions, healthcare, or other supports for migrant workers. Joshua and Pangani set off dynamite. Fortuné and Amadou guided steel I-beams into place.

Fig. 7. Workers on truck leaving construction site, Cape Town, South Africa. Photo by author.

When I asked Amadou if he thought he and Fortuné received adequate pay, Amadou responded that Cape Town gave them more opportunities than their home countries. "We're not poor and not rich," Amadou said. "We're just earning enough to get by and send some home." Then he added, "But we'll never be as rich as Jeff Bezos!"

Bezos's wealth at that time was $214 billion, with daily earnings of around $321 million. He spent $5.5 billion for a four-minute ride into space and more than $500 million on a yacht. For $5.5 billion, by my calculation, he might have built brick housing for 20,000 Cape Town residents the previous year,[36] planted up to 5 billion trees globally, or paid hundreds of millions more tax dollars to governments internationally and increased wages for people working for Amazon developers.

Many Capetonians also thought along these lines. One opinion piece in the city newspaper compared Bezos to British industrialists who drove Welsh miners to their deaths and to Cecil Rhodes, who sent Africans in the late nineteenth century to his diamond and gold mines "underground to be killed in large numbers by what are euphemistically called 'accidents' and 'occupational diseases.'"[37]

Many Capetonians also wondered how many South Africans, as opposed to migrants from other countries, were actually employed by the project. At that time, unemployment had reached a staggering 29 percent, with pandemic lockdowns severely affecting hiring processes.[38] In an effort to demonstrate their commitment to hiring South African citizens, Amazon's developer co-hosted a job enrollment campaign in August.

Hundreds of people gathered at the enrollment site. This group was not the typical all-male assembly of construction workers arriving on unlicensed transportation; instead, it included men and women in their twenties, thirties, and forties. Some attendees traveled by city buses, while others arrived in private cars. Many had learned about the event through social media and personal connections and expected to be hired on the spot. However, upon arrival, they discovered that the drive was not intended to offer immediate jobs; instead, it was simply collecting names to create a database. This database would be used by Amazon and other future tenants when they were ready to hire.

One Capetonian man I met the following Monday morning, in his 40s, was utterly devastated. He had put his name in the database and brought his identification card to start working that Monday. But the contractors turned him away, saying they had enough workers for the day. He sat on the hill with his knees bent and hands near his head, holding his identification card. "I came all the way, paying the bus fare," and now he did not have a job to cover even his bus fare back.

At the job campaign event, Amazon's developer also relaunched its plan to establish a cultural heritage center, appearing to unify rather than divide indigenous First Nations and the Khoi and San people. The developer's spokesperson, Jody Aufrichtig, reaffirmed that the project had gone through extensive public approval procedures and asserted that the opponents would not be able to stop it. The developer's tactics of unfavorably reporting on the opponents' activities undercut the latter's fundraising efforts and ability to maintain momentum.[39]

Several months later, after the South African High Court ruled against the plaintiff OCA, the developer complained to the fundraising platform that the plaintiff's case and the entire antidevelopment OCA campaign were fraudulent.[40] The hosting platform froze the activists' campaign site and threatened to advise their donors that they could ask that their money be returned, severely disadvantaging the activists' financial wherewithal to continue with the court proceedings. The OCA agreed to pause its efforts but did not concede its case.

With their savvy public relations departments, US corporations and their subsidiaries are skilled in furthering such divisions within communities to further their development and land acquisition goals. In this South African case, developers' interests pitted indigenous groups against one another and took comments made out of context, then attributed those comments to the OCA to create animosity among the leadership. Facing extreme and unenviable pressure to unify its constituents, and flatly out of money, the OCA chose, "after much agonizing," to withdraw from the case.[41] In its closing letter to its constituents, the OCA asked, rhetorically, "Do we regret taking up the case?" and answered:

> This has been a long and bruising road and one which has seen opponents of the development vilified, threatened, defamed, libelled, subjected to anonymous smears and intimidated; our funding platform was targeted; we have seen a generously funded media machine fabricate propaganda against us on a mass scale. But we regret none of it because it was a fight for justice that had to challenge the power of rich men, the new VOC (Dutch East India Company), supported by Amazon, one of the wealthiest corporations in the world, to make decisions about land that is environmentally significant and a sacred heritage site for Indigenous peoples.[42]

By June 2023, the OCA had paused its legal action; it had run out of money and owed the developers 96 percent of its crowdfunding money in legal fees, which the developers then waived in exchange for the OCA dropping legal action against them.[43]

HIDING BEHIND A CLOUD

The Amazon-in-South-Africa case is a striking illustration of how foreign investors develop strategies to expropriate land and degrade the environment at the expense of cultural heritage and indigenous land rights. But to understand the full extent of Amazon's impact in South Africa, one must recognize that Amazon's developer built on this land for a particular kind of business, one that extends its market power through digital data mining and artificial intelligence.[44]

Although Amazon's developer generates some profit through land capitalization (as through buying land, then charging Amazon rent to use the site), property rental constitutes only a small part of shareholders' returns on investment. Amazon derives the full scope of its profits by using the site to strengthen its hold of the reigns of the e-commerce market in South Africa and the world. It does this through an array of corporate market strategies. The site offers the company specific opportunities to generate business by leveraging South Africa's laws and appealing to US property laws, helping it capture and convert digital data into capital for further investment. Operating in South Africa helps Amazon contain costs for its US owners by working through intermediaries who manage non-US legal cases. Indeed, as the name Amazon World Services indicates, AWS has a globally encompassing mission. To me, Amazon's expansion into South Africa not only raises concerns about a foreign corporation operating on culturally significant land but also illustrates how some global investors see Africa's digital data as a new resource of revenue growth.[45]

Amazon's domination in digital markets also raises significant concerns about data privacy and questions about what Amazon will do with the data it collects.[46] Some people may say that if Amazon does not monopolize the digital computing market, other companies with less interest in protecting consumer data will drive the industry. However, that argument does not preclude a different, more politically democratic, and economically equitable way to manage intellectual property and redistribute profits. In the current scenario, an Amazonian megalithic company arguably surpasses a government's ability to regulate activities within its sovereign borders. Ceding data to third parties is a concern not only in the United States but also in regions where countries may not have implemented legislation to secure data protection and privacy.

In the face of criticism that Amazon's market domination undermines people's ability to protect their interests—or their government's ability to do so—Amazon may respond by pointing out that it is not breaking any laws, but simply using the law—particularly US intellectual property law—to run its business. But such US corporate "lawfare"—using US intellectual property law to promote an unjust system—turns the law itself into another alibi to shield corporations from serious constraints on destructive business practices. "The law is on our side," the controlling entity affirms; "we are not breaking any rules." But this renunciation of blame, in my estimation, violates the code of ethics that Amazon has established for itself.[47]

AWS's expanded Cape Town site in Observatory provided a prime location for growing Amazon's African continental cloud computing. In 2023, AWS issued its "Investment in South Africa Economic Impact Study," boasting of Amazon's "ripple effects" and "local community impacts" across the continent.[48] On the surface, the Cape Town headquarters was to be another new hub for integrating up-continent online retailers and businesses with an international consumer market. However, on scrutiny, the impact statement indicates that AWS trades in more than "material" or "tangible" commodities. Like the intangible, immaterial "heritage" its developer discounted as "notional," the product that AWS trades in is much more profitable than items it sells online: digital data, which, according to US property law, remains under Amazon ownership.

When Amazon announced its expansion in Cape Town, many people working in the private sector were pleased and supportive. Internet development is crucial to transforming business operations by boosting internet speed and usage. Without mentioning Amazon, media outlets quickly repeated claims about the value of distributing data storage on globally connected servers; and it was about this time, as I recall from my morning routine in Cape Town, that disc jockeys and morning radio hosts on stations like Cape Town's Metro FM and *Cape Talk* began chatting about the benefits of cloud computing, helpful in converting radio channels to webcasts via websites. But also, at that time, most people in the general public and the media focused on the Cape Town site as a retail space for restaurants, a hotel, shops, even a private school—not on cloud computing—and even fewer knew that Amazon World Services was already operating in South Africa.

Back in 2016, AWS had opened a site in Johannesburg to move customers to the cloud, bypassing data storage on individual computing servers physically located in South Africa. The following year, AWS "expanded into Africa" (the expansionist language is Amazon's[49]) by connecting consumers directly to cloud computing, and eventually it launched "Amazon CloudFront" in Johannesburg and Cape Town to transfer data at high speeds.

"Think of cloud computing as like a handshake," one South African former Amazon employee, Jaco, told me over a meal in a restaurant. Instead of storing data on a single server, cloud providers distribute data across multiple data centers worldwide. "If one center goes down—let's say due to a crash or because it's scheduled for maintenance—cloud providers can redirect data from one center to another."

From Jaco's perspective, Amazon's capability to provide ground-based and, eventually, satellite-distributed connectivity would be a valuable asset for businesses in South Africa. However, while Jaco is likely correct that AWS will benefit some South Africans, he overlooks that AWS also owns the data passing through its proprietary platforms, which raises concerns about data privacy and user rights.

Per US property law, Amazon retains ownership of digital data that people generate when using its platforms, such as (in the United States) Alexa Internet or Amazon Prime. Much as, for instance, Coca-Cola remains the owner of its proprietary recipe licensed for use to overseas subsidiaries (discussed in chapter 1), and US biotechnology companies such as Corteva Agriscience retain ownership of genetically modified crops and farm input formulas (discussed in chapter 2), so Amazon retains sole intellectual property rights to user data generated on its digital platforms including Amazon Prime Video in South Africa. (Amazon Prime retail shopping is unavailable in South Africa, but the company is working on it.) By owning this data, Amazon can license its use to other companies, generating profits for itself.

In addition to licensing the data it gathers through its platforms, AWS also sells or freely offers products directly to South African consumers. These include an online "AWS InCommunities" product marketed as an educational game for children. RANGER challenges children to "catch a poacher with a net to save a rhino" while ostensibly teaching young people how to problem solve and code on their phones.[50] In the Amazon game, students catch a poacher for claiming ownership of that which does not belong to the poacher—not unlike white settlers poaching indigenous land four centuries ago, though RANGER does not consider that historical overlap. Instead, there is a less tangible form of digital data poaching. South Africans' use of the platform generates data that, when clustered and recoded, Amazon can use to scope new markets and sell to other companies. Some would counter that Amazon should not own that data; it should not poach from online users who do not know how their data profits others. AWS follows this practice everywhere, but South African media that covered the project neglected to note this data collection. The *New York Times* also ignored this aspect in its article about the project.[51]

While some governments contest the right of AWS, a US-based company, to collect and bundle non–US citizens' data, not all countries do, deferring to US laws on the issue. And according to US law, AWS holds the right to store data in the United States that it collects globally. With appropriate warrants, the South African government can demand that AWS return some data, but in general South African officials agree to the US technology behemoth's terms because they hope to keep Amazon invested in South Africa. This course of action—agreeing to US-based multinational corporations' terms to keep them invested in the country—occurs across the continent and indeed around the world, to the detriment of local competitors' and governments' abilities to advocate for their citizens' privacy and consumer rights.[52] In addition, since most of the taxes imposed on Amazon's revenue from its South African business are collected in the United States rather than South Africa, the international business model prevents the South African government from receiving tax revenues from consumer spending to support domestic programs.

By its own proclamation, Amazon World Services trades on the world's turf. Amazon's online US corporate ethics statement ("Our Positions") declares: "We are committed to helping build a country *and a world* where everyone can live with dignity and free from fear" (my emphasis). Amazon continues: "We will use our position as a large employer to support innovative housing affordability initiatives. And, in locations where we have a sizeable presence, we will invest directly in efforts where we believe our financial support will make a difference." Other Amazon's "Our Positions" bullets state authoritatively:

- The inequitable treatment of Black people is unacceptable.
- Human-induced climate change is real and serious, and action is needed from the public and private sectors.
- We strongly support the rights of immigrants and immigration reform.
- All people should have access to housing they can afford.

Yet low-cost labor undertaken primarily by Black and Colored South Africans, destruction of a fragile ecosystem, and the indirect hiring of immigrants and housing-insecure people all characterized Amazon's development project in South Africa. Tactics along the lines of creating a code of ethics called "Our Positions" hid the obvious fact that "white local developers, foreign investors like Amazon, and government officials stand the most to gain from the development."[53] Rather than offering a solution to poverty, the Amazon project appeared to many to be eerily reminiscent of colonial-era land expropriation that took place centuries ago.

BOTTOM LINE: PEOPLE TALK

Officially, Amazon Inc. never commented on the South African court case or environmental and First Nations interests. Perhaps Amazon's developer did not know who its subcontractors hired or where those migrant laborers were from—possibly not even those subcontractors knew (such are the measures for securing jobs when people need them).

Jeff Bezos, the CEO of Amazon Inc., the "cornerstone tenant" of the development project, received a letter from the OCA via registered mail. The letter warned against building on land sacred to First Nations and on a sensitive ecological floodplain (figure 8). But Bezos did not respond.

South Africans of many social and political demographics closely follow stories in the South African media about the United States, including Amazon labor relations.[54] For example, when Amazon employees in the United States voted to unionize and press for improved working conditions and higher pay, and a judge ruled in their favor,[55] the South African media picked up on the news. One Capetonian, commenting on Amazon's

60 Trill Road
Observatory
7925
7th October 2020

Mr Jeff Bezos
CEO: Amazon
410 Terry Ave, N Seattle
WA 98109-5210

Dear Mr Bezos

The River Club project: Proposed construction of Amazon's new regional headquarters in Cape Town on land sacred to First Nations and a sensitive ecological floodplain

I write to you as the chair of the Observatory Civic Association, a local organisation representing residents and businesses of the suburb of Observatory in Cape Town, where the owners of the Liesbeek Leisure Property Trust (LLPT) propose to construct a massive 150 000m² Mixed Use development on land that is sacred to First Nations and is a sensitive ecological floodplain

We wrote to you previously by email on the 18th March 2020 to alert you to this situation at that stage, to which we did not receive a reply. By registered mail, we want to ensure that you are able to make an informed decision, based on due diligence, as to your investment in the River Club project.

As anchor tenant in this development, we believe your investment will forever associate Amazon with everything you would not wish to stand for: environmental destruction, greed over protection of heritage and the environment and a complete abdication of any commitment to addressing climate change.

We urge you to reconsider your involvement in the project and withdraw. We would love to hear a public statement from Amazon agreeing with us and the tens of thousands of South Africa who believe this development is simply wrong.

I explain this all in more detail overleaf.

Best wishes

Leslie London

Leslie London

Fig. 8a. October 7, 2020, letter from the Observatory Civic Association to Jeff Bezos. Source: Leslie London.

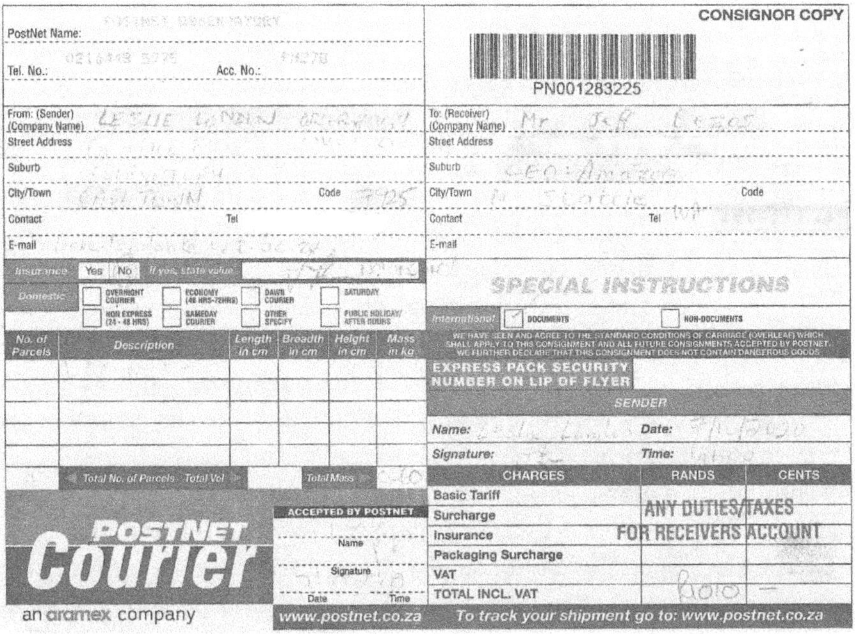
CONSIGNOR COPY

PN001283225

PostNet Name:

Tel. No.: Acc. No.:

From: (Sender) (Company Name)

Street Address

Suburb

City/Town Code

Contact Tel

E-mail

Insurance Yes No If yes, state value

Domestic: OVERNIGHT COURIER; ECONOMY (48 HRS-72HRS); DAWN COURIER; SATURDAY; NON EXPRESS (24-48 HRS); SAMEDAY COURIER; OTHER SPECIFY; PUBLIC HOLIDAY/ AFTER HOURS

No. of Parcels	Description	Length in cm	Breadth in cm	Height in cm	Mass in kg

Total No. of Parcels Total Vol Total Mass

To: (Receiver) (Company Name) Mr

Street Address

Suburb

City/Town Code

Contact Tel

E-mail

SPECIAL INSTRUCTIONS

International: DOCUMENTS NON-DOCUMENTS

WE HAVE SEEN AND AGREE TO THE STANDARD CONDITIONS OF CARRIAGE (OVERLEAF) WHICH SHALL APPLY TO THIS CONSIGNMENT AND ALL FUTURE CONSIGNMENTS ACCEPTED BY POSTNET. WE FURTHER DECLARE THAT THIS CONSIGNMENT DOES NOT CONTAIN DANGEROUS GOODS

EXPRESS PACK SECURITY NUMBER ON LIP OF FLYER

SENDER

Name: Date:

Signature: Time:

CHARGES	RANDS	CENTS
Basic Tariff		
Surcharge	ANY DUTIES/TAXES	
Insurance	FOR RECEIVERS ACCOUNT	
Packaging Surcharge		
VAT		
TOTAL INCL. VAT		

ACCEPTED BY POSTNET

Name

Signature

Date Time

POSTNET Courier an aramex company

www.postnet.co.za To track your shipment go to: www.postnet.co.za

Fig. 8b. The courier's receipt documenting delivery of the letter. Source: Leslie London.

extensive history of racialized and questionable labor practices in the United States, where racialized capitalism is barely spoken about, wrote: "Amazon's well-documented brutal conditions of warehouse work do not show it to be a tenant capable of contributions to apartheid reparations" in South Africa. "Apartheid spatial reparations," the writer continued, "require careful spatial planning . . . to repair both ecological and economic harms built into the city's design since the 1600s, in which the Liesbeek River has been a central player as a boundary line between wealth and poverty."[56] In South Africa, AWS has built its headquarters and its cloud computing business there on a legacy of land expropriation and resource extraction that fueled the colonial conquest of Africa through the late twentieth century. Despite the formal end of colonial political and military control, Amazon's investment model in South Africa underscores how this pattern of unequal economic relations continues in the twenty-first century.

REPRISE

Like the Coca-Cola Foundation in Tanzania and Corteva Agriscience in South Africa, the Amazon-in-South-Africa project is a prime example of a US corporation operating through a private contractor or subsidiary. In each of these cases, US corporations have portrayed themselves as "charitable" in helping "impoverished" or "underresourced" Africans, a subtle rehash of deficit theory. They use the job creation and investments narrative to paint a picture of community salvation. However, in every case, the corporation also conveniently overlooks the broader context of its operations, focusing instead on the details that make its project appear generous. The companies' self-serving narratives portray them as saviors sacrificing for "poor Africa."

Through mediators, "cheap" labor, and the media, Amazon constructs a narrative that investors are eager to manage. However, the untold truth is that the developers' consolidated land acquisition for financialization operates under a veil of an intangible strategy. Many aspects of value in a construction project begin with intangibility: a promise of earnings, a future with jobs, a space where, in the developer's view, nothing now stands but where a better world will unfold.

Whether knowingly or not, new land tenants are stepping into a landscape shaped by past social forces and memories. These intangible aspects, vividly remembered if not physically visible, are a constant presence in the minds of locals, with daily reminders all around.[57] The names of places indicate who has lived there; contemporary family names identify forebears, and the ideologies of attachment to the land all articulate how people connect to one another, including with the deceased.[58]

In South Africa, land acquisition triggers a sense of historical déjà vu whereby many feel they are reliving the displacement experienced by their ancestors.[59]

Writing about the world financial system as an intangible social reality, anthropologist Frances E. Mascia-Lees has emphasized how racialized and economic disparities between colonizers and colonized people continue into the twenty-first century.[60] American public affairs scholar Manning Marable refers to this situation as "global apartheid," or "the racialized division and stratification of resources, wealth, and power" that separates Europe and North America "from the billions of mostly black, brown, indigenous, undocumented immigrant and poor people across the planet."[61] In South Africa, memories of apartheid and land loss support the narrative that the Amazon expansion represents whiteness and is a foreign invasion posing a threat.[62]

To comprehend how this intangible system rests on overlapping ideological "jurisdictions," many anthropologists turn to Achille Mbembe's work on deterritorialized sovereignty.[63] Mbembe discusses *deterritorialization* as a process whereby different state, traditional, religious, and other jurisdictions coexist to create borders separating autochthons from foreigners. Deterritorialization helps in exploring the entanglement of social boundaries that span judicial-political geographies. At the nexus of physical and social territories, "ordinary" and "powerful" groups entwine and reproduce or transform power. Mbembe points to regimes in colonial-era and postindependence Africa and to private security and surveillance forces, which he calls "private indirect government," to argue that sovereign power creates a particular closeness between ruler and ruled, a form of "conviviality" that goes beyond any simple binary that paints some as winners and others as victims.

Mbembe does not name global corporations engaged in mass data collection and sale (Industry 4.0) as a form of private indirect government, but he might have. Transnational technology companies such as Amazon World Services imprint themselves politically, economically, and socially in overlapping jurisdictions that span continents. Because this technology connects a constellation of territories, Industry 4.0's infrastructure operates through specific people, policies, and protocols. Using fees and laws, the developer in Observatory fenced in and enclosed opponents. While no overt plan or protocol drove the project, a closeness or conviviality among investors, including LLPT's stakeholders, did.

The political economy of this world financial system overlays corporate activities onto deterritorialized legal structures that reproduce and sustain global inequities. In the event, chumminess in the form of a *private capital investment disposition* greases the world's proverbial construction sites. Some Khoi investors accepted the project. "In the instance of the River Club [Amazon project], it is our belief," Chief Khoisan of the pro-development group said, "that we have removed ourselves from the evil gridlock of government paper pushing," adding that the developers, unlike the government, responded to their pain.[64] Others, most living close to the engineering tremors, felt extreme unease at the devastation.

The Coca-Cola Company hid its water extraction and pollution in Tanzania by sending profits to its charitable foundation in Atlanta. The Amazon case illustrates that hiding behind a private subsidiary or subcontractor obfuscates what is happening in communities. Similarly, Corteva Agriscience's claims of creating more sustainable farming across the African continent distorts that monocropping and seed monopolies undermine small-holding farmers and their communities. What all three cases have in common is that US corporations collaborate with local, provincial, and national officials in presenting private benefits as a public good. In this Amazon case, private investors consolidated alienated public land (bought at a bargain basement price) and transferred ownership to a private trust that then leased office space to Amazon.

Amazon implies its neutrality by hiding behind US tax and property law, claiming no South African jurisdiction, which advances Amazon's work by default. In the event, influential leaders with capital to invest collaborate with US investors for mutual benefit.

US corporations are not exceptional in benefiting from waging "lawfare." Nor are corporations entirely to blame. But the case of Amazon shows how transnational investors, local developers, and City of Cape Town officials used their resources to draw opponents over to their side.

4   Big Pharma, Big Donors

On a warm Southern Hemisphere day in Cape Town in early January 2022, I met with Lawrence, a police officer, whom I had first met the previous year. We spent some time that day discussing the COVID pandemic, which was spreading worldwide. There was still much uncertainty about what the pandemic meant for communities and people's long-term health. At the time, US and European pharmaceutical companies were feverishly producing their new COVID-19 vaccines, but African countries were largely unable to purchase them or produce any on their own.

"The worst part is," Lawrence said, with frustration bordering on anger, "these international companies are playing Russian roulette with our lives."

Despite making significant profits at the time, US pharmaceutical companies declined to share COVID vaccine formulas with low- and middle-income countries. Concerns about intellectual property rights, quality control, profitability, and existing contracts with wealthier nations contributed to this reluctance. This decision hindered global vaccination efforts and exacerbated the disparities in access to lifesaving medicines.

"Big Pharma companies have taken ownership of the vaccine," Officer Lawrence continued, using the term "Big Pharma" to refer to multinational companies wielding powerful pro-industry influence over governments. "They won't share their recipes with African scientists. They take us for granted, play God with our lives, and treat us like guinea pigs," he rumbled.

Lawrence had good reason to distrust the decisions and motivations of Big Pharma. Large pharmaceutical companies have a history of engaging in unethical and harmful practices in Africa. In the past, foreign biomedical companies conducted experiments and tested developmental formulas on African people before selling their products to higher-paying markets outside Africa.[1] Lawrence's referenced this history with his "guinea pigs" remark. Indeed, the history of foreign pharmaceutical companies in Africa has often been scandalous and disturbing, and it continues to cast a long shadow over people's views of those companies.

Like e-commerce and data-mining companies such as Amazon and water-extracting companies such as Coca-Cola, the biomedical industry often presents a narrative of "helping" that can obscure the complexities of their operations in Africa. While the formal era of colonial rule has ended, foreign-owned biomedical companies still navigate a landscape shaped by historical dynamics, sometimes leveraging altruistic narratives to advance their interests. Additionally, foreign private foundations often collaborate with peers in industry, leading to the extraction of resources and knowledge. This dynamic can create a sense of frustration and distrust among medical professionals and the general population in Africa, highlighting the importance of ensuring that African voices are integral to discussions about healthcare and development.

One philanthropic organization collaborating with the biomedical industry in Africa, which health officials often criticize, is the Gates Foundation, co-founded in 2000 by Bill and Melinda Gates.[2]

During our conversation in Cape Town, Lawrence expressed his frustrations and opinions about the operations of the Gates Foundation in Africa. "I've done my research," he said. "Bill and Melinda have this big global foundation in America that they're using to make money, *MON-EY*, from us Africans."

Lawrence's concerns about foreign pharmaceutical companies and US foundations—particularly the Bill & Melinda Gates Foundation and its allied Global Fund—reflect the sentiments of many scientists and doctors across Africa.[3] Their concerns extend beyond COVID. Fourteen months after that meeting with Lawrence, while I was in Tanzania riding to the airport, I spoke with Dr. Urassa, a fifty-five-year-old Tanzanian doctor with an MD and PhD in medicine and a post in the Tanzanian Health Ministry. He expressed frustration with pharmaceutical companies' self-serving approach to working in African countries. Specifically, he highlighted their refusal to grant African scientists, doctors, and public health officials access to the data those companies compiled, from (among other sources) the services and medications they provided to treat HIV/AIDS, tuberculosis, and malaria.[4]

"US pharmaceutical companies have no desire to end diseases in Africa," Dr. Urassa said. "They want to send their medicines here and take control of our public health systems so they can collect data to study and tweak their formulas. If they really wanted to help us, they'd share more information." Urassa's criticism pointed to Big Pharma's role in trading medicine for data and using data to create huge profits for shareholders and, ultimately, to wield political influence over governments.

Dr. Urassa, too, named the Gates Foundation and US pharmaceutical companies as co-conspirators controlling the Tanzanian public health system. "While many people in these agencies are generous and good-willed," he observed, "they are not part of the leadership team, and they don't know the larger picture of the pharmaceutical industry."

Established in 2000 by Microsoft founder Bill Gates, the Gates Foundation is one of the largest charitable foundations in the world, holding more than $70 billion in net assets in 2023.[5] Between 2021 and 2022, the foundation assisted the Geneva-based organization Gavi, the Vaccine Alliance, which it cofounded in the early 2000s, in delivering 4.1 million doses of Pfizer COVID vaccines to Tanzania.[6]

In donating vast sums to global health charities, Bill and Melinda Gates appeared to have been securing their legacies as selfless benefactors, nurturing the health and well-being of future generations. But there is, I suggest, more than altruism behind their work. They invest in a circular market economy that also benefits their trust financially (figure 9). A trust is a larger, controlling entity that supersedes a foundation and provides gifts to individuals, groups of individuals, and foundations. As donors, the Gateses contribute their earnings to the Bill & Melinda Gates Foundation

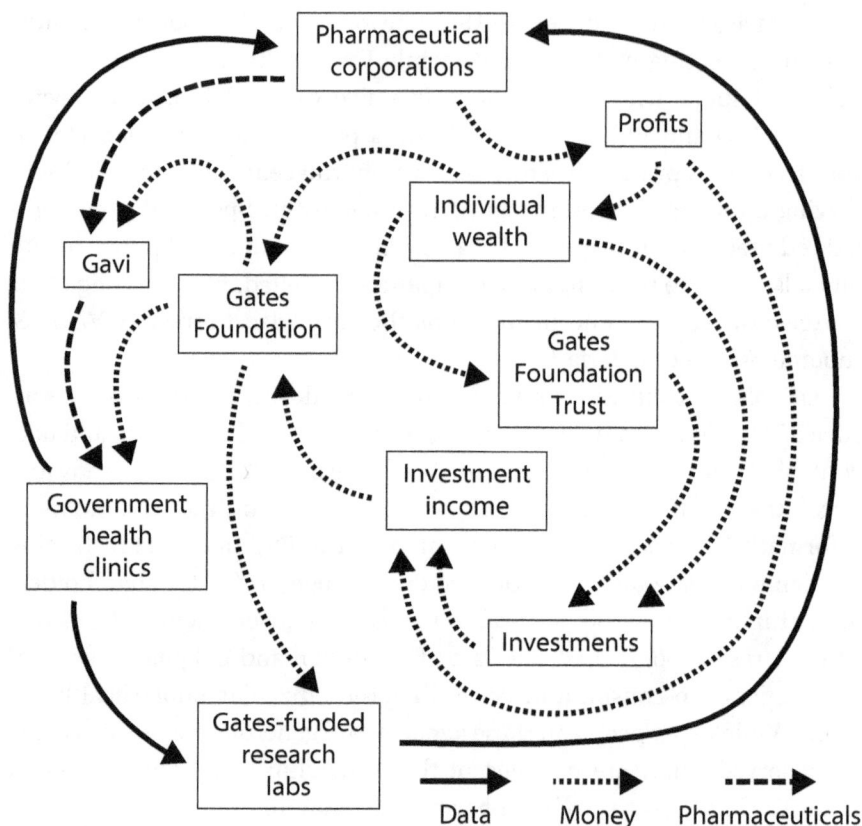

Fig. 9. The circular pharmaceutical economy. Because the Gates Foundation partners closely with the Global Fund, the latter is not represented separately in this figure but should be understood to be represented within the Gates Foundation node. Drawing by author.

Trust. This trust then collaborates with an asset management company that invests the Gateses' money in Berkshire Hathaway, which invests in Pfizer.[7] Pfizer sells pharmaceuticals internationally to high-income countries, making money for the Bill & Melinda Gates Foundation Trust. Beneficiaries of the trust include but need not be limited to the Bill & Melinda Gates Foundation. Generally, a donor establishes a trust to transfer wealth to children and avoid paying gift and estate taxes.

To avoid paying taxes on investment earnings in the form of dividend income, the Bill & Melinda Gates Foundation Trust donates or delivers "gifts" to the Bill & Melinda Gates Foundation. The Bill & Melinda Gates Foundation (simply the Gates Foundation since 2024, as I call it hereafter) donates that untaxed trust income to charities, including Gavi. Then, using untaxed Gates Foundation funds earned partly from Big Pharma companies, Gavi (a nongovernmental organization in Switzerland) pays Pfizer to send vaccines to Africa.[8] Pfizer and the Gates Foundation then present this provision of vaccines in Africa as altruism. But according to Dr. Urassa, these vaccines come with stipulations. For example, government doctors, such as Dr. Urassa, are not allowed access to even basic health data from the uses of these products, including changes in body weight and blood counts.[9] Pfizer also requires health workers who administer these vaccines to allow the company's research and development team to collect and use data in creating new products for the market. In essence, billionaires' untaxed trust money controls African doctors who use companies' pharmaceuticals that enrich billionaires' trust funds, and a big pharmaceutical company gets free data it can use to tweak and improve its formulas. Meanwhile, needing vaccines and other medications, the Tanzanian government has little power to advocate against these rules.

The frustration that Dr. Urassa and Officer Lawrence expressed about the selfishness of the Gates's charity is shared by some other public health officials in African countries. "Donor data vacuuming" is not unique to the Gates Foundation's work in Tanzania.[10] In Côte d'Ivoire, Kenya, Lesotho, and Mozambique, foundations control health information access, flow, and use. In 2021, thirteen African governments representing more than ten thousand public health clinics on the continent received money from the Gates-supported Global Fund to reduce rates of COVID infections as well as HIV, tuberculosis, and malaria. But, according to Urassa, the Global Fund prohibited clinicians working in those clinics from accessing their own citizens' health records. Data about patient health outcomes and medications' efficacy could be reported only to the Global Fund, the pharmaceutical company, or Gavi—according to the terms those Gates-allied organizations set prior to providing medicines.[11]

"These agencies deliver medicines, but they don't allow our government or doctors to keep track of basic health data from our citizens who participate in their programs." I had to ask Dr. Urassa to repeat this several times because I could not believe it. He clarified: Any Tanzanian clinic whose doctors or nurses treat patients enrolled in Gates-funded health campaigns are not permitted to report data from those campaigns to the Tanzanian government; they must report data directly to the donor organizations or companies.[12] Consequently, Dr. Urassa, a medical doctor and Tanzanian government health official, cannot get population-wide data on mortality rates or causes of death for patients enrolled in the Global Fund–backed Gavi health programs.

"Imagine not even giving your hosting country that information!" he said. "I work for the health ministry, and even I don't know how many people die from AIDS who are on new medicines." He added, "The Global Fund used to provide such data on their website, up to 2013. But since then, there is no information, not in their annual reports or meetings with our government."

Moreover, health clinics funded by the Global Fund cannot share basic body mass index (BMI) information for patients enrolled in the programs it supports. "If I had even the minimal BMI numbers for all HIV-positive patients every time they checked into a donor-funded health clinic, I could correlate their changes in BMI with registration at the AZT clinic [the clinic that administers Azidothymidine, which delays the development of AIDS] even if I never knew the cause of mortality directly. Why don't these agencies want us to know the efficacy of the medicines they give us?" he asked. "I can only infer they don't want to partner with us to cure diseases in Africa, but they want to keep sending us medicines."

Dr. Urassa verified Lawrence's streetwise hunch about the biomedical industry that pharmaceutical companies control distribution and supplies and withhold information about medicines' efficacy from African scientists in order to continue collecting data from host countries.

But there was more.

"On top of all this, we don't even know what we are getting," Dr. Urassa continued. "Governments participating in donor-funded global health programs do not have access to the recipes, the formulas, for the drugs we receive because the pharmaceutical companies own the biotechnology." Companies like Pfizer, Abbott, Moderna, and others retain the intellectual property rights to the patented formulas for COVID vaccines and HIV antiretroviral medicines.[13] Every time one of their products is provided or purchased, even with donor funds, the corporations benefit financially.

This profit comes not only from the sale of the vaccine or medicine but also from the potential to collect population-level data from Tanzania. They may use this data to refine their formulas for more lucrative markets while withholding this information from the Tanzanian government and health professionals. The Gates Foundation and others give to Gavi, which donates medicines to countries but also advises which formulas to use. Pfizer and Moderna used Gavi's funds to send COVID vaccines to Tanzania and other African countries. Again, not wanting to benefit competitors by sharing formulas with public health scientists, pharmaceutical companies kept their recipes secret and proprietary.[14]

"And because they own the formulae, we never know what we're getting. We are the end users [of pharmaceuticals]," Dr. Urassa remonstrated, "and we don't even know what we are using." Nor do most Tanzanians know they are serving as guinea pigs. Most do not sign or receive a consent form, and, especially in rural regions, where 60 percent of the population lives, many people are not well versed in the health and science research frameworks needed to make informed decisions about medicines.[15]

"They're making money," Officer Lawrence assured me that day in Cape Town. "Everybody is making money at the expense of the general public." He lamented that the South African media insisted people buy sanitizers and masks when most couldn't afford food. "People have lost their jobs, and they want them to buy sanitizers?" Similar concerns about profiteering and job loss circulated in the United States; they were not unique to Africa.

Many were also rightly frustrated with the way government agencies and multilateral organizations set rules that disadvantage African countries. Lawrence, who had indeed done his research, called out the World Health Organization, the United Nations agency responsible for setting policies and procedures to manage global public health. "Who is WHO?" Lawrence asked. "Who 'owns' it? Again, I have done my research. The WHO is under the control of Gavi and the Gates Foundation."

Although funding for the WHO comes from many countries, Lawrence is correct that the Gates Foundation has been intricately involved in the WHO's work. During the first year of the COVID pandemic, the Gates Foundation—along with Gavi and others—gave $1.4 billion directly to the WHO to create a distribution network for COVID-19 vaccines, particularly in Africa.[16] However, that network fell under the direction of nongovernmental organizations (NGOs) including Gavi, not the WHO, and failed to meet its initial distribution goals because of the decentralized NGO system. Many observers and doctors criticized the Gates Foundation and other donors for unduly influencing WHO policy.[17] This critique also came from US health officials. As one former senior US health official put it: "They [Gavi and the Gates Foundation] have very, very powerful influence within multilateral organizations—equal to or above governments."[18]

For people aware of how this system works, including Lawrence and Dr. Urassa, the situation is infuriating. "Who do they think they are?" Lawrence asked. "A government? A country?" Of course, he already knew the answer: the Gates Foundation is not a government agency and it does not represent a people. The Gates Foundation's work, promoted by the foundation as humanitarian in intent and outcome, comes with rules that stipulate how its donations are used. The foreign donor–controlled system appears to prevent African public health officials from tracking the effects of those medicines on their citizens, all while generating financial benefits for the companies and foundations' donors. Like Amazon, Coca-Cola, and Bayer Monsanto, the Gates Foundation shields from public view its own wealth-reinforcing contributions, using an alibi of serving the public good while operating in ways that clearly work against that objective.

MEDICAL MISTRUST AND SUSPICION OF BIG PHARMA

During the global COVID-19 pandemic, the Gates Foundation, more than any other private entity, leveraged its wealth to influence the pharmaceutical industry and international health policy. To Lawrence and Dr. Urassa, the Gates Foundation and Western agencies placed Africa and African governments on the wrong side of history. When Melinda Gates warned that if the world did not act fast enough, there would be dead bodies on the streets of African countries, people in Tanzania took offense at her underestimation of the continent's twenty-first-century infrastructure.[19] Others heard her words as a prediction that Africans certainly would die, a shadow under which no one wanted to live. Still others objected to Melinda Gates's assumption that the Gates Foundation would act as

Africa's savior, likening it to the claims of missionaries and the narrative in Kipling's "The White Man's Burden." They argued that her reasoning reflected a long-standing belief—an excuse story, an alibi[20]—that wealthy westerners have a responsibility to intervene in Africa.

Racialized tensions developed over centuries of medical experimentation in Africa as millions of people on the continent were subjected to biomedical experiments, making them human fodder for research on various epidemics and diseases. In light of this history, the Gates Foundation's intervention looked, to Lawrence, Dr. Urassa, and many others, much like painful colonial déjà vu. During the German occupation (1884–1916) and under British colonial rule (1916–1961), foreign administrations coerced Tanganyikans—people living in what is now known as Tanzania—into surrendering their blood and other bodily fluids to international researchers. These researchers conducted tests that included deliberately exposing research subjects to microfilaria infection caused by roundworms and drawing midnight blood samples from every patient admitted to a Dar es Salaam hospital for a six-month period. In 1937, German occupiers of Namibia subjected Namibian children to forced sterilization experiments.[21] Colonial governments carried out "research" of this kind across the continent in hospitals, clinics, labs, and medical colleges where victims were explicitly selected based on race. Medical researchers used Black and Colored bodies for experiments without most people's knowledge or consent. All of these investigations, like the ignominious "Tuskegee Study of Untreated Syphilis in the Negro Male," conducted in the United States between 1932 and 1972, reproduced and rested on an ideology of white superiority that subjected nonwhite people to experimentation.[22]

In the past, as today, significant funding for public health research and medicine came from wealthy private philanthropists. In 1939, the Rockefeller family, which then owned Standard Oil (predecessor of ExxonMobil and Chevron), created a business alliance among multiple companies called the Drug Trust. The Trust, which included the German chemical industry Farben (today Bayer), Kellogg's (the food company), and the pharmaceutical corporation Bristol-Myers Squibb, financed medical research and pharmaceutical development in Africa.[23]

In Nigeria in the 1940s, to test a new treatment for yellow fever, Rockefeller scientists introduced the disease into an area where people had likely never been exposed to the virus.[24] By the 1950s, six hundred Nigerians had died of yellow fever, and in Ethiopia in the 1960s a devastating outbreak killed thirty thousand people. Manufacturing an outbreak to develop and market a vaccine (the virus is now nearly eradicated) is the epitome of medical imperialism. It shows why people in Africa today are critical of the "humanitarian" missions of foreign foundations like the Gates Foundation and the tactics of pharmaceutical companies working in countries on the African continent. Deliberately creating life-threatening danger for profit matches our understanding today of a crime against humanity, an inhumane act intentionally causing serious injury to bodily health in a civilian population.[25]

Health officials in South Africa and Tanzania—and, indeed, in many other countries—have been forthright in voicing their concerns about these kinds of crimes. As Sarah Cooper, senior scientist at the South African Medical Research Council's Cochrane Centre, told the media at the height of the COVID-19 pandemic: "Over the last few decades, there have been various incidents of medical research conducted in Africa which have involved gross human rights abuses."[26] These incidents include, for example, a 1996 West African meningitis epidemic during which the American pharmaceutical corporation Pfizer tested an experimental medication, Trovan, on two hundred children in Kano, Nigeria, without their parent's consent.[27] Pfizer's experimentation was egregiously unethical and created a context of fear and distrust that put people's health at serious risk afterward. For example, although the polio vaccine is safe and saves lives, five northern Nigerian states in 2003 boycotted the Western-made polio vaccination, remembering the 1996 Pfizer catastrophe. In the 1990s and again in 2014, East Africans boycotted oral polio vaccination for a similar reason.[28] In 1994, the US National Institutes of Health funded AZT trials to reduce mother-to-child HIV transmission for approximately 925 women in Côte d'Ivoire, Burkina Faso, Malawi, and Uganda, many of whom did not fully understand the implications of their consent, including whether they received a placebo and what that would mean. During the trial, some women transmitted HIV to their unborn children, causing public outrage in local, national, and international communities and driving American doctors to call for a change in US overseas research policies.[29]

In early 2020, AstraZeneca and the University of Oxford conducted human trials of a COVID-19 vaccine in South Africa. The experiments fueled some South Africans' concerns that people of color were again, as during the colonial era and at the height of the 1990s HIV/AIDS pandemic, being used for experimental testing. The government assured those concerned that the country would receive one of the first batches of vaccines once they were ready. But that never happened.[30]

Reports of HIV-positive women sterilized without their knowledge have emerged in Kenya and other countries. Kenya's Family Planning Guidelines require informed and voluntary permission for sterilization. But more than a decade ago, a US-based 501(c)(3) organization named Children Requiring a Caring Kommunity [sic], called Project Prevention on its website, offered $40.00 to women in Kenya living with HIV who agreed to being fitted with an intrauterine birth control device.[31] Some of that organization's charitable donations came through the AmazonSmile Foundation, another 501(c)(3) entity, this one much larger, created by Amazon Inc.[32]

AmazonSmile allowed a shopper on Amazon to select a charitable organization of their choice, then donated 0.5 percent of their purchase to that charity.[33] Children Requiring a Caring Kommunity, operating as Project Prevention in Kenya, convinced a handful of Kenyan clinicians to fit women with an IUD.[34] However, while implanting the device, it appears that some clinicians sterilized women without those women's consent and misled them into thinking that HIV-positive women needed to stop having children. Indeed, Project Prevention's work in the United States advises HIV-positive women to consider sterilization,[35] lending plausibility to the possibility that Kenyan clinicians adopted this perspective. A few years after the project opened, more than forty HIV-positive Kenyan women went to court to seek compensation, some of them naming other nongovernmental health providers as well. Additional women filed suits in Zambia, South Africa, Malawi, and Namibia. Finally, in 2023, after eight years of litigation, the Kenyan High Court ruled that the women's forced sterilization violated their human rights. But it did not mention the two US-based 501(c)(3) charities that provided the financial backing for Project Prevention's dangerous approaches to treatment in Kenya.[36]

A US-GATES BIOMEDICAL EMPIRE

Foreign pharmaceutical companies in South Africa are facing criticism for what many South Africans see as a long history of unjust and immoral practices. Despite its industrial capacity, South Africa does not have a robust vaccine manufacturing industry, which has been a source of frustration for the country's leaders.

Back in Cape Town in 2022, during the COVID pandemic, while Amazon was rapidly building its African continental headquarters there, the US-based company NantWorks launched a new vaccine-manufacturing facility in Cape Town, the first to promise end-to-end manufacturing for COVID vaccines in South Africa. At about that same time—from November 2021 to early January 2022—many governments, including the United States, restricted travel to and from South Africa, where scientists first isolated the COVID Omicron variant in November, due to concerns about its spread.

South African president Cyril Ramaphosa, himself heavily invested financially in US companies,[37] countered Western media and governments' characterization of the Omicron variant, arguing that the international travel ban unjustly stigmatized the African continent. "Africa's old colonial masters," Ramaphosa said, saw Africa through a racist lens and perpetuated a narrative of fear of encountering a "diseased black body" on the continent, even while COVID was prevalent worldwide and the Omicron variant was already spreading rapidly in the United States. Despite protests from South Africa's leaders, the Western media continued to portray South Africa and its people through this lens of fear, illustrating Ramaphosa's point.

Disregarding Western stereotypes, Ramaphosa championed the NantWorks venture as "a bold step to unite biotechnology and pharmaceutical companies, government agencies, non-profit organizations, and academia."[38] Although NantWorks was a US company, its CEO, Patrick Soon-Shiong, was a South African. Soon-Shiong was born in South Africa to ethnic Hakka parents who fled China during the Japanese occupation, and it was his family foundation that financed the African Union's then-new vaccination program, Accelerate Africa's Access to Advanced Healthcare (AAAH). At AAAH's opening celebration in Cape Town,

President Ramaphosa introduced Soon-Shiong, who had flown in from the United States, as a South African "coming home" to his native country.[39]

Pfizer's reputation in South Africa was still so tainted by its dishonest vaccination of children in Nigeria in 1996 that a business associated with a South African CEO seemed more trustworthy in 2022 than a giant US pharmaceutical company. However, debates about the importance of having the vaccine also intersected with concerns about existing social problems, including extreme wealth and income inequality and the lack of basic services in many parts of the country, particularly in impoverished areas of Cape Town.[40] The previous year, a WhatsApp text circulated widely suggesting that—reflecting Lawrence's view—the World Health Organization and the South African government immorally prioritized "the jab" over water and electricity for the "poor, unemployed people who live in unfinished RDP [Reconstruction and Development Program] houses and shacks."[41] South Africans also questioned whether they were getting accurate information from the media and whether their voices were being heard. A few weeks after the WhatsApp message circulated, South Africans interpreted Facebook's and YouTube's removal of posts about vaccines as "suppressing free speech" and as "typical of the capitalists [who seek] to control the Covid-19 vaccine narrative."[42] South Africans' many years of fighting apartheid was morphing easily into a critique of the privatized corporate control of healthcare and medicine.

The criticism of foreign pharmaceutical companies intensified in the months that followed. On November 12, 2021, when it was reported that "Pfizer has made billions in profits from their Covid vaccine," many social media users began referring to US pharmaceutical corporations as "modern-day drug dealers."[43] Many accused the company of running "a money scheme" to line the pockets of US shareholders. The South African government echoed that message when it announced that "Pfizer is profiting from vaccine sales." Despite much fanfare, a year after its official opening in South Africa, the NantWorks project that Ramaphosa had championed as bringing vaccine production to South Africa had still not moved forward. As a result, South Africa, like many other countries, relied heavily on foreign pharmaceutical companies and donors, including Pfizer and the Gates Foundation, for vaccines. But this reliance on the very foreign companies and foundations that South Africa had learned to distrust was extremely frustrating to many in the country.

One South African university professor told me that Ramaphosa's earlier focus on Soon-Shiong's company had been driven simply by "a bit of South African nationalism"—not necessarily because Soon-Shiong was born in South Africa but because Soon-Shiong's vaccine production project there offered South Africa an alternative to the Gates-Gavi-WTO-Pfizer empire. Ramaphosa had hoped that having external funding to start an in-country pharmaceutical company would help push back against the foreign control of South Africa's healthcare system. But in the end, the South African government's efforts to work outside the orbit of the Gates Foundation were unsuccessful.

MEDICAL NEED, VULNERABILITY, AND QUESTIONS OF RESPONSIBILITY

Despite some African governments' and healthcare officials' displeasure with the way foreign-owned pharmaceutical companies and the Gates Foundation operated in their countries, many people living there nevertheless continued to rely on the medications and services those companies offer. This included Amadou and Fortuné, briefly introduced in the previous chapter. Both from the DRC, Amadou and Fortuné worked as undocumented laborers at the Amazon construction site in Cape Town. Before working there, both had been employed in the hospitality industry until the COVID lockdown closed restaurants and hotels. While working on the Amazon construction project, both fell ill with COVID-like symptoms.[44] "I had no money, I couldn't work, but I needed medicines," Amadou recalled. "And I needed bus fare to get to the clinic." At first, he started making a few Rands on the street, "selling this and that."

One day, he heard about a new COVID vaccine trial being run in the city that was enrolling healthy adults and medically stable, HIV-positive adults.[45] The trial also permitted non-HIV-positive people to participate. But for Amadou, in addition to getting the vaccine, a key selling point was that the trial offered money to anyone willing to participate. "I said to myself, yeah, I'll take anything," he told me; "if they pay me to take an experimental drug, I'll take it." The South African government permits this kind of trial participation payment, and Amadou received a stipend to cover his travel costs and pay him for his time participating in the trial, though Amadou did not tell me how much he received.[46]

The trial in which Amadou participated was for a new mRNA vaccine designed by a US-based company to combat HIV.[47] The program was funded by the Gates Foundation, who trumpeted it as the "first-in-Africa clinical trial of mRNA HIV vaccine" in South Africa and Rwanda.[48] The United States Agency for International Development and the US President's Emergency Plan for AIDS Relief provided additional support for the trial. Because Amadou had no health insurance or other social safety net, should the clinical trial he signed up for go awry, he would have no recourse to the courts.

It is debatable whether health clinics and physicians know if people like Amadou who sign up for experimental drug trials in South Africa are undocumented or not.[49] But it is clear that many undocumented people eager to access the medicines and services find ways to get what they need when they are in difficult or troubling situations, and it is not impossible to borrow a citizen's identity card.

Although pharmaceutical manufacturers and trial administrators prioritize participants' welfare, they also typically inform participants about potential unknown risks. In the case of the Gates Foundation–funded vaccine trial in which Amadou participated, the US company noted in its publicity materials that it "neither promises nor guarantees" success from its clinical trials "because they involve known and unknown risks."[50] The company advised study participants to locate further information about "uncertainties described under the heading 'Risk Factors'" in the company's "most recent Annual Report on Form 10-K filed with the US Securities and Exchange Commission." While this disclosure of uncertainties is commendable, I am confident neither Amadou nor other participants like him would have known how to find a US pharmaceutical corporation's annual 10-K form on file with the US Securities and Exchange Commission.

Medical sociologist Barbara Katz Rothman argues that the US-based medical industry's expansion of economic activities beyond national boundaries constitutes a biomedical empire: a transnational entity that extends US contractual terms and protocols into another sovereignty and thereby controls people from birth to death.[51] A US pharmaceutical company's presumption that SEC regulations are known to or even apply to non-US study participants such as Amadou and Fortuné, Congolese with limited rights in South Africa, would seem to be an example of one of Rothman's three elements of a biomedical empire: namely, that the US biomedical industry defines the conditions under which a non-US government and non-US participants receive experimental medicines.

Yet, within South Africa, South African law, not US law, governs study participants' engagement with US medical trials, creating an ambiguous space between what, for example, a US company or the donor funding the clinical trial might say should happen and what actually happens in South African clinics.

Typically, the details of overseas projects funded by the pharmaceutical industry and donor agencies are known only to officers in those private agencies. And those details are rarely shared. "We don't have democratic accountability mechanisms that allow us to scrutinize those interactions" among the pharmaceutical industry, donor agencies, and governments, said Katerini Storeng, associate professor at the University of Oslo's Center for Development and the Environment and head of a research project on public-private partnerships for pandemic preparedness.[52] Meetings such as those between the Gates Foundation and the WHO, which cocreated the COVID-19 health response policy, are seldom subject to open-access record policies.

Rohit Malpani, a public health consultant who worked for Médecins Sans Frontières, Oxfam, and the WHO, also questions the transparency of the US pharmaceutical industry and donor agencies. "The Gates Foundation sits on boards of other agencies and shapes the policies and practices of multilateral organizations, but these entities are not permitted to examine or engage with the Foundation in the same way that the Foundation examines and engages with them,"[53] he explained in an interview with the online American news outlet *Politico*. Other US foundations contribute to global health programs, but none come close to the Gates Foundation in the amount or in the donations they can leverage to influence international health policy. In 2021 the Rockefeller Foundation committed US$35 million to COVID response efforts in Africa but did not have influence on the WHO to the extent that the Gates Foundation did, and does.[54] The Ford Foundation committed US$1 million in direct support of the Africa Center for Disease Control between 2020 and 2022, and the Carnegie Corporation contributed $2.16 million between 2020 and 2022 to support higher education research and reporting in South Africa on the pandemic.[55] In comparison, the Gates Foundation, in 2020 alone, gave more than $250 million to promote vaccine health in Africa and, in that year, leveraged its Gavi connections to influence the WHO's distribution policy.[56]

Speaking to the issue of the circularity by which donors' investments benefit foundation trusts and foundation trusts leverage foundations' work, Malpani continued his description of the Gates Foundation's opacity: "We still need the Foundation to publish more detailed information on its investments, and on how it evaluates the success or otherwise of its programs."[57] Access to the Gates Foundation Trust's investment decision-making practices is necessary for WHO constituents and allied physicians to correctly assess the degree to which the Gates Trust earns dividends by investing in the pharmaceutical industry and then how those industry earnings inform the foundation's funding practices.

Like internationally connected doctors and WHO consultants, nationally prominent physicians like Dr. Urassa are not privy to the Gates Foundation's decision-making process. But to properly evaluate citizens' health status and healthcare in their countries, doctors need access to drug formularies and clinical trial results. Without this information, they in effect operate using not a lamp but a penlight. Imagine going to a clinic stocked with medicines that another country's scientists are studying, or being employed as a doctor but being unable to report patient data to anyone but wealthy donors or overseas organizations. The result would be the same as closing your (and your doctor's and government's) eyes and unthinkingly trusting in a distant so-called benefactor. But that is how the global health system works.

Describing the twenty-first-century biomedical industry as a "vast and influential" governmental force, sociologist Barbara Katz Rothman echoes historian Helen Tilley's proposal that Africa has been a "racial laboratory" where colonizers segregated medical services and applied racial categories to physical reproduction.[58] This furthering of a neocolonial project is not just a theoretical point but a present reality. Big Pharma, which may *act* like a quasi-sovereign entity, is first and foremost a cultural phenomenon. It shapes perceptions, converts medicines to data, data to money, and money into power and influence.

As a cultural phenomenon, the donor-pharmaceutical complex depends on (some people's) particular shared sense of morality. However, this shared sense of morality is not a natural occurrence but a crafted narrative. Like the mobilizing myths at the heart of many social institutions, Big Pharma deploys images of kindness and generosity that evoke and imply a powerful sense of cultural agreement about wealth as power and the power of the wealthy to assist "the poor." To go beyond the contours of this Big Pharma imperial alibi, we must unpack the presumed shared sense of social ethics that quietly exploits public views—specifically, the racialized stereotypes companies use about Africa to rationalize their methods of operations there.

THE USE OF COLONIAL STEREOTYPES TO ADVANCE BIOMEDICAL RESEARCH AND PROFITS

Health disparities and racism in healthcare emerged conspicuously in Africa around the beginning of the twentieth century.[59] Using a discourse of cultural superiority that highlighted their own beneficent capacity to provide the "help" they thought Africa needed, foreign investors helped convince colonial governments to allow them to experiment in Africa. As these companies conducted their experiments, they extracted the knowledge and profits they gained from them, while integrating a system of foreign medical investment that relied on racialized stereotypes and economic inequities that continue to structure biomedical investment and health care on the African continent. Today, US-based donors like the Gates Foundation continue to rely on Americans believing that "Africa needs help" and its people need saving. But that belief is founded on an outdated premise that Africa is backward and needs assistance to catch up with modernity.

No one is returning to the tired, clearly racist trope that Africa is "primitive." But Western media continue to paint Western donors as selfless benefactors, as competent foreign actors able to serve the unmet needs of African people. This narrative, however, ignores the larger truth that this "selfless giving" is in fact an alibi for companies and foundations to maintain control over their operations and intellectual property so as to extract private wealth for their investors and financial supporters.

Messages in the Western media portraying Africa as backward are as common as ever today, and they are consistently linked to foreign biomedical operations on the continent. Melinda Gates's comment, mentioned above, about the need to act to prevent people from dying on the streets in Africa during the COVID epidemic is a good example. But there are many more. In 2020, Agence France-Presse published an article around the world that called Bill Gates the "new bête noire," or "black beast," in Africa. Although the French term *bête noire* is commonly used to refer to a powerful figure, it carries racial overtones. And context matters. By highlighting Bill Gates's activities in Africa, the report was clearly drawing on that racial overtone—one tightly linked to a long history of framing Africa as "the dark continent," a colonialist expression used in the nineteenth century to describe Africa as mysterious and technologically backward. Today, for many, the term "bête noire" reinforces notions of superiority while portraying people of color as subordinate.[60]

These stereotypes in the Western media reinforce racist ideas about Africa that ultimately serve the needs of many foreign companies. The BBC (British Broadcasting Corporation), for example, aired a report portraying Bill Gates as "the voodoo doll of Covid conspiracies," describing him as wrongly "accused of rolling out a tetanus vaccine in Kenya that includes abortion drugs" and of testing "vaccines on children in Africa and India, leading to thousands of deaths and irreversible injuries."[61] These claims are not true: Bill Gates did not in fact roll out a tetanus vaccine that included abortion drugs or test vaccines on children. However, the report perpetuated damaging stereotypes about African culture. For example, it mocked vudú—a serious, syncretic African diasporic religion[62]—while failing to even mention the documented history of actual medical interventions in the past that did experiment on African bodies to ill and often deadly effect. Those experiments helped drive the distrust about foreign interventions in Africa in the first place. "Africa is backward" has remained a subtext in the media insofar as it has continued to serve those who profit the most from usurping the land and natural resources of the continent and experimenting on its citizens.

Bill Gates himself has also drawn on these stereotypes in his efforts to promote his activities in Africa, sometimes implying that "Africa is backward." In an interview with the British broadcast channel Sky News about whether pharmaceutical companies should make COVID vaccine formulas publicly available, Gates responded with a firm "No." He explained that the limitation in manufacturing capacity, rather than patents on intellectual property, hinders scalability. He also implied that Africans may not be able to manufacture vaccines reliably.[63]

Gates's comment infuriated many people in South Africa, who, in effect, asked, How could one of the wealthiest people in the world withhold vaccine knowledge from Africans? How could Gates possibly suggest that *not* lifting pharmaceutical companies' intellectual property protections would *not* save millions of lives? People wondered why Gates, who is publicly generous in giving money to global health causes, did *not* want to see vaccine recipes shared so that governments and doctors could treat people amid a worldwide pandemic.

On the face of it, Gates's statement seemed incredible, and it led many people, including Lawrence, my police officer acquaintance in Cape Town, to speculate that, while Gates may well be interested in responding to global health emergencies, he's also benefiting financially from that portion of pharmaceutical profits that comes to the Gates Family Trust as returns on its investments and possibly (depending on their investments) to Gates's private wealth.[64] Plus, the profit margins on the COVID vaccines for Pfizer and Moderna were so astronomical that many health officials, including some in the United States, considered the common argument for pharmaceutical patents—that such patents will encourage pharmaceutical companies to risk investment capital on new drugs in the future—to be unreasonable in this case. Pfizer had already profited so handsomely by 2021 that releasing the vaccine formula would still have allowed the company huge benefits. Within the week after making these comments, facing outrage from within and beyond the global health community, mainly outside the United States, Gates retreated from his declaration. Despite backtracking, his comment led to lingering reputational damage for him among many people like Lawrence and health professionals like Dr. Urassa.

While people reeled at Gates's shocking suggestion that protecting pharmaceutical profit margins was more important than the lives of millions of people, Pfizer's prescription and Moderna's vaccine profits surged—43 percent for Pfizer and 95 percent for Moderna from December 2020 (four months prior to Gates's comment) to December 2021—and Pfizer's spending on vaccine research and development increased to almost $14 billion in 2021.[65] Then, a month later, in early 2022, Pfizer topped the industry's list of prescription sales, with $37 billion generated by the COVID vaccine, an amount that could have funded sustainable water projects across the continent or pharmaceutical factories on half the continent.[66] It was in South Africa—which had the capacity and facilities—where antiviral trials against COVID first began, in April 2020. Nevertheless, and although Pfizer held onto its intellectual property for maximum profits, the company eventually did sell its mRNA vaccine to South Africa, where it earned significant profits from its effective, if not somewhat controversial, antiviral therapy for COVID.

Gates's harnessing of vaccines to global philanthropy fueled the African general public's mistrust of medical experimentation and donors' political powers. During the COVID pandemic in the United States, harmful stereotypes about Asians spread on social media and in public discussions. These stereotypes not only caused significant harm but also reinforced a misguided sense of cultural superiority among those perpetuating them. Similarly, the justifications for the ways pharmaceutical companies depicted Africans—particularly South Africans who were on the front lines of COVID vaccine testing, often relied on Western stereotypes. The historical context suggests that African individuals could be viewed as subjects for testing by Western companies, yet they could access these medical products only through the perceived "goodwill" of Western countries.

BIG DATA AND A CIRCULAR PHARMACEUTICAL ECONOMY

The Gates Foundation's $70 billion endowment has targeted HIV and AIDS, tuberculosis, malaria, and now SARS-associated coronaviruses, including COVID-19, in Africa. The foundation emphasizes that, by pouring most of its contributions into the fight against high-profile killers, Gates grantees have extended lives and reduced maternal and infant mortalities.[67] Although developing philanthropic projects that support urgent healthcare needs can significantly impact people's lives, not everything about donations is good, and charitable gifts are not free. Donating vast sums to charity diverts scrutiny from billionaires making or seeking to create excessive wealth while others face health and financial insecurity.

Among the top six US billionaires to profit during the COVID pandemic, Bill Gates ranked third to Elon Musk (first) and Jeff Bezos (second). Profit itself is unobjectionable, but the amount and percentage growth is beyond reason. Between March 18, 2020, and March 10, 2022, Bill Gates's wealth increased 32 percent, from $98 billion to $129.5 billion.[68] Of course, Gates's wealth derives most directly from the big-tech industry, not from biotechnology sales or production. He and Melinda Gates donated $255 million to coronavirus relief programs worldwide in 2020, second only to Jack Dorsey, then Twitter's CEO.[69] Bill and Melinda Gates are seemingly solidifying their legacies by donating substantial sums to charity. However, they invest in a circular market economy that concurrently yields big returns on investments for them.

Bill Gates understands that knowledge is power; he has made a fortune developing computer software and has invested in knowledge-driven solutions to inform healthcare treatment. His foundation uses data-driven decision-making strategies to guide investments and tailor the work of philanthropy. Gates's Global Fund promotes accountability but does not make all its data publicly available. It requires transparency from recipient governments yet itself lacks transparency. For example, the fund offers an online Data Explorer platform, that shows how many people have been treated instead of how effective those treatments were, which is the information Dr. Urassa needs.[70] While the Global Fund works through in-country coordinators, those coordinators, like Dr. Urassa, do not have access to biometric data. Consequently, healthcare information remains proprietary, leading to a lack of transparency and restricting the critical knowledge needed for effective, sovereign healthcare governance.

Moreover, the circularity of the money is head-spinning. The Gates cofounded Gavi, the Vaccine Alliance in 2014 to increase low- and middle-income countries' access to immunizations. In 2020, Gavi launched the COVAX COVID-19 vaccination plan and, in May of that year, gave $750 million to AstraZeneca to purchase 300 million doses for

| | | PC: 509(A)(1) | DELIVERY OF SOLUTIONS TO IMPROVE GLOBAL HEALTH | 1,360,000,000 |

Top of figure navigation:

≡   **ProPublica**   Donate

← Back to main page for BILL & MELINDA GATES FOUNDATION   Form 990PF ▾

GAVI ALLIANCE
CHEMIN DU POMMIER 40 1218 GRAND SACONNEX
GENEVA
SZ

Fig. 10. Entry from the Gates Foundation's US Internal Revenue Service Form 990, showing $1.36 billion in contributions to Gavi, the Vaccine Alliance. Source: ProPublica Nonprofit Explorer, https://projects. propublica.org/nonprofits/.

delivery to low- and middle- income countries. Shortly thereafter, it signed an additional purchase agreement with Pfizer. In 2021, the Gates Foundation gave $1.36 billion to Gavi to help fund vaccinations (figure 10) and $260 Million to the Global Fund to fight AIDS, T.B., and malaria. In 2021, it donated $4 Million for health-related causes to institutions in Tanzania and $44 Million to health-related entities in South Africa. Despite Gates's significant donation to Tanzania, most of those funds went to labs endorsed by Gavi (the organization funded in part by the Gates Foundation), not to government-run public health labs.

As we entered the parking lot of Kilimanjaro International Airport, after talking nonstop during the hour-long trip, Dr. Urassa summed up: "Money from the Gates Foundation goes to the Global Fund or Gavi, then money goes to Tanzania, which sends it to the drug maker where that company pays Pfizer for the right to produce its product."

Urassa agreed that donations are good, but "they should be given directly to public health systems, [so] we can manage our own data and health records, and we can begin to see health care sovereignty." But, instead, "Gavi or a similar agency labels these funds as a *donation,* making them tax-reduced or tax-free to Gavi, located in Switzerland," where banks provide their depositors high levels of privacy.[71]

I understood Dr. Urassa's point; he knew that American audiences often accuse African officials of taking money from public coffers, but he made it very clear to me that the greater beneficiaries of the money and data sharing in this system were the Gateses and Big Pharma, not anyone in his country.[72] When the inequitable distribution of resources occurs in the United States, US media and UN agencies call the deed "siphoning" or "misallocation" of funds, essentially whitewashing illegality.[73] Yet, as the watchdog group Transparency International affirms, "far too often, globally-trading companies resort to bribery" and "secretive contracts" in order to make deals with officials and governments. The Transparency International report specifically names Pfizer and Moderna.[74]

REPRISE

Over the past decade, the Gates Foundation, a significant contributor to the pharmaceutical industry, has emerged as a pivotal force in supplying medicines to Africa. This influence has transformed African health officials' governmental control of national health and demographic systems, aligning them with Gates's interventions. In this landscape, American pharmaceutical manufacturers have reaped substantial benefits, while African citizens have drawn parallels between the Gates Foundation and the colonial-era laboratories of experimental medicine.

My analysis of the Gates-US–Big Pharma complex uncovers a fundamental issue: the disparity between its social mechanisms for advancing its objectives and its justifications for exploiting public perspectives. These justifications often blur the line between ethical and legal actions. For instance, African governments and scientists may grant corporations free access to public infrastructure and resources, a practice that is legally protected but ethically questionable when *not* reciprocated by sharing recipes. Alibis of "caretaking" or "serving the common good" frequently allow companies and corporate foundations to undertake activities that create products and services that may be in demand. However, those alibis also enable these entities to shield from public view elements of their operations that may be harmful. Pharmaceutical companies, along with private foundations associated with their work, exhibit a business model similar to that of agribusinesses and other resource-extracting industries.

As with so many other people I spoke with as part of my work, Lawrence and Dr. Urassa underscored the basic theme that few Americans understand in this global system, not because it's complicated but because so many Americans view Africa as a disconnected, "Third World" continent, so far away.

Are Lawrence and Urassa correct? Is an American biomedical and corporate empire profiting from research and by testing new drugs in African
countries? Are donors and companies not actually interested in ending
diseases on the continent but instead in using the populations to gather
data on the effects of new medications and vaccines from which it can
make even more money?

Certainly, the Gates Foundation's charitable contributions and the
Global Fund's and Gavi's filtering money to pay US-based pharmaceutical
companies recalls the parable of the thief, the goose, and the public common wherein the villainous biomedical empire steals the public health
goose from the common (see the preface, where this lyric is quoted) and
government officials such as Dr. Urassa dare not conspire to break the
laws that pharmaceutical companies and donors make.

While the influence of a US megaphilanthropist in African public
health systems may seem comprehensive and impossible to contest, it is
not beyond challenge. Fostering education and critical thinking—among
people in countries where the companies are based and elsewhere where
they operate—in order to empower individuals to question and reshape
the world through reasoned debate will be an important part of any last-
ing solution. Concretely, strengthening governance structures within
national boundaries will enable people to hold governments accountable
and ensure their interests are represented in negotiations with investors
and multinational corporations.

Officer Lawrence and Dr. Urassa provide firsthand insights into people's perspectives regarding the Gates Foundation. The significance of
their views lies in their potential to inform public health policies and
interventions aimed at addressing human needs and social justice. By
examining global health governance from the ethnographically grounded
perspectives of people on the receiving end of philanthropic giving,
rather than analyzing corporate websites and media as so much scholarship has effectively done, this chapter highlights that recipients recognize
that global health partnerships are highly unequal. Donors' and foundations' reports, media releases, and websites often overlook the perspectives of those they seek to help. This oversight restricts the knowledge
necessary for fostering meaningful discussions about effective public
health delivery. Incorporating the voices and experiences of those

directly affected is essential for creating a more equitable and effective public health framework.

Officer Lawrence and Dr. Urassa's words are direct. They question what is global in the arena of global health, what is ethical about medical ethics, the depth of development in international development, and the scope of the public in public health policy. Their incisive analyses of global health power and politics also register protests against the rules of engagement that favor the donors at recipients' expense. Perhaps because they spoke in settings where they clearly were in charge—on an officer's beat in South Africa, among friends in Tanzania—and not at a board meeting hosted by donors' spokespeople, they spoke their minds, putting politeness aside. Their outrage not only illuminates the inherent conceits and alibis undergirding "global health partnerships" but also shows how to speak out in the interest of equitable partnerships—directly, publicly, and decisively.

In line with recent research on the role of businesses in privatizing water, speculating on agricultural production, and converting rural and heritage landscapes into real estate and digital commodities, this review of the Gates Foundation's financialization of global public health yields three interconnected observations. First, the concept of partnership conceals deeper fractures; second, donations, gifts, and charitable giving serve as alibis for donors' financial speculation; and third, donor speculation occurs at the expense of people in formerly colonized territories who generate the data that donors use to build their wealth. Yet donors, including the Gates Foundation, do not acknowledge or remedy that history or their role in its perpetuation. This revelation raises deep and alarming concerns about the potential negative consequences of such corporate-led forms of development on global public health.

Awareness of donors' tactical uses of alibis and understanding of the potential for donors' gifts and alibis to mask underlying ethical questions are crucial if public health programs are to deliver on promises of equity and are to appropriately assess and acknowledge the genuine impact of gifts. More ethnographically grounded accounts focusing on thoughtful people's knowledge are thus essential for unraveling the hidden negative consequences of global health philanthropy. To meet that need, more people like Officer Lawrence and Dr. Urassa should spill the tea on the effects of gifts.

5 Ed-Tech Philanthropy versus the Common Good

No gift is free. Gifts require the return of loyalty. Private charitable gifts take decision making away from the state and recipients and turn citizens' loyalties to the benefit of donors. Donors represent gifts as free, but all gifts require reciprocity.

The Gates Foundation's work in the healthcare sector, discussed in the previous chapter, is an important example of how gifts can benefit a donor. Similar to the operations of the Gates Foundation or corporate investments in water, land, or agriculture, philanthropic initiatives in the education sector hinge on narratives, or alibis, that shape perceptions and enable benefactors to obscure the more problematic aspects of their projects.

This final chapter brings into view one more important example of the use of corporate alibis, in the realm of US-based ed-tech philanthropy. Together with the earlier chapters, the examples here show how corporate donations sometimes can create the façade of progress while entrenching the very disparities they claim to address.

ALL THAT GLITTERS IS NOT GOLD

At 10:30 a.m. every weekday, Mandisa Nkosi takes a break from preparing students' lunches at Starling Vocational Technical School in Vineyard Valley. She sits on a chair to sip rooibos tea. The school's whitewashed buildings sparkle in contrast to the unpainted houses belonging to students' families, perched at various angles on the hill behind the school.[1]

Vineyard Valley is a popular destination for international tourists. Wine tastings, wine cellars, vineyard tours, and award-winning South African pinotages draw up-market visitors from North America and Europe. But, for many people living in the area, life is difficult. With 50 percent of the population unemployed in the Cape Winelands District Municipality, parents in the community worry about what their children will do after finishing school.

"Twenty years ago, everyone picked grapes on the boss's farm," Mandisa tells me, gesturing toward Vineyard Valley. "Now, there are so many people looking for jobs. And our children don't want to work in the fields. They want to work in businesses and factories, and for that, they need technical skills."[2]

Only 41 percent of the nonwhite community in Vineyard Valley has permanent employment, mainly in the agricultural sector, and an additional 9 percent work during harvest season.[3] Parents and grandparents of Starling's students used to work in the vineyards in exchange for flasks of wine. Called the *dop* system (*dop* being slang for "alcoholic drink" in Afrikaans), the payment practice trapped people in poverty and alcoholism. Labor laws have changed, but the nonwhite community continues to face many challenges, including drug dependency, alcoholism, and low rates of school completion.[4]

In response to growing unemployment and increasing social and economic inequality, anger and frustration have risen among residents of Vineyard Valley. About a decade ago, teenagers living there rioted and destroyed commercial property. The South African media portrayed Vineyard Valley as gang ridden and dangerous. The tourist industry suffered. The police intervened, businesses blamed parents, and parents, including Mandisa, impugned a system that didn't give their children equal opportunities to attend schools that would prepare them for jobs.

Responding to the crisis, a wealthy South African winemaker donated money to build Starling Vocational Technical School. But the project became more than local philanthropy, and Starling Vocational Technical School became more than a vocational-technical academy. It became part of a larger business venture involving a US corporate giant—Dell Technologies.

Starling Vocational Technical School in Vineyard Valley is a collaboration between the South African government and the Texas-based Michael & Susan Dell Foundation.[5] For several years, the Dell Foundation has channeled money to Starling Vocational Technical School through the D. G. Murray Trust (DGMT), a South African investment company; in 2021, donations totaled $2.1 million, two times the school's subsidy from the South African government.[6] Collaboration schools, like charter schools in the United States, are government-funded entities managed by a self-appointed governing body and exempt from many public school laws and regulations. They are organized around a particular teaching philosophy or programmatic objective; Starling's mission is to provide a vo-tech education to underserved youth in Vineyard Valley.[7] An initial public policy goal in authorizing collaboration schools was to improve students' academic performance and reduce socioeconomic inequalities between rich and impoverished communities. However, research shows that partnership schools may not definitively improve students' educational outcomes.[8] At best, the schools become integrated in the community and advance regional economic interests. At worst, they prioritize projects that primarily benefit donors, financially or otherwise, including, as this book discusses at length, in ways that can be morally, ecologically, and economically problematic.

Founded in 1999, the Michael & Susan Dell Foundation invests wealth derived largely from Dell Technologies into education and health programs in India and South Africa. In the case of Starling Vocational Technical School and other collaboration schools, the D. G. Murray Trust, a South African company (like a quasi-subsidiary or broker through which the foundation communicates) invests Dell's twice-untaxed dividends (once in the United States and again in South Africa) to buy school supplies and equipment and hire teachers, staff, and contractors. The Dell Foundation's charitable responsibility statement indicates that a significant "transformation" in African education operations is under way "in poorer communities" and that Dell is helping to promote it.[9] Dell's use of the word "transformation" here is telling because, as discussed below, the foundation's focus on funding digital school management tools, though presented as a charitable project for "poor communities," appears to be less about transforming education to improve the lives of students and communities than about boosting a commercial and technological transformation in South Africa that will enhance industry in ways from which Dell potentially stands to profit.

Although the Dell Foundation focuses its philanthropic work on schools in impoverished communities, its gifts link closely with projects that further Dell's educational technology industry. For example, the Dell Foundation in South Africa supports YearBeyond, a mentoring program that builds technical skills for school graduates who will work as "data administrators" and in corporations. It also sponsors Injini, a nonprofit ed-tech operator providing start-up capital for digital businesses.[10] In 2020, the Dell Foundation funded "access to affordable credit and savings products," creating a debt-incurring digital lending program presented to the public as "supporting improved livelihoods for low-income South Africans." Other Dell-funded projects champion "the creation and implementation of an education data system in South Africa that will advance student outcomes through district management tools and best practices sharing" and promote online schooling, digital technology training, and South African ed-tech companies.[11] In offering on-the-job mentoring and skills training, these programs operate, I argue, as an alibi: by presenting the funding as charity, the companies can divert scrutiny from what these programs are also often creating—significant potential benefits for the donors' and their industries.

At Starling Vocational Technical School, the D. G. Murray Trust uses Michael & Susan Dell Foundation funds to help sustain a 51 percent private sector majority on the school board. That majority has close ties to ed-tech operators and start-up companies.[12] It lobbies the Western Cape public education department for exemptions for Starling Vocational Technical School as a collaboration school, including allowing the school to hire (and fire) teachers using the board's (not the government's) criteria, paying teachers less than they might be paid at fully state-funded schools, and foregoing enrolling teachers in professional development programs, as other schools are required to do.

When I spoke with the principal and teachers in March 2022, Starling was lobbying the provincial government to approve a privately owned company to provide internet service for the school.[13] Extant government policy required schools to contract with government-approved internet providers for reasons of accountability and digital security. However, in seeking to separate from the government-supplied service provider, the government argued, Starling students, teachers, staff, and administrators would no longer be accountable for the transmission of any unauthorized content. Teachers, for example, could use the internet to develop private businesses, the school could use it to surveil the teachers and track students and staff online.

"No way could you put security cameras in public school teachers' classrooms," Dr. Vandana Sayed, a lecturer at a South African university, told me. "The teacher unions forbid it." But, as a collaboration school, Starling Vocational Technical School was not obligated to employ licensed teachers. Thus, union policies about teacher surveillance did not apply. Instead, contracting with a privately owned internet service provider would allow Starling's administration and school board to keep track of the school's digital data, including teachers' and administrators' uses of school technology, and to help the school augment its already substantial use of technology for surveillance and fundraising.

Consistent with the entrepreneurial ethos of the ed-tech industry, the Starling school board recruits instructors from the private sector, many with no classroom teaching experience, and offers stock options in local companies to supplement teachers' salaries. Although the school does not explicitly promise that employment will help teachers move into ed-tech companies, it provides an avenue for some to connect with digital industries. One teacher, Delgado, admitted, "Sure, the stock options were attractive, but the real reason I took this job was to use it as a stepping-stone to build my own company." Delgado started his career as a factory floor manager and then quit because, he said, "I wasn't going anywhere."[14] Delgado's long-term goal was to own and operate an ed-tech company. His interest in teaching was to learn from the board and the school tech providers about the education system's commercial angle. He took the job to understand how the school's purchasing processes worked, so he could break out and become an independent operator. Other teachers had already left Starling Vocational Technical School to set up companies. Indeed, the school administration encouraged teachers to be entrepreneurial. "Initially, we wanted this school to be named 'Start-Up Academy,'" a member of the school board told me.[15] "But the Western Cape education department said they couldn't do it because they don't have that as a category. So we had to call ourselves a vocational-technical school to check the box of what the government wanted."

The academy was to have trained students to use technologies in the digital sector and, eventually, to create a pathway for graduates to work with firms that teachers and the local business community in Vineyard Valley cocreated. To mobilize this plan, the school's governing body in the first two years purchased high-bandwidth digital technologies dovetailing with the ed-tech start-up industry. But many of the products they purchased seem clearly aimed less at helping the students than in helping the ed-tech industry: surveillance cameras installed in classrooms, an airport-like security system whose cameras scanned students for contraband, a state-of-the-art software system to keep track of purchases in case of theft, and drones that flew overhead and recorded the school's rugby matches for absent donors. All these not only policed students and socialized them for a consumer electronics market that they likely wouldn't be able to afford, but also used school funds to contract with local ed-tech companies.

A SHADOW INDUSTRY OF INVESTORS

For US-based technology and digital service corporations like Dell Technologies and Amazon, schools often serve as test beds, allowing companies to pilot their products in real-world educational environments and strengthen relationships between the company and educators. As schools adopt more technology, ed-tech companies can use their experience and case studies to enter new regions or markets, in some cases eventually analyzing digital data for broader market gains and selling insights to other businesses, investors, or policy makers. Mining digital data offers a major opportunity to create new intellectual property, which—as with Corteva Agriscience's proprietary bioengineered seeds, and the patient health data collected at Gates–funded clinics in Africa for the exclusive use of US corporations—investors can use to expand into new markets.

International debate continues over digital data privacy laws and the need for stronger regulation of secondary use of data collected through digital technologies.[16] Like other tech companies, Dell Technologies creates new software that it licenses for use by schools, consumers, online learning platforms, and various organizations around the world. These technologies gather data that, in some cases, tech companies can retain. By compiling user data on tech companies' proprietary platforms, corporations can obtain essential information needed to create new products and expand their markets. The technologies can track keystrokes, geolocation, browsing histories, and other electronic bits and bytes, all of which the company can use to develop new products or permit other companies to develop new products. This data serves as the "raw digital material" used to manufacture and sell "prediction products" to buyers interested in probabilistic behavior information, such as other surveillance industries or advertisers.

Data mining is pervasive—it happens everywhere digital technologies operate.[17] It functions differently in different countries, and its social, economic, and ethical implications vary depending on the context in which it occurs. For example, when a US company collects and stores data from users in the United States, the social and ethical questions differ from those that arise when the same company collects and stores data from users overseas. In the latter scenario, data mining by ed-tech companies can evoke parallels to colonial-era wealth extraction and further perpetuate global wealth disparities.

Although this form of business—collecting digital data and creating value from it—is deeply integrated into today's world economy, it is a business model that is often critiqued. Sociologist Gargi Bhattacharyya calls financiers' uses of personal digital data to create wealth for billionaires "digital capitalism," and philosopher Shoshana Zuboff refers to the unseen—often unknown—collection and commodification of personal information "surveillance capitalism."[18] Zuboff adds that surveillance capitalism rests heavily on a governance model steeped in policing and monitoring, as pursued in some programs of education (broadly defined). Technologies that allow people to track their own and others' movements have many applications, including, at Starling Vocational Technical School, instructing students, supervising workers, tracking data use, and monitoring spaces. While corporations and venture philanthropies like Dell Technologies and the Dell Foundation frequently promote their products as offering students new economic opportunities, their initiatives simultaneously facilitate the immersion of users into panopticon-like frameworks that are predominantly governed by, and advantageous to, ed-tech industries.

I am not the only one to draw attention to a shadow industry of investors, venture philanthropists, and private equity firms operating behind many students' classroom experiences. Tyler Hook's research documents the corporatization of education in Liberia, where "investors and organizations decide what is best and formulate [education] policy to fit their objectives."[19] Krystal Strong and Christiana Kallon Kelly show how corporate philanthropic institutions such as the MasterCard Foundation Scholarship Program strategically fund "Africa's growing leadership pipeline."[20] These and many other studies document a clear and unsettling story: Big Tech consistently uses charity it funnels from the United States to underfunded overseas education systems in Africa to generate returns and profits for US corporations and industries by quarrying and extracting students' and schools' digital data, sourced from those companies' un- or undertaxed charities. Ed-tech companies all around the world use this data-mining model to run their businesses, and US companies are the dominant global players. But due to the enduring impact of colonial and apartheid histories in some communities in Africa today, foreign corporations mining data in Africa to generate wealth for investors raises serious ethical concerns that may be less prevalent, or at least different, in other countries, such as the United States.

US tech companies—Dell, Google, Microsoft, Apple, Amazon, and others—have significant interests in school systems worldwide.[21] Many produce networked platforms or software tools, two of the largest of which are Google Workspace for Education and Google Classroom. These Google entities operate in some of the best-resourced South African private schools, including the Oprah Winfrey Leadership Academy for Girls and in some public-private collaboration ventures like Starling Vocational

Technical School. Thousands of local South African technology businesses and start-up companies use US hardware and technologies. One of the biggest is Get Smarter, recently bought by US-based 2U. Others are Siyafunda, which uses US-linked mobile technology to work in nine hundred South African schools, and Fundi Bots and Genius, which use networked platforms to facilitate courses in science and technology.

Small-scale South African operators deal with complex chains of technical, legal, and economic dependencies that US corporations and investors often control. According to Purdue University researchers, "The global market for big data analytics was valued at $271.83 billion in 2022" and "is expected to increase to an estimated $745.15 billion by the year 2030."[22] US investors and industries have significant control of South Africa's digital infrastructure and given the growth of data mining and Amazon's expanded cloud storage on the African continent, they are poised to get bigger.

A BRIEF EXCURSION: ELITE BENEFACTION AT A GLANCE

For readers who wish to know "how we got here," a brief excursion into history may be helpful. Distribution practices from which today's philanthropy emerged—which includes the philanthropy model of Dell's Starling Vocational Technical School and other philanthropic ventures like the Gates Foundation—derive from a system that is now thousands of years old: Greco-Roman law. The legal basis for charities was first outlined in ancient Greece and Roman tax law, and it has since been carried worldwide through waves of imperialism and settler migration.

Elite benefaction in the sense enshrined in US tax codes and international protocols derives from an age-old Greco-Roman sense of aristocratic prerogative. It became well established in Hellenistic kingdoms and continued under the Roman Empire (31 BCE–18 CE). Although gifting became legally codified, it was not well suited to Athenian democracy, in that Athenians recognized that elite benefaction to the poor cemented political-economic inequality within a commonwealth. Elite benefactors constituted nonrepresentational administrations; they operated like unelected governments. Regardless, the rules and terms of elite benefaction became codified and continued under the Roman Empire.[23] As Rome colonized western Europe, a similar system of elite benefaction through gift giving emerged and interfaced with patron-client feudal systems and the medieval Christian Church, which in turn gave way to charitable organizations and guilds in seventeenth- and eighteenth-century Europe.

As Europe went on to occupy parts of Africa, a similar system of colonization through charity took hold in colonized lands. Religious missions offered gifts in aid of hospitals and schools. Like the early missionaries, the British Colonial Office and British civil society organizations considered Black Africans to be in need of saving. Political philosopher John Stuart Mill, writing in 1859, argued that a doctrine of liberty applied "only to human beings in the maturity of their faculties" and that "backward states of society" such as different "races" in India and Africa could not govern themselves.[24] At the end of the nineteenth century (as mentioned in the previous chapter) English poet Rudyard Kipling wrote the poem "White Man's Burden." "Go send your sons," he intoned, to "serve . . . new-caught, sullen people, half devil and half child," referring to indigenous populations.[25]

Roman-derived civil law, in effect in most nation-states today, including the United States and most African countries, allows charitable trusts to avoid paying taxes on a portion of their annual earned income. In both the United States and South Africa, when wealthy people die and pass wealth to their heirs, the state claims a portion of that wealth as an inheritance tax.[26] This inheritance tax, essentially a leveling mechanism, redistributes wealth societally. To avoid losing control of their wealth, however, wealthy families set up charitable trusts; those trusts invest the family's wealth in stocks and bonds that earn an income. A portion of the income earned through investing funds kept in a trust remains tax-free, provided the trust donates that income as a charitable gift to a nonprofit entity. In the United States, foundations must give to nongovernmental organizations and typically engage third-party investment agencies to invest their wealth and manage investment-earned income. This philanthropic model—taken from ancient Roman law, then increasingly cultivated by nation-states around the world in the twentieth century—is at the heart of philanthropic projects like the Starling Vocational Technical School, which is heavily funded by tax-exempt investment earnings of ultrawealthy donors.

In South Africa, the D. G. Murray Family Trust manages the posthumous wealth of Douglas George and Eleanor Murray, South Africans whose ancestors immigrated from Europe. In 1902, Douglas Murray's father established the Cape-based construction company Murray and Stewart, which, in 1967, merged with another company to become Murray and Roberts. In 2020, the D. G. Murray Trust managed R433,901,072.[27] More than half of those investments came from external partner funds, including the Michael & Susan Dell Foundation, one of whose namesakes is the twentieth-wealthiest person in the world and founder and CEO of Dell Technologies. As noted, in 2022, the Dell Foundation contributed R36 million to the D. G. Murray Trust to "increase adoption of the Partnership Schools model" in South Africa.[28] It donated a similar amount to Acorn Education in South Africa to "develop a network of high-quality Partnership Schools." The D. G. Murray Family Trust partners with Acorn to operate eleven Western Cape collaboration schools. While these dispensations are legally classified as charitable donations, labeling them purely altruistic is not entirely accurate, as the benefits of these "gifts" circuitously flow back to the donors' industries.

THE ED-TECH PHILANTHROPIC ALIBI

Dell Technologies and other tech companies have become digital-mining businesses, not only sourcing cobalt and other minerals needed for lithium batteries (as discussed in the preface) but also positioning themselves to gather data from tech users. When collaboration schools receive or purchase goods that align with donors' businesses, as when Starling Vocational Technical School receives gifts from Dell, collaboration schools facilitate corporate donors' business interests. Likewise, when donors give to recipients whose work augments donors' means of production—such as Starling's training in computer use and socializing students into digital surveillance technologies—donors' philanthropy becomes a tactical form of investment called *venture philanthropy*: earning a profit by donating to charity.

Venture philanthropists themselves describe the strategy differently, however. They frame investment-based charity as an intelligent way to make their donations count, and they claim that traditional sources of charity are shrinking. Yet venture philanthropists have also contributed to the shrinkage of traditional philanthropy. They have not donated directly to social causes like donors in previous generations.[29]

Philanthropic efforts in the twentieth century, exemplified by figures like Andrew Carnegie, Andrew Mellon, and more recently, Oprah Winfrey, were driven by diverse motivations ranging from personal background to social priorities. Carnegie focused on education due to his experiences overcoming poverty through schooling, Mellon aimed to preserve his family's legacy, while Winfrey's initiatives reflect her commitment to community empowerment and social equality. These philanthropists relied on corporate tax breaks and supported corporate board members', not workers', interests, as do today's venture philanthropists. However, traditional philanthropists did not, in general, construct circles so that their charities went to projects that in turn benefited their industries (which support their charities), as ed-tech venture philanthropies do. Venture philanthropists donate funds to organizations, social entrepreneurs, and community initiatives. They offer beneficiaries a variety of investment options typically connected to philanthropists' businesses. Much as Starling Vocational Technical School offered teachers stock options in school-connected start-up companies, venture philanthropists offer recipients the chance to partly own the donors' subsidiaries or related companies.

Stemming from the digital technology boom of the 1990s in the United States, US venture philanthropies build supply chains and business infrastructures *and* lock users into technologies that benefit US corporations.[30] For example, a corporate-to-philanthropy-to-corporate circle extracts cobalt from the DRC, donates digital technologies and sponsors start-up companies on the African continent, then locks users into US markets that supply and create digital platforms. Through these platforms, corporations mine digital data in order to build mass surveillance and probabilistic industries that, in turn, potentially augment the donors' wealth. This manifold ed-tech cover gift constitutes the *ed-tech philanthropic alibi*.

Put simply, ed-tech digital venture philanthropy papers over investors' potential profit; investors capture and enclose markets within the garden walls of their industries; they extract digital data from students and end users; and they gain coveted unearned social prestige for "rescuing" public systems they have also gutted.

VENTURE PHILANTHROPY: UNTAXED WEALTH MASKING INVESTMENTS AS DONATIONS

Using corporate wealth to support education is not new. Cecil John Rhodes, the British-born mining executive who played a central role in Britain's colonization in southern Africa and who, in the 1890s, was prime minister of Cape Colony (part of today's South Africa), created large educational philanthropic enterprises with his wealth, including the Rhodes House and the Rhodes Scholarship fund at Oxford University. Fifteen years before Rhodes died, he effectively monopolized the gold and diamond fields in South Africa. Then he used his initial mining wealth to secure political power there and, backed by the British government, launched conquests northward on the continent. Rhodesia and Northern Rhodesia (now Zimbabwe and Zambia, respectively) were named for this mining magnate and politician.[31]

Similarly, US companies operating across southern Africa in the early twentieth century, particularly the Carnegie Corporation, used their profits to fund libraries, schools, and rural development programs on the African continent. In South Africa, the Carnegie Corporation of New York partnered with the white South African Nationalist Party to support technical education for "Coloured" and Asian students and, later, to fund a study of white poverty in South Africa. The partnership did not, at that time, address opportunities for Black South Africans. When Andrew Carnegie died in 1919, his foundation was worth $350 million (the equivalent of $6.5 billion in 2024).[32] A decade later, the Carnegie Foundation's "First Inquiry into Poverty in South Africa" recommended segregating white from Black South Africans to "improve" the lives of whites, which would become part of the intellectual justification for the apartheid regime that would be implemented in 1948.[33] The philanthropic foundation thus supported programs that advanced and reinforced systemic inequalities.

Unlike the Dell Foundation and other ed-tech venture philanthropies today, however, Carnegie generally did not use charity to support programs immediately tied to the donor's industries. Arguably, Rhodes set up the Rhodes Scholarship fund at Oxford University to train a colonial administration service that would perpetuate his political and economic goals, including maintaining British control of the southern African continent.[34] However, his philanthropy, once given, did not redound directly to his projects.

In giving gifts to ultimately benefit givers' industries, today's philanthropies differ from those of previous centuries. Venture philanthropic entities associated with twenty-first-century digital finance and speculative trading anticipate a business return on donations. Venture philanthropy treats schooling as a "social investment" that starts with a business plan and leverages spending in ways compatible with the business interests of the strategic donor. In this sense, donations are investments. Social critic Kenneth Saltman calls this corporation-to-philanthropy-to-corporation cycle a "circle of privatization." Public subsidies to private businesses encourage "private giving that influences, leads, and directs public education initiatives. These financial redistributions, in turn, redistribute public governance in privatized ways."[35] This circle differs from traditional philanthropy but, like it, appears designed to save "impoverished Africa," while reinscribing, if indirectly, racialized socioeconomic hierarchies by making billions of dollars on the backs of the "poorer communities" it claims to help.

Not all contemporary models of charity circle back to the donor's sources of profit making, of course. Are today's philanthropies conquering other people's lands to increase their industry's valuation? A more nuanced answer to this question, with some caveats, is to look at another, different model of US corporate foundation charitable giving.

A BETTER KIND OF PHILANTHROPY?

Wiping sweat from her brow, Hennie, the breakfast cook at Riverside Hotel, eyes a roomful of well-dressed guests sitting in front of a picturesque window overlooking a flower garden in this horseracing corner of Gauteng Province, the wealthiest region of South Africa.

The hotel, Hennie says, is packed twice a year, once during March school break, when wealthy families enroll their children in riding lessons, and again at the end of the year, when students graduate from the Oprah Winfrey Leadership Academy for Girls (OWLAG), located on the edge of town. OWLAG is in the town of Henley on Klip. Founded in 1904 by an Englishman, Horace Kent, on land once under the exclusive control of Zulu and indigenous Africans through the eighteenth century, Henley on Klip sits astride the confluence of two rivers, now flooding as a result of climate change and sending a stench through part of the town. But the Oprah school is on a drier parcel, a thickly wooded square kilometer of land, ringed by a five-meter-high electric fence conspicuously marked with no-trespassing signs and security cameras.

As Hennie takes a break from plating bacon and eggs, she recalls how much more difficult life was before OWLAG opened. "Twenty years ago, this was a quiet place. Now, the school holds its graduation ceremony in the area, and tips are good, thousands and thousands of rands some days," she says, widening her eyes to show the size.[36]

OWLAG, a predominantly Black, well-resourced boarding school for girls ages fourteen to eighteen, opened in 2007 for economically disadvantaged students, though locals like Hennie see it as accessible these days primarily for the rich. "My kids go to a grade-B elementary school. There's no way they can qualify," she says. "I'm bottom middle-class. I have a house and a job, but I live where the schools are bad. To get into OWLAG, you first need a sponsor, a fairy godmother, to send your kids to a good primary school, then maybe they will get the test scores needed to qualify for the Oprah Academy."

Many townspeople told me similar stories of a quiet life in the early 2000s, then a sudden economic boom when the school was being built, designer classrooms went up practically overnight, and parents arrived in their Audis. You also hear gratitude that the town (population six thousand) is again on the map and that the school serves as a model for closing the apartheid-era entrenched gap between historically well-resourced white schools and historically impoverished Black schools.

Legend in South Africa has it that the American television celebrity Oprah Winfrey, born of disadvantaged roots but spirited and high achieving, spoke with the first democratically elected Black South African president, Nelson Mandela, in 2000 about opening a school to help girls like herself. Oprah gave $40 million to the school, which would have been enough to rebuild many of the public secondary schools in Johannesburg at the time, albeit to a less glamorous standard. A media frenzy erupted around the school, generating criticisms and controversies in the international press. Coverage spanned from the extravagant amenities provided for the girls, such as indoor and outdoor theaters and a beauty salon, to the near-total isolation of the students from their parents and families.[37]

However, by the mid-2010s, international interest began to wane, and local discussions shifted to focus on students' social demographics, including their social class and how attending the school might influence their positions within the gendered hierarchies of South Africa. Additionally, there were discussions about whether being a student there could lead to generational power shifts within their families. Oprah's school generated controversy and praise, yet few questioned her motives. As a highly respected public figure known for her philanthropic efforts and commitment to education, particularly for underserved communities, Oprah's reputation as a compassionate leader likely led people to view the school, overall, as a worthy cause rather than scrutinizing her intentions.

Nevertheless, ongoing contention at the school centers on progressive social values, which often conflict with the beliefs of students' families. For example, Noxolo Ntaka, an alumna of OWLAG who conducted research on the educational and employment experiences of alumnae, documented some of the stress and anxiety that students subjectively experienced when navigating and bridging their home and school environments. Drawing on the scholarship of Frantz Fanon, W. E. B. Du Bois, and Ferial Haffajee to analyze graduates' experiences, Ntaka observed that "the alumni of OWLAG face a contrasting struggle, one that is linked to being a black woman in the context of their socio-economic identity."[38]

When they became "Oprah girls," Ntaka recorded, students entered a world materially and socially removed from their families. "One of the hardest parts was the feeling that I was living two different realities," Refilwe, from Mafikeng, told Ntaka. "You had the academy where everything was basically perfect, [except for] the pressure of being an 'Oprah Girl.' It was overwhelming at times. You'd think about what's going on at home and begin to lose track of what you're supposed to be focused on."[39]

Speaking of her own experience at the school, Ntaka noted that this lack of comprehension went both ways. Her family, she said, likewise "could not understand what was going on with me" when she returned home during holidays. "I had changed, and I was struggling to adapt back into who I was before I had left."[40] As a boarding school, OWLAG socialized students around the clock. Students remained at school for three consecutive months, then returned home for one month per term.

The students who attended the school, many of whom were the first generation in their families to complete school, sometimes faced conflicts at home with their parents, especially their fathers, highlighting the complexity of creating a school that has imported American social and gender values into a region where such values are less centered. Bongeka Zuma, for example, experienced tensions between her home and the school when she began to receive opportunities historically reserved for men. Her father was skeptical. "When I got into the Oprah school, a lot of my teachers had to calm him down," Ntaka quoted Bongeka as saying. Bongeka's father believed that he was the best person to socialize and discipline his children. When he saw that even the school's top teachers were women, he had second thoughts about his daughter attending. "My teachers were worried my father wouldn't allow me to go because he wouldn't want me to be raised by someone else—outside of him—not really out of love but more so out of being able to control me and the way that I am brought up. They had to come to my home bazomtshela bona [to tell him] about the school and emphasize ukuthi [that] it's an all-girls school with predominantly womxn teachers."[41]

Many people would argue that these controversies were part of the purpose of the school—to bring attention to the need to support and empower Black women who may be struggling in a patriarchal society. Refilwe, Bongeka, and other students, Ntaka notes, learned at the academy that they "had the agency to act" and "the autonomy to think" for themselves.[42] Concomitantly, they adopted a demeanor that their families sometimes considered arrogant and off-putting.

While the school did not replace students' families, it created a space where the students, as "Oprah girls," could reposition themselves in relation to economic opportunities and social settings that, while new and exciting, created a form of double consciousness. "Double consciousness provides a framework with which we can understand the duality that comes from our consciousness when walking between the 'white' and 'Black' world," Ntaka wrote. "However, this duality of consciousness is further broken down when we consider that these womxn not only navigate white and black—with all the economic associations that come with it—but also have to manage and grapple with who one should be at home and at school."[43] The new social subjectivities that "Oprah girls" struggled with and learned to embody were precisely those some community members objected to.

I heard some of these criticisms of the school in my conversations with townspeople about whether the school should better conform to South African than American standards of teaching and discipline. OWLAG publicity puts students at the center of the school and champions the school for fostering discussion and debate rather than rote learning or passive silence. "But that method may be too American," Hennie and others told me. Dozens of OWLAG employees over the years quit the school, quietly wondering if the "Oprah method," as one café owner described it, is best for them as teachers or for the students. The family model that pervades the school does not work for everyone. Teachers unable to lead by example and not, metaphorically speaking, "by the cane" often choose or are asked to leave.[44]

Other critiques of the school's importation of American values centered on the American idea of celebrity. Teachers and parents indicated that OWLAG's approach, at times, is too American celebrity driven. Not unlike the "Oprah girls" who walk down a narrow path that puts them between two competing contexts, their families and the school, some teachers, parents, and community members expressed discomfort in having to balance the benefit of the school with the potential cost to their own autonomy in determining how to fund and run it. "Celebrity humanism" fills a gap in "systems under duress from funding cuts and lack of support," Alexandra Cosima Budabin and Lisa Ann Richey note in an analysis of how celebrities have disrupted the politics of development in the Democratic Republic of the Congo.[45] But in OWLAG's case, celebrity humanism rivals, if not undercuts, the South African government's own mandate to provide education and leadership training for all South Africans.[46]

At the same time, many people in the local community with whom I spoke also noted that the most significant benefit of OWLAG is the money the school brings to the community. However, this kind of benefit can also create dependencies among local communities and states on foreign support, dependencies that may feel uncomfortably reminiscent of those that emerged during colonialism.

Several years ago, anthropologist James Ferguson suggested that entering relationships of hierarchical dependence may be desirable in cases where alternatives are few or nonexistent.[47] Hierarchical dependencies, he argues, provide a source of recognition and belonging. Others, however, have argued that this perspective simply "downplays the role of colonial, global, and regional entanglements in creating the inequalities that lead toward particular geographies of dependence."[48] Taken at face value, Ferguson's claim implies that South Africans find fulfillment and benefit when they depend on other people. Yet, as Danielsen notes, in the landscape of postapartheid South Africa, people might appear to seek out relations of dependence while also articulating strong critiques of those relationships.

Danielson's point about the copresence of contrasting elements in tension finds a poignant reflection in the case of the Oprah Winfrey Leadership Academy for Girls. While the school represents an opportunity for many young women, its success emerges from the broader context of inequality that shapes access to wealth and to education. The story of OWLAG encapsulates a broader narrative of striving for progress while confronting the legacies of inequality, inviting ongoing conversation about how best to bridge these divides for future generations.

NO FREE GIFTS

Charitable gifts may (or may not) help the neediest. But, in all events, charity is not and cannot be designed to alter the macrostructure of political economic inequality. Charity cannot be so designed, because private donors' control of education (or of health, food production, or communication) competes with a system of government to the extent that donors hold disproportionately greater power than most citizens to bring about change through action and economic influence.

In the words of anthropologist Mary Douglas, "Charity is meant to be a free gift, a voluntary, unrequited surrender of resources. Though we laud charity as a Christian virtue, we know that it wounds." Douglas worked for many years in a UK-based charitable foundation that gave away a "large sum" of money annually "as the condition of tax exemption."[49] She reported that newcomers to the office sometimes learned that "the recipient does not like the giver"; that is, that the impoverished receiver of the donation may not like the donor, no matter "how cheerful" and pleasant the donor may be. According to Douglas (with whom I agree), a donor may claim to make gifts "free," without strings attached, and without any expectation of material or immaterial return. However, any donation of money or resources, whether from corporate venture philanthropists or celebrity donors, may be intended to return at least one thing: loyalty, public-facing support for the donor's generosity.

At Henley on Klip, the local community carefully courts Oprah's money, even if many residents question the school. Back in Cape Town, in the offices of the D. G. Murray Trust, South African administrators report to the Michael & Susan Dell Foundation in the United States, whose officers in turn report to the US government that "the foundation reviewed the grant reports submitted by the Grantee, but did not undertake any verification thereof, as there was no reason to doubt their accuracy and reliability."[50] Similar statements appear on virtually all corporate philanthropic 990 tax forms, including Dell, Gates, Microsoft, and Pfizer. The language fulfills a legal obligation to report to the American public that US foundations sending funds overseas disburse their money ethically and lawfully.

I have no reason to question the legality of any activities I describe here. The law and tax processes favor corporate philanthropists and celebrity donors. But, as in the saying about the law benefiting those who seize the commons and about the thief who needs a goose to eat, the cycle of obedience traded for generosity undergirds—as rhythm invisibly braces up poetry—a political economy that reproduces inequality.

Corporate venture philanthropy cycles donations into a market economy that reinvests charitable ventures into ed-tech industries. Celebrities give, it would appear, in order to secure their public legacy without prominently guaranteeing longer-term investment prospects. The former quietly boosts tech empires; the latter builds altruistic activities alongside egos and brand legacies. Both approaches come with pros and cons. However, there is a better way to share the commons, which requires neither thieves nor villains, donors nor recipients, but just a more distributive and democratic political economy.

Sustained governmental financing for education requires adequate domestic revenue, not charity. US ed-tech venture philanthropy hurts education systems overseas by undermining faith in government, labeling public systems as inefficient, building private industries around US ed-tech philanthropy, and extracting digital "capital" that accrues primarily to Big Tech corporations in the United States. Economists estimate that at least 6 percent of GDP is needed to finance universal education in any country.[51] That means national governments need a tax base, and that means that the mobilization of money for taxes for schools needs to go hand in hand with other efforts, including changing the tax structures in the United States and elsewhere that hide corporate US low- and no-taxed wealth, in the billions or trillions, in contributions that in the end build their industries.

Corporate ed-tech philanthropy undercuts democratically supported government-led solutions to community problems and moves the world toward oligarchic governance. To paraphrase education economist Steven Klees: of course, there have been sensible, even progressive charitable trusts in the past and today. But philanthropy is embedded in an ideology that deprecates governments and extols the benefactor and the market.[52] A political-economic worldview that sees the free market as the main mechanism for securing social solidarity, and that severely restricts the government, is antidemocratic, as the Athenians knew. It perpetuates a ranked society by restricting social power in a highly stratified social system to a narrow political class.

REPRISE

Corporate donations are alibis for diverting scrutiny from extreme concentrations of untaxed private wealth. The fact that US corporate philanthropies use gifts to increase stock dividends in the United States is one thing. The fact that they also do it overseas, to me, is criminal.

Spurred by a strong tradition of resistance to institutionalized inequalities, recent research across the social sciences has begun to elucidate how wealthy entities harness the power of state institutions to bankroll their private wealth.[53] In "The 'New' Imperialism: Accumulation by Dispossession," David Harvey argued that when financiers have no place to productively invest, they face an overaccumulation crisis and begin to deregulate publicly protected entities that freeze up investors' wealth, such as labor unions, health and safety laws, environmental protections, and supply chain costs.[54] Harvey focused on workers' struggles but much has changed since he wrote twenty years ago.

In today's world, the erosion of public trust in elite benefaction can be overshadowed or overlooked by ostensibly positive changes such as the construction of new schools and the provision of laptops to teachers and students. While these improvements may seem beneficial, they do not fundamentally address deeper issues of inequality and trust in authority. Instead, these superficial advancements can distract from more serious underlying problems. Charitable giving can create a "protective covering," diverting scrutiny from the more significant matter that government coffers are underfunded.[55] Whereas older family trusts and noninvestment charities such as Oprah's construe themselves as kinship groups, "families of like minds" espousing shared beliefs,[56] today's clearinghouses like the Dell Family Trust and D. M. Murray Family Trust take a market-oriented approach to financializing charity. Like lenders in the financial world, donors offer hope for something better. However, that "something better" is invisibly packaged in the capital market that returns dividends to lenders.

To reiterate, *both* venture philanthropy and traditional philanthropy such as Oprah's create dependency. While they may be established and run by those with good intentions, they undermine solidarity between the public and governments. "In being directly cued to public esteem, the distribution of honour, and the sanctions of religion," charities minimize the state's ability to instill solidarity and draw people away from government.[57] In giving to the poor, they pull citizens' allegiance over to private agencies.

Corporate ed-tech philanthropy conducts business through data extraction; it is wealth generation labeled "charity." On the scale we see, corporate philanthropy weakens tax bases. A mechanism for private enrichment washing money through public systems, ed-tech philanthropy depends first on the minerals required for tech companies to exist (the lithium) and then on "poor communities" in Africa to accept gifts that are also used to extract raw data from unpaid, often unknowing end users. Corporations may say they step in to support "weak" or "corrupt" governments, claiming that "corruption is holding Africa back."[58] But as I see it, corruption is the system of wealth extraction and data expropriation that masquerades as charity. Such extraction is all the more egregious when, as in the case of ed-tech venture philanthropy, it is built on the backs of, yet claims to help, "impoverished African children."

Conclusion

A US CORPORATE ROUNDUP

This book focuses on how US corporations use corporate alibis to shield themselves from public scrutiny for environmentally and socially destructive business practices in Africa today. It has documented how companies and charitable organizations employ hidden tactics such as greenwashing, working through subsidiaries, and setting up philanthropic charities to extract wealth for shareholders across numerous industries, including agribusiness, e-commerce, biomedicine, and education. Companies such as Coca-Cola, Corteva Agriscience, Amazon, and Pfizer use a variety of types of alibis, including legal and communications-based defenses, to avoid accountability for resource-destroying and unethical business practices, often by hiding behind their charitable industries or working through subsidiaries. Corporations use the language of "doing good" when they invest in locations like those in Tanzania and South Africa and others discussed in this book—highlighting how their investments will "help" communities they consider impoverished or in lands they consider "empty." However, corporations are not in the business of doing good or helping communities. Instead, they invest in their own market missions and use the language of "helping others" to divert scrutiny from both the profits and the negative impacts of their investments.

Both private companies and philanthropic foundations connected to private companies construct and use these strategies. The Gates Foundation ostensibly uses an alibi of philanthropic work to obscure practices that contribute to the financial expansion of the Gates family. A pertinent example is the Foundation's investment in Pfizer via Berkshire Hathaway during the COVID pandemic, which coincided with the Foundation's efforts to facilitate the distribution of Pfizer vaccines in Africa. This dual role raises questions about the interplay between charitable endeavors and profit-driven motives.

In digital commerce, such alibis provide companies with similar opportunities. Amazon World Services (AWS) and Dell Technologies both proffer technologies and financial support to the public through initiatives such as AWS's InCommunities RANGER program and the Dell Foundations' backing of educational institutions and ed-tech startups in South Africa. However, these ostensibly altruistic "technology gifts" can also be used to extract the intangible intellectual data of children and educators for corporate profit without needing to acknowledge any conflict of interest. If a government official used or sold data the government had secretly collected from private citizens for private gain, that practice would, appropriately, be called corruption. In the private sector, however, such taking and reprofiting from "raw" digital data is protected by US intellectual property laws. This legal protection in the United States helps companies demand other countries' governments—such as in South Africa, as discussed with the Amazon case, or as in Tanzania in the case of the Gates Foundation's refusal to share public health information—also protect those foreign companies' right to own and retain raw data collected in African countries, something African governments agree to because they want to attract and keep US investors. The irony, indeed, the moral offense of this scenario, is that those investors undermine the governments' power.

Alibis help corporations channel profits through foundations to avoid obligation for taxes needed by governments. Many also take advantage of underfunded governments and income-insecure people and communities— and work through subsidiaries—to make their extractive practices appear generous. When KFC asked food-insecure and low-wage customers in South Africa to donate their change to the KFC Foundation—money that was supposed to be used to help food-insecure people in Africa—it simultaneously was in a position to classify these donations as corporate tax write-offs. Asking customers to support corporate philanthropy may be leveraging an effective alibi of "doing good" while simultaneously profiting from a social issue. Furthermore, KFC historically invoked the practice of using a subsidiary to deflect responsibility for de facto profiting during years the US government imposed economic sanctions against the pro-apartheid South African government. Although KFC's action may not have broken the law, it went against the spirit of the US economic sanctions.

As the range of examples discussed in this book shows, the use of alibis is not limited to one industry or one country or region. It is built into corporate investment practices, and it is an essential tool for multinational corporations today—no matter where they operate. The use of these alibis in South Africa, Tanzania, and other countries by companies like Coca-Cola, Corteva Agriscience, Amazon, and Apple, shows the central role these alibis play for corporations today.

In law, an alibi is a plausible defense against having been present where and when a crime occurred. In the sense I use it in this book, it is an excuse warranting interrogation. US and international law may be on the side of US investors, corporations, and their philanthropies, but that does not mean their practices are moral or ethically supportable. Indeed, the US corporations I name in this book may have laws on their side, but their operations in Africa seem to reflect ongoing inequalities linked to historical patterns of exploitation.

Cedric Robinson describes wealth generated by the labor of enslaved people during the African slave trade as "racial capitalism."[1] Since the colonial era to the present, Robinson elaborates, wealth extraction and exploitation have been deeply entwined throughout history. Robinson's term "racial capitalism" is also interwoven with the complex history of property law, as Cheryl Harris has written—including intellectual property law, which, as this book explains, is deeply embedded in US corporations' wealth extraction processes. Both Robinson and Harris outline the social, cultural, and historical conditions that create the context for the corporate alibis discussed in this book. Robinson's geographic focus on the African diaspora in the Americas and Harris's analysis of the relationship between law and power establish a foundation for this book's *corporate alibi* analytic intervention. Foreign wealth extraction in Africa continues to exploit the legacies of property and historical injustices, highlighting how the ongoing processes of wealth extraction shape today's globalized economy.

Today, people across the globe are increasingly aware of the structural inequalities arising from extreme wealth concentrations, which impact both public and private life in the United States and beyond. This heightened awareness has influenced consumer behavior, prompting companies to adapt their public-relations strategies to address these concerns. As a result, it is rare to find US corporations that do not acknowledge the importance of social equity in their practices; most now incorporate language related to social and economic justice in their marketing materials. For instance, Amazon's "Our Positions" message serves as its ethical statement to the US audience, declaring the company supports affordable housing for workers and the rights of immigrants. However, such statements often lack substantive action and genuine commitment, leading to skepticism about the authenticity of these corporations' dedication to meaningful social change. Consequently, while some firms may make superficial efforts, the challenge of addressing these inequities remains a complex issue.

Drawing on the pivotal contributions of a diverse array of researchers, this book analyzes the connections among corporate wealth extraction in Africa, historical inequities, and the legacy of colonialism. Ikaika Ramones and Sally Engle Merry have scrutinized the intricate interplay between settler-colonial capitalism and indigenous populations, illuminating what Marshall Sahlins earlier called the "structure of the conjuncture" that governs the multifaceted interactions of participants in economic exchanges.[2] This book examines key sites of exchange in this "structure of conjuncture"—the exchanges between US corporations or philanthropies and communities in Africa—to highlight how these corporate alibis play a role in structuring and restructuring global inequities. From the school funded by Oprah Winfrey and Dell's Starling Vocational Technical School, brokered by the D. G. Murray Trust; to exchanges involving Pfizer, international health organizations, and national medical centers in Tanzania; to the relations between community and indigenous activists and Amazon World Services in Cape Town; to the interactions between small-holding African farmers and US agribusinesses and water-guzzling monopolies—

these sites of interaction between local communities and foreign companies and philanthropies all constitute liminal spaces wherein power struggles for control of resources generally favor the Goliaths of the world, not the Davids.

The corporate alibis outlined in this book are today a key part of the strategy that the Goliaths use in this quest for power, a strategy built on a paradox. I call this paradox the *kindness conceit*. It accompanies investors' extraction of raw materials from the African continent to create surplus wealth that impoverishes others. Tania Li and Paige West have separately analyzed an implicit operating principle of today's global economy: not only does extraction dispossess people of their resources but the commodification of labor and resources, as the principle underwriting "development," frames dispossession as good for communities.[3] Li's essay "Indigeneity, Capitalism, and the Management of Dispossession" unearthed the paradox at the heart of post–World War II international development policies: on one hand, they lauded "cultural diversity" and, on the other, painted indigenous worlds as "poor," needing markets. The use of alibis by corporations today offers powerful examples of this paradox in action.

The surplus wealth that today's global capitalist system generates for investors is more than even billionaires can spend, and even more than can be reinvested in extractive industries. Surplus wealth is so great in the largest US multinational corporations that—like the Dell Foundation with its Starling Vocational Technical School funded through a South African trust—multinational corporations invest, philanthropically, *in their own businesses.* They provide the so-called seed corn funds that will germinate as industries on the African continent. Such corporate colonization of Africa's food, agriculture, health, and education zones recalls Namita Dharia's argument that the extractive, dispossessing aspects of capitalism mesh with and create seemingly equal parts of love and opportunity— again, the "kindness" aspect that, in my use, provides the alibi that extractors cannot possibly cause harm when people embrace the extraction model so fully.[4]

Today, the unprecedent levels of wealth concentration among global corporations like those discussed in this book dwarfs the GDP of nation-states around the world, including many in Africa. This market power has enabled companies to gain great leverage over governments in countries where those companies wish to operate. This power has in turn diminished nation-state sovereignty and people's trust in government. While an older literature on global finance and the globalization of culture celebrated the unprecedented mobility of ideas and money, unleashed in the wake of digital technologies,[5] another literature has lamented this loss of nation-state sovereignty as a result of the progressive undermining of governments.[6]

Sovereign states rely on other states to claim their own sovereignty and independence. Economic globalization, once seen to strengthen recognition among states of one another's authority as a basis on which treaties and contracts could be signed and enforced,[7] fell prey to other forces that have diminished the authority of states, including South Africa and Tanzania, where corporations and philanthropies like the Gates Foundation, the Coca-Cola Foundation, and the others discussed in this book maintain significant operations. Highlighting their role—and the alibis and tropes they rely on to maintain their philanthropic and business practices—is important for understanding how the ongoing effects of globalization, neoliberalism, and deindustrialization are unfolding among communities where these organizations operate today.

In Africa, and worldwide, corporations have had a detrimental impact on governments, the planet, and people's abilities to control the resources needed to sustain their livelihoods. Both the gifts and charitable donations through philanthropic foundations attached to corporations and their local subsidiary companies operate hand in glove, pairing the "value-neutral free market system" with gifts and philanthropic charity. The alibis that foreign corporations and investors in Africa use—enabled through this philanthropy and their subsidiaries—are at the heart of the discourse enabling extractive and destructive practices in Africa.

However, it is also true that US corporations' power to buy or undermine governments and their capacity to set up effective alibis to camouflage their actual purposes is limited and sometimes enabled by influential stakeholders on both sides of the Atlantic. Indeed, government officials and other groups and entities play a crucial role, often due to wealth, in influencing the distribution of resources, the types of industries that thrive, and trade practices and regulations. At the same time, while corporations can weaken and undermine governments and alienate populations from the state, governments are essential players not only as tax collectors but also in providing access to infrastructure and enforcing legal frameworks for curtailing the privatization of resources. They zone and approve projects, build bridges and roads that serve industries, provide industries with information and financial advice, and, though often overlooked, set the laws that regulate and protect businesses from infringement by competitors.

A substantial criticism of corporate influence within governments is that it creates the potential for regulatory capture by industries the governmental agencies are supposed to scrutinize. When that happens, the industries supposedly regulated by the government take control of the agencies they are nominally under, and the regulator may actively benefit favored firms. Ultimately, any study of the corporate wealth extraction and corporate capture of governments is also a study of governments' relationship to businesses and the creative ways people, including some in government, shape and bend the "world system" to match their interests and agendas. The corporate alibis that this book has outlined across multiple business sectors are examples of how this molding works.

At the same time, nongovernment officials, non-elites—including small-scale farmers, laborers, health workers—are not powerless. Africa is not in the "global shadows" of a neoliberal world order; it is part of that order.[8] African small-holding farmers are not victims unable to effect the terms and outcomes they wish to see. On the contrary, through their day-to-day relationships with others and the land, many small-holding farmers in Tanzania and South Africa critique and resist the technologized, anthropocentric view of the environment as distinct from people's interactions and social relations. In these farmers' "mobilizing myths," social history and the physical environment are integrated, as they were for Bibi Alilya and as they continue to be for her grandchildren. In my formulation, power and domination are not contrasted with but are coextensive with practices and discourses of resistance and activism.

In this book's introduction, I mentioned Bakhtin's notions of simultaneity and heteroglossia as useful for thinking about foreign corporate practices in Africa today, specifically for grasping how corporate messaging exhibits a copresence of contrasting elements in tension and the multiplicity of socio-ideological discourses. The corporate messaging of greenwashing and the reliance on "communicative opacity" in advertising discussed earlier help companies paint over likely negative outcomes of their activities with positive, optimistic notions of "the good." Recognizing how these discursive elements can remain in tension is, in the end, essential for understanding how corporations are able to maintain such problematic business practices.

I also quoted at the start of this book a CEO in the Florida agribusiness industry, who suggested that "someday, we will not need governments; corporations will do everything," proposing that an investment-based, corporate-driven financial market could take the place of a government's policies, actions, and affairs. This vision conflates corporations' profit interests with the public's social and environmental concerns. It is an example of the easy slogans of corporate jargon and alibis that provide cover for flawed analyses according to which shareholders' interests are the same as those of the public. Corporate governance is not government governance. Investment markets require growth; government concerns are more holistic. Importantly, regulations can mitigate the adverse effects of unbridled commerce, including environmental damage and labor abuse, keeping firms from finding loopholes. At the same time, today, the locus of power in the food, water, health, and education sectors is shifting at a dizzying speed—moving away from public management to private enterprise. The furious pace of corporations' expansion into these connected sectors in Africa and elsewhere—and the legal and corporate alibis that are so integral to this expansion—demands our immediate attention from conceptual, practical, and political standpoints.

A US corporate-led future on its current course will continue to generate inequalities, deepen livelihood stresses and food insecurity, and harm environments. Yet choosing *not* to unpack the cover stories and alibis US corporations promulgate in the name of "helping" or "developing" Africa is to ensure an ongoing environmental, diplomatic, and societal collision course. History shows that knowledge is power, and people can work for the better almost overnight when confronted with knowledge and when people still hold political power. Organizing, pressuring lawmakers, voting, and insisting corporations pay more taxes can foster new transformations. The profound changes the world has seen since the most recent pandemic, including changing our interactions quickly and working together, show that anything is possible tomorrow.

Notes

PREFACE

1. See "Greenhouse 100 Polluters Index," Political Economy Research Institute, University of Massachusetts Amherst https://peri.umass.edu/collection /greenhouse-100-polluters-index/, accessed March 3, 2025; "Toxic 100 Water Polluters Index (2024 Report, Based on 2022 Data)," Political Economy Research Institute, University of Massachusetts Amherst, accessed March 3, 2025, https:// peri.umass.edu/index-edition/toxic-100-water-polluters-index-2024-report-based -on-2022-data/, accessed March 3, 2025. "Violation Tracker: Offense Groups," Good Jobs First, accessed March 3, 2025, https://violationtracker.goodjobsfirst .org/.

2. However, a recent decision by the US Supreme Court drastically curtailed the power of the Environmental Protection Agency to protect drinking water and wetlands. Many states are working to bolster their own protective regulations See Sackett et al. v. Environmental Protection Agency et al., 598 U.S., https://www.supremecourt.gov/opinions/22pdf/21-454_4g15.pdf. Moreover, many cases are settled out of court and typically not in the best interests of the communities impacted. See Dave Yost, Ohio Attorney General, "AG Yost Seeks Answers as One-Year Anniversary of East Palestine Train Derailment Approaches," news release, February 2, 2024, https://www.ohioattorneygeneral .gov/Media/News-Releases/February-2024/AG-Yost-Seeks-Answers-as-One-Year- Anniversary-of-E; and "Judge Gives Preliminary Approval to $641 Million Flint,

Michigan, Water Settlement," Reuters, January 21, 2021, https://www.reuters
.com/article/us-usa-michigan-flint-water-idUSKBN29Q2WZ/.

3. Geoffrey Heal, "Are US Corporations above the Law?" Columbia Business
School Insights, July 11, 2021, https://business.columbia.edu/insights/business-
society/are-us-corporations-above-law.

4. "Supreme Court Backs Nestle, Cargill in Child Slave Labor Suit," Associated Press, June 17, 2021, https://www.politico.com/news/2021/06/17/supreme-
court-ruling-child-slave-labor-495022.

5. Marcoux, "Coca-Cola's Cape Town Crisis"; Steve Kretzmann and Raymond
Joseph, "Coca-Cola, the City of Cape Town and Day Zero Tariffs," *News24*, South
Africa, May 9, 2020, https://www.news24.com/news24/southafrica/news
/coca-cola-and-cape-towns-sweetheart-day-zero-deal-20200509.

6. Gloria Dickie, "Pollution Killing 9 Million People a Year, Africa Hardest
Hit—Study," Reuters, May 18, 2022, https://www.reuters.com/business
/environment/pollution-killing-9-million-people-year-africa-hardest-hit-
study-2022-05-17/; Fuller et al., "Pollution and Health"; "Violation Tracker:
Offense Groups."

7. Dolan, Huang, and Gordon, "The Ambiguity of Mutuality"; Orock, "Less-
Told Stories about Corporate Globalization."

8. For examples, see "Training AI Training Takes Heavy Toll on Kenyans Working for $2 an Hour," *60 Minutes*, CBS News, November 24, 2024, https://www.
cbsnews.com/video/ai-workers-kenya-60-minutes-video-2024-11-24/, Isobel
Cockerell, "Legendary Kenya Lawyer Takes on Meta and ChatGPT," *.coda*, October 22, 2024, https://www.codastory.com/authoritarian-tech/mercy-mutemi-
meta-lawsuit/. See also Niamh Rowe, "'It's Destroyed Me Completely': Kenyan
Moderators Decry Toll of Training of AI Models," *The Guardian*, August 2,
2023, https://www.theguardian.com/technology/2023/aug/02/ai-chatbot-
training-human-toll-content-moderator-meta-openai; and Billy Perrigo, "OpenAI
Used Kenyan Workers on Less than $2 Per Hour to Make Chat GPT Less
Toxic," *Time*, January 18, 2023, https://time.com/6247678/openai-chatgpt-kenya-
workers/. Facebook, too, employed low-wage laborers in Kenya to remove illegal or
banned content from Facebook, paying as little as $1.50 per hour. See Billy Perrigo,
"Inside Facebook's African Sweatshop," *Time*, February 22, 2022, https://time.
com/6147458/facebook-africa-content-moderation-employee-treatment/.

9. ChatGPT's content moderators working in Kenya for $2.00 per hour would
have needed to view traumatizing material sixty-two hours per week, four weeks
per month, to afford even basic living expenses. "Poverty and Equity Brief: Africa
Eastern and Southern," World Bank Group: Poverty and Equity, April 2023,
https://databankfiles.worldbank.org/public/ddpext_download/poverty/987B9C90-
CB9F-4D93-AE8C-750588BF00QA/current/Global_POVEQ_KEN.pdf; Simon
Ayub Lilian Wanjala, "Average Salary in Kenya Monthly and Annually per

Person in 2024," *Tuko News*, June 12, 2023, https://www.tuko.co.ke/343265-average-salary-kenya.html.

10. Dell, Apple, and Google quoted in "Apple, Google, Microsoft, Tesla, and Dell Sued over Child-Mined Cobalt from Africa," *CBS News*, December 17, 2019, https://www.cbsnews.com/news/apple-google-microsoft-tesla-dell-sued-over-cobalt-mining-children-in-congo-for-batteries-2019-12-17/.

11. The judge's ruling, quoted in (by Danielle Toth), "Judge Dismisses Child Labor Class Action Against Apple, Google Alphabet, Microsoft, Dell and Tesla," Top Class Actions, November 3, 2021, https://topclassactions.com/lawsuit-settlements/employment-labor/judge-dismisses-child-labor-class-action-against-apple-google-alphabet-microsoft-dell-and-tesla/. The Child Labor Class Action Lawsuit is *Jane Doe 1, et al. v. Apple Inc., et al.*, Case No. 1:19-cv-03737, in the US District Court for the District of Columbia.

12. Cooper, Alber, and Njoya, *Education Alibi*.

13. The enclosure and privatization of the commons is famously analyzed by Karl Marx in *Capital*, vol. 1, pt. 8, chs. 26–28, 33, and David Harvey in *New Imperialism* (2003) and *Brief History of Neoliberalism* (2007).

INTRODUCTION

1. Lyimo et al., "Cancer Mortality Patterns in Tanzania."

2. Following US legal practices that treat corporations as juridical persons, I use the pronoun *who* when I refer to a corporation or corporations. See Hartmann, *Unequal Protection*.

3. Overseas (or foreign) subsidiaries are companies owned by an enterprise based in another country. Overseas subsidiaries must comply with the law of their local jurisdiction and are responsible for their own assets and taxes. See "Subsidiary," Encyclopedia.com, updated May 18, 2018, https://www.encyclopedia.com/social-sciences-and-law/law/law/subsidiary.

4. Chang et al., "International Trade Causes Large Net Economic Losses"; Sy and Tinker, "From Exxon *Valdez* to Oriental Nicety."

5. "Greenwashing: The Deceptive Tactics Behind Environmental Claims," United Nations: Climate Action, accessed March 3, 2025, https://www.un.org/en/climatechange/science/climate-issues/greenwashing.

6. "About Us," Bezos Earth Fund, accessed March 3, 2025, https://www.bezosearthfund.org; Bezos Earth Fund, "Bezos Earth Fund Announces $100 Million for AI Solutions to Tackle Climate Change and Nature Loss," *PRNewswire*, April 16, 2024, https://www.prnewswire.com/news-releases/bezos-earth-fund-announces-100-million-for-ai-solutions-to-tackle-climate-change-and-nature-loss-302118384.html.

7. See Sigal Samuel, "How Should Billionaires Spend Their Money to Fight Climate Change? I Asked 9 Experts," *Vox*, November 12, 2019, https://www.vox .com/future-perfect/2019/11/12/20910176/billionaire-philanthropy-charity-climate-change.

8. Sigal Samuel, "Donating $10 Billion Isn't the Best Way for Jeff Bezos to Fight Climate Change," *Vox*, February 19, 2020, https://www.vox.com/future-perfect/2020/2/19/21142312/jeff-bezos-climate-change-ten-billion-philanthropy. Amazon that year emitted 68.82 million metric tons of carbon. For 2023 and 2024 country emissions, see "Total CO2 Emissions per Year (MtCo2/day) in All Sectors," The Carbon Monitor, updated December 28, 2024, https://carbonmonitor .org. The Carbon Monitor is part of the Carbon Monitor Project housed at the University of California–Irvine under the direction of Steven Davis. For Amazon 2023 emissions, see Susanna Twidale, "Amazon's Total Emissions Fell in 2023 As It Meets Renewable Power Goal," Reuters, July 10, 2024, https://www.reuters .com/business/environment/ amazons-total-emissions-fell-2023-it-meets-renewable-power-goal-2024-07-10.

9. Jedy-Agba et al., "Trend in Cervical Cancer Incidence." Chlorinated hydrocarbons are used in "chemical products such as pharmaceuticals, plastics, and solvents." "Learn about Effluent Guidelines," EPA: United States Environmental Protection Agency," accessed March 3, 2025, https://www.epa.gov/eg /learn-about-effluent-guidelines. See also. "Cervical Cancer," World Health Organization: African Region, accessed March 3, 2025, https://www.afro .who.int/health-topics/cervical-cancer. I do not know that Gloria's occupational exposure caused her cancer; however, her family suspected that Gloria's occupational exposure was the cause, given that regulations of the solvent were lax or nonexistent.

10. Grant and Keohane, "Accountability and Abuses of Power in World Politics"; Gustafsson, Schilling-Vacaflor, and Lenschow, "Politics of Supply Chain Regulations."

11. Fieldwork notes, October 2018.

12. On economic redistribution, see Guest, *Cultural Anthropology*.

13. Adu Sarfo and Tweneboah, "Mineral Wealth Paradox"; Githiria and Onifade, "Impact of Mining on Sustainable Practices and the Traditional Culture of Developing Countries"; Morgan, Farris, and Johnson, "Foreign Direct Investment in Africa."

14. See "US Annual Foreign Direct Investment in Africa 2000–2023," Statista, August 5, 2024 (update January 2025), https://www.statista.com/statistics /188594/united-states-direct-investments-in-africa-since-2000/ (data for the Statista report are sourced from the US Department of Commerce, Bureau of Economic Analysis, "Balance of Payments and Direct Investment Position Data," released August 2024). I extrapolated from projected investment to round the $987.17 billion to $1 trillion for 2024.

15. Morgan, Farris, and Johnson, "Foreign Direct Investment in Africa."

16. US Department of State, Bureau of African Affairs, "2022 US-Africa Leaders Summit Overview," accessed January 6, 2025, https://www.state.gov /2022-u-s-africa-leaders-summit-overview/.

17. Kikayo Akeredolu, "African Perception of the United States in an Evolving Geopolitical Landscape," Woodrow Wilson Center: Africa Up Close, July 27, 2023,https://www.wilsoncenter.org/blog-post/african-perception-united-states-evolving-geopolitical-landscape.

18. "Global Wealth Report 2024," USB, accessed March 7, 2025, https://www .ubs.com/us/en/wealth-management/insights/global-wealth-report.html; *The World Inequality Report 2022*, World Inequality Lab, March 7, 2025, https:// wir2022.wid.world/.

19. Nielsen et al., "The Role of High-Socioeconomic-Status People."

20. "Warmer temperatures lead to drying," as Tiffany Means simply puts it, in "Climate Change and Droughts: What's the Connection?" *Yale Climate Connections*, May 11, 2023, https://yaleclimateconnections.org/2023/05/climate-change-and-droughts-whats-the-connection/.

21. See "How Enablers Facilitate Illicit Financial Flows: Evidence from Africa," Transparency International, December 5, 2023, https://www.transparency.org /en/news/how-enablers-facilitate-illicit-financial-flows-from-africa; Antonio Cascais, "Chasing Africa's Tax Dodgers," *In Focus*, June 17, 2021, https://www .dw.com/en/africas-problem-with-tax-avoidance/a-48401574. The UN Trade and Development (UNCTAD) organization notes, "Due to the lack of domestic transfer pricing rules in most African countries, local judicial authorities lack the tools to challenge tax evasion by multinational enterprises." See "Africa Could Gain $89 Billion Annually by Curbing Illicit Financial Flows," UNCTAD, September 28, 2020, https://unctad.org/news/africa-could-gain-89-billion-annually-curbing-illicit-financial-flows.

22. McNamee and Miller, *Meritocracy Myth*; Fuhrer, *Myths That Made Us*.

23. For example, Arndt, "Linking Wealth and Power"; Beckert, "Varieties of Wealth"; Hay, "Economic Wealth and Political Power in the Second Gilded Age"; Rossi, "Impact of Individual Wealth on Posterior Political Power."

24. On this topic, see the excellent dissertation of Maria Hengeveld, "Girl Incorporated."

25. Giridharadas, *Winners Take All*.

26. On securing consent without the use of force ("hegemony"), see Gramsci, "State and Civil Society," 206–76. On accumulation by dispossession (creating wealth on the backs of impoverished people), see Harvey, "The 'New' Imperialism." My analysis goes beyond Harvey's to show how gifts hide or disguise accumulation by dispossession.

27. Steuart Pennington, "Let Hope, Not Doubt, Shape South Africa's Future: #ThisIsUs World Food Day 16 October," *Home of Great South African News*,

October 14, 2021, https://www.sagoodnews.co.za/let-hope-not-doubt-shape-south-africas-future-thisisus-world-food-day-16-october/. The quote "by customers rounding up the cost of their meals" comes from "Purpose That Feeds the Future: 2021 Global Citizenship and Sustainability Report, Yum!, accessed January 6, 2025, https://www.yum.com/wps/wcm/connect/yumbrands/8aba36f2-f631-40c8-925a-671ea74692a3/R4G-Report-printer-2021-v6.pdf?MOD=AJPERES&CVID=o9apqa8ead-2021-responsibility-report.pdf.

28. According to a South African research agency, around 26 percent of South African adults bought food from KFC between April 1 and April 30, 2024. See "Colonel's Corner," Eighty20 Consulting, May 7, 2024, https://www.eighty20.co.za/fact-a-day/colonels-corner/. See also Shaun Jacobs, "South Africans Love KFC," *Daily Investor,* November 9, 2023, https://dailyinvestor.com/south-africa/36981/south-africans-love-kfc/.

29. "Apple, Google, Microsoft, Tesla, and Dell Sued over Child-Mined Cobalt from Africa," *CBS News*, December 17, 2019, https://www.cbsnews.com/news/apple-google-microsoft-tesla-dell-sued-over-cobalt-mining-children-in-congo-for-batteries-2019–12–17/. For an inside look into the mining industry in the DRC, see Smith, *Eyes of the World.*

30. The Child Labor Class Action Lawsuit is *Jane Doe 1, et al. v. Apple Inc., et al.,* Case No. 1:19-cv-03737," in the US District Court for the District of Columbia. See Danielle Toth, "Judge Dismisses Child Labor Class Action Against Apple, Google Alphabet, Microsoft, Dell, and Tesla," Top Class Actions, November 3, 2021, https://topclassactions.com/lawsuit-settlements/employment-labor/judge-dismisses-child-labor-class-action-against-apple-google-alphabet-microsoft-dell-and-tesla/.

31. Marber, "Globalization and Its Contents."

32. Marber, "Globalization and Its Contents."

33. Dahl, "Can International Organizations Be Democratic?"; Suris, *Networking Futures,* 1–60, 287–302.

34. Trouillot, "Culture on the Edges."

35. Scheper-Hughes, "Propositions for a Militant Anthropology"; Tax, "Action Anthropology."

36. Bakhtin, "Discourse in the Novel," 281. Uma Pradhan's work on the simultaneity of national and ethnic identity in Nepali students' language practices helps me apply Bakhtinian thinking here and below. See Pradhan, *Simultaneous Identities.*

37. Chukwumerije Okereke argues that companies use Africa as a testing ground for unproven technology even though they deny it. See Okereke, "My Continent Is Not Your Giant Climate Laboratory," *New York Times,* April 18, 2023, https://www.nytimes.com/2023/04/18/opinion/geoengineering-climate-change-technology-africa.html.

38. Heteroglossia does not require that a particular aspect (e.g., southern colonel) be read as important and relevant in every setting. Instead, the concept points sociologically to many readings across different audiences.

39. Ortner, "Dark Anthropology and Its Others," 47.

40. Robbins, "Beyond the Suffering Subject."

41. Luhrmann, "Anthropology as Spiritual Discipline," 26.

42. Tett, *Fool's Gold.*

43. Ortner asks a similar question, in "Dark Anthropology and Its Others," 60.

44. Welker, *Kretek Capitalism.*

45. "Coca-Cola Donates Sh61 Million to Mitigate Drought," Kenya News Agency, December 21, 2022, https://www.kenyanews.go.ke/coca-cola-donates-sh61-Million-to-mitigate-drought/.

46. "Worst Drought on Record Parches Horn of Africa," NASA Earth Observatory, 2022, accessed March 3, 2025, https://earthobservatory.nasa.gov/images/150712/worst-drought-on-record-parches-horn-of-africa.

47. "Immediate Global Action Required to Prevent Famine in the Horn of Africa," FEWS Net (Famine Early Warning System Network), November 7, 2022, https://fews.net/unprecedented-sixth-consecutive-season-drought-forecast-horn-africa-hunger-surges-humanitarian.

48. Jacob Kushner, "Coca-Cola's River Cleanup Work in Tanzania Shows Mixed Motives," *The World from PRX,* July 30, 2016, https://theworld.org/stories/2016/07/30/coca-colas-river-cleanup-work-tanzania-shows-mixed-motives; "West Africa Is Drowning in Plastic: Who Is Responsible?" *Bloomberg,* August 19, 2022, https://www.bloomberg.com/features/2022-coca-cola-nestle-west-africa-ghana-plastic-waste-recycling/.

49. Steven Mufson, "The Trouble with Chocolate," *Washington Post,* October 29, 2019, https://www.washingtonpost.com/graphics/2019/national/climate-environment/mars-chocolate-deforestation-climate-change-west-africa/. Compare Dolan, Huang, and Gordon, "The Ambiguity of Mutuality"; Freidberg, "Metrics and Mētis"; Roll, Dolan, and Rajak, "Remote (Dis)engagement.

50. "Six Workers Killed in Newmont Mining Accident in Ghana," Global Greengrants Fund, April 11, 2018, https://www.greengrants.org/2018/04/11/mining-accident/; "Sustainable Mining," Newmont, https://www.newmont.com/sustainability/default.aspx, accessed March 3, 2025.

51. For a theoretically rich analysis of the pharmaceutical industry's harmful effects on people in India, see Rajan, *Pharmocracy,* and, for Nigeria, see Peterson, *Speculative Markets.* For a classic and highly readable account of the powerful roles financial interests play in controlling global public health, see Farmer, *Pathologies of Power.*

52. The longevity and breadth of my research enables me to track changes and themes that a snapshot of life would not.

53. One website declares that "Africa Is a Country," https://africasacountry
.com/, accessed March 3, 2025. It confronts and addresses the stereotype that
Africa is a single country. Yet it challenges this "wrong" global view by recognizing that Africa preceded and culturally "exists" beyond historically imposed
nation-state boundaries.

54. Mtei, *Goatherd to Governor*.

55. I am conversant in Kiswahili, the national language of Tanzania, having
studied the language formally at an advanced level, and I used it exclusively in
my early research. I am a beginning speaker of the Xhosa language, one of twelve
official languages of South Africa, having studied it through an accredited
trainer yet found that most Xhosa speakers preferred to speak English.

56. Callander, Foarta, and Sugaya, "Market Competition and Political
Influence."

CHAPTER 1

1. Boccaletti, *Water*. For an analysis of how regulators' formulae translate into,
for regulators, a picture of social harmony, see Ballestero, *Future History of Water*.

2. Gerrard, "Public-Private Partnerships."

3. Compare Orlove and Caton, "Water Sustainability," 402, 408.

4. Lyatuu, *Watch Your Steps!*, 29.

5. Wittfogel, *Oriental Despotism*.

6. On responsibilization, see Cooper, Alber, and Njoya, "Introduction." See
also Pyysiäinnen, Halpin, and Guilfoyle, "Neoliberal Governance and 'Responsibilisation' of Agents." *Responsibilization* refers to the transfer of responsibility
to individuals for problems they did not create, particularly in the context of
shifting responsibility from powerful actors (governments, corporations) to individuals. In this case, Bulelwa did not create the water problem, but my question
suggested she was responsible for handling it.

7. For in-depth discussions of the "Day Zero" water crisis in Cape Town, see
Dugard, "Water Rights in a Time of Fragility"; Mokoena, "Questioning Day
Zero"; and Wingfield, "'Working Time' in Environmental Activism."

8. Compare Strang, "Water Rights." See also van Koppen , Schreiner , and
Mukuyu, " Redressing Legal Pluralism."

9. Peters, "Conflicts over Land"; Woodhouse, "New Investment, Old Challenges."

10. Chitonge et al., "Silent Privatization of Customary Land"; Kwayu, "Taxing
the Rich"; Lofchie, "The Political Economy of Tanzania"; and Orock, "Less-Told
Stories About Corporate Globalization."

11. As did many Tanzanians during the years of transition to independence.
See Brennan, "Blood Enemies."

12. Bessire, *Running Out*; Perramond, *Unsettled Waters*; Strang, "The Taniwha and the Crown"; Harnish, Cliggett, and Scudder, "Rivers and Roads."

13. The basic income grant is discussed in Ferguson, "Uses of Neoliberalism." Business advocates in South Africa have argued against implementing the grant. See "Poverty and a Basic Income Grant: Six Questions about a BIG," CDE (Centre for Development and Enterprise), June 2022, https://www.cde.org.za/wp-content/uploads/2022/06/BIG-full-report-pdf.pdf.

14. The act was amended in 2013. For details, see Warikandwa and Osode, "Indigenisation Jurisprudence and the Renewed Fight Against 'Fronting.'" See also Alessandri, Black, and Jackson, "Black Economic Empowerment."

15. Gajadhur and Nicolades, "A Reflection on Corporate Social Responsibility in Africa." See also Ndong Ntoutoume, "Challenges of CSR in Sub-Saharan Africa."

16. See, for example, "Youth and Community Fund," at "Community Projects," Siza Water: A SAWW Company, https://www.sizawater.com/community-projects, accessed March 3, 2025; Republic of South Africa, Department of Water and Sanitation. See also du Plessis, "Progressive Deterioration of Water Quality Within South Africa," in *South Africa's Water Predicament.*

17. United Nations Educational, Scientific, and Cultural Organization (UNESCO), "Is Wastewater the New Black Gold?," Africa Renewal, United Nations, accessed January 5, 2025, https://www.un.org/africarenewal/news/wastewater-new-black-gold.

18. David Mosse, in *Cultivating Development,* has noted that a "new functionalist" logic of investment "substitutes false objects with real ones—development with social function (for instance, the extension of bureaucratic power)—and therefore destroys its object" (6; citing Latour, "When Things Strike Back"). To apply these concepts to Africa: sustainability discourse replaces development with investment capital and destroys what needs sustaining.

19. For additional discussion of sustainability in Yohane's water system, see Stambach and Kwayu, "Witness to a Passing."

20. Bibi did not explicitly explain this change. She stated it as a fact, invoking *Iruwa tu*, "God only," for knowing its causes, possibly reflecting companies' active attempts to frame global warming as an inevitable event, not the increase in the Earth's average atmospheric temperature corresponding to industries' centuries-long releasing carbon dioxide by burning fuel.

21. "National Irrigation Act No. of 2013," National Irrigation Commission, United Republic of Tanzania, accessed September 14, 2024, https://www.nirc.go.tz/publications/policies-and-acts.

22. For a valuable discussion of entrepreneurial water users and vendors, see Smith, *Every Household Its Own Government,* 27–54.

23. Kilimanjaro Drinking Water is also a registered trademark of the Coca-Cola Company.

24. Pallangyo et al, "Obesity Epidemic in Urban Tanzania."

25. Byala, *Bottled.*

26. See, for example, Nash, "Consuming Interests"; Kaplan, "Fijan Water in Figi and New York"; Foster, "Corporations as Partners"; Drew, "Coca-Cola and the Moral Economy"; Gill, "Limits of Solidarity."

27. Thu Huyen My Nguyen, "Net Income of Coca Cola from 2019 to 2023," Statista, November 1, 2024, https://www.statista.com/statistics/1522083/coca-cola-net-income.

28. Coca-Cola, "Sustainability," accessed March 3, 2025, https://www.coca-colacompany.com/sustainability.

29. Coca-Cola, "Business and Sustainability," accessed August 2, 2023, https://www.coca-colacompany.com/sustainability.

30. United States Environmental Protection Agency, "Enhanced Aquifer Recharge Research," EPA, updated January 9, 2024, https://www.epa.gov/water-research/enhanced-aquifer-recharge-research. I have no direct evidence that Coca-Cola's recharge waters carry chemical or microbial contaminates.

31. See Louwyck et al., "The Water Budget Myth and Its Recharge Controversy," which reasons that linear rates of extraction differ from nonlinear rates of replenishment and which does not appear to account for the even more difficult matter of modeling the interactions of the injected fluid with the chemistries of metals and radionuclides of the surrounding aquifer rock, a matter flagged in: "Aquifer Recharge and Aquifer Storage and Recovery," EPA: United States Environmental Protection Agency, accessed January 5, 2025, https://www.epa.gov/uic/aquifer-recharge-and-aquifer-storage-and-recovery#impact_usdw.

32. United States Agency for International Development, "USAID and Coca-Cola Partner to Improve Water Access for 70,000 Tanzanians," press release, June 19, 2018, https://www.usaid.gov/tanzania/press-release/usaid-and-coca-cola-partner-improve-water-access-70000-tanzanians.

33. Roberts, "Development Capital."

34. Coca-Cola, "Business and Sustainability"; United States Environmental Protection Agency, "Enhanced Aquifer Recharge Research."

35. "Worldserve International: Full Text of 'Full Filing' for Fiscal Year Ending Dec. 2023" (Form 990), ProPublica, accessed January 5, 2025, https://projects.propublica.org/nonprofits/organizations/431535009/202433199349303583/full.

36. My reasoning here is based on a hypothetical. I do not have evidence of a specific conflict of interest.

37. Dietrich, *States, Markets, and Foreign Aid.*

38. "Partners: Waterboys.ORG," WorldServe International, accessed January 5, 2025, https://www.worldserveintl.orgpartners/#waterboys; "Our Partners," Waterboys, accessed March 3, 2025, https://waterboys.org/partners-charities/.

39. United States Agency for International Development, "USAID and Coca-Cola Partner to Improve Water Access for 70,000 Tanzanians," press release, June 19, 2018, https://www.usaid.gov/tanzania/press-release/usaid-and-coca-cola-partner-improve-water-access-70000-tanzanians.

40. For information about Dodoma University students' water problems, see "Aweso aitaka Duwasa kumaliza tatizo la maji UDOM," Radio TADIO: Dodoma FM, January 23, 2024, https://radiotadio.co.tz/dodomafm/2024/01/23/14138/; and Jasusi (@Chahali), "#Tanzania: University of Dodoma student arrested after sharing photos showing acute water shortage problem at the uni," Twitter (now X), January 22, 2020, https://twitter.com/chahali/status/1220022311740375040.

41. Global Water Institute, "Water and Development Alliance," Ohio State University, accessed March 3, 2025, https://globalwater.osu.edu/our-work/water-and-development-alliance.

42. See Maureen Langlois, "Engineering Capstone Team Visits Partner Village in Tanzania," Ohio State University, June 17, 2016, https://globalwater.osu.edu/news/engineering-capstone-team-visits-partner-village-tanzania; Global Water Institute, "Corporate Partners," Ohio State University, accessed March 3, 2025, https://globalwater.osu.edu/our-partners/corporate-partners.

43. Massuel and Riaux, "Groundwater Overexploitation."

44. Sawyer, "Corporations," 2.

45. Eva Nilsson's research shows that Tanzanian officials seek to control international corporate social responsibility (CSR); however, in the words of one ruling-party member of Parliament, "I feel embarrassed that we have CSR in the law. Every time I meet with experts on this, I try to say that it is too narrow to rely on this revenue stream." Nilsson, "Instrumentalization of CSR," 1189.

46. Mzee Jacob Nkya Kiungayi, quoted in Meena, *Mount Kilimanjaro*, 44.

47. Andrew Connelly, "MacKenzie Scott Is Shaking up Philanthropy's Traditions: Is That a Good Thing?" *Goats and Soda*, NPR, January 10, 2023, https://www.npr.org/sections/goatsandsoda/2023/01/10/1147903370/mackenzie-scott-is-shaking-up-philanthropys-traditions-is-that-a-good-thing.

48. Village Enterprise, "A $7M Gift from MacKenzie Scott Will Help Village Enterprise End Extreme Poverty for 20 Million People in Africa," *PR Newswire*, March 29, 2023, https://www.prnewswire.com/news-releases/a-7m-gift-from-mackenzie-scott-will-help-village-enterprise-end-extreme-poverty-for-20-million-people-in-africa-301783905.html.

49. Connelly, "MacKenzie Scott Is Shaking up Philanthropy's Traditions"; Global Water Institute, "Our Partners," Ohio State University, accessed January 5, 2025, https://globalwater.osu.edu/our-partners; Village Enterprise, "Our Partners and Funders," accessed March 3, 2025, https://villageenterprise.org

/about-us/our-partners-and-funders/. As I discuss in chapter 3, the community and First Nations South Africans appealed to Scott in their case against Amazon for having put 150 million tons of concrete into wetlands. Scott did not respond.

50. The Water Footprint Network reports that, on average across world regions, "one glass of wine (125 ml) costs 110 litre" of water. "Product Gallery," Water Footprint Network, accessed January 5, 2025, https://www.waterfootprint.org/resources/interactive-tools/product-gallery/. I converted metric units to imperial units.

51. See "Cape of Good Hopes," Meininger's International, June 11, 2018, https://www.meiningers-international.com/wine/analysis/cape-good-hopes.

52. See William Alan Reinsch, "What's AGOA-ing On," CSIS: Center for Strategic and International Studies, August 5, 2024, https://www.csis.org/analysis/whats-agoa-ing.

53. Mariana Álvarez, "World Water Report Warns of Imminent Water Crisis," UNESCO, updated March 22, 2023, https://www.unesco.org/en/articles/world-water-report-warns-imminent-water-crisis. For an example of this outrageously inaccurate claim about the world's water supply, see Biswas and Tortajada, "Water Crisis and Water Wars": "As every school kid knows water is a renewable resource. . . . [It] can be used, and the wastewater generated can be treated and reused. Properly managed, this process can continue indefinitely" (727).

CHAPTER 2

Epigraph: A Tanzanian friend showed me this package in 2018. Photo of text and bag in author's files.

1. Information from Kilimanjaro coffee farmers, fieldnotes, 2018 and 2023.

2. Kilimanjaro coffee farmers, interviews with author, recorded in fieldnotes, 2023.

3. Robbins, "Monocropping"; Zhao et al., "Long-Term Coffee Monoculture Alters Soil," 2.

4. Burden-Stelly, "Modern U.S. Racial Capitalism," 8.

5. Gathii and Tzouvala, "Racial Capitalism and International Economic Law," 200.

6. In reporting on the catastrophic landslides and flood, NASA's Earth Observatory noted that "climate change has amplified rainfall and floods, heatwaves, drought, and wildfires" in the Southern Hemisphere. Quoted in Hansen, "Deluge in South Africa." Referring to the 2022 floods in South Africa's KwaZulu-Natal and Eastern Cape provinces, the United Nations Office for Disaster Risk Reduction (UNDRR) reported that "the disaster underlines once again the increasing hazards posed by intense rainfall in a changing climate." See UNDRR, "South Africa."

7. Axelrod, "Corporate Honesty and Climate Change"; Ritchie, Rosado, and Roser, "Environmental Impacts of Food Production"; Ayesha Tandon, "Climate Change Made Extreme Rains in 2022 South Africa Floods 'Twice as Likely,'" *Carbon Brief: Clear on Climate*, May 13, 2022, https://www.carbonbrief .org/climate-change-made-extreme-rains-in-2022-south-africa-floods-twice-as-likely/.

8. World Health Organization, ": Fact Sheet: Protecting Health from Climate Change," March 2016, https://www.who.int/docs/default-source/wpro---documents/hae---regional-forum-(2016)/climatechange-factsheet-rfhe.pdf.

9. Axelrod, "Corporate Honesty and Climate Change"; Paul Griffin, Richard Heede, and Ian van Der Vlugt, "The Carbon Majors Database," Climate Accountability Database, February 17, 2017, https://climateaccountability.org/pdf/CDP_ CAI%20CarbonMajorsDatasetRpt%20v1.0%20Mar17.pdf; Tandon, "Climate Change Made Extreme Rains in 2022 South Africa Floods 'Twice as Likely.'"

10. Albertus, "Why Land Reform Matters in South Africa." Piers Pigou writes, "When the institutionalised racial segregation and discrimination known as apartheid officially ended, whites owned 87 per cent of the land. The newly empowered ANC promised to redistribute 30 per cent of commercial farmland within five years. It managed a paltry 1 per cent by 1999 and only 9.7 per cent by 2018." Pigou, "Land Reform in South Africa." Precise data on the return of land is unavailable, however. Cousins, "Land Reform in South Africa."

11. Ricciardi et al., "How Much of the World's Food Do Smallholders Produce?"

12. Reyes-García, "Traditional Crop Management"; Govindrajan, *Animal Intimacies*, 18.

13. Coomes et al., "Farmer Seed Networks Make a Limited Contribution to Agriculture?"; Maxted et al., "Towards a Methodology"; Musacchio, "Key Concepts and Research Priorities"; Reyes-García, "Traditional Crop Management."

14. For example, neonicotinoids are more toxic than previous generations of insecticides and persist longer in the environment. DiBartolomeis et al., "An Assessment of Acute Insecticide Toxicity Loading (AITL)." The intensive use of pesticides in countries with minimally trained workforces and weak regulatory measures may result in farmers' acute poisoning. The resulting social, medical, and health costs to farmers and health systems could outweigh the financial benefits of higher crop yields from using insecticides.

15. Ferguson, *Global Shadows*, 203.

16. "The dissolution of DowDuPont completed on June 1, 2019. Please visit the websites of the independent companies to learn more about each." http:// dow-dupont.com.

17. Winter and Morris, "Mistbelt Grassland Fragmentation in the Umvoti Conservancy."

18. Corteva Agriscience, "Extension Workers Improve Life for African Farmers," accessed March 3, 2025, https://www.corteva.com/who-we-are/outlook/agricultural-extension-lending-a-helping-hand-in-africa.html.

19. Jeandré van der Walt, "Health and Safety Do's and Don'ts for Farmers," *Farmers Weekly*, February 12, 2021, https://www.magzter.com/es/stories/Business/Farmers-Weekly/Health-And-Safety-Dos-And-Donts-For-Farmers.

20. Leslie London points to "inequity in employer-employee power relations." London, "Human Rights, Environmental Justice, and the Health of Farm Workers," 62.

21. Corteva Agriscience, "Fighting Malnutrition in Africa," accessed December 22, 2024, https://www.corteva.com.

22. Mususa, *There Used to Be Order*, 13.

23. Corteva Agriscience, "Corteva Agriscience Invests in Africa [and] Middle East Seed Treatment Capability," accessed December 22, 2024, https://www.corteva.com.

24. Stoller, "About Stoller," accessed March 3, 2025, https://stollerusa.com/about/#:~:text=About. See also Corteva Agriscience, "Corteva and Stoller Exclusive Agreement to Sell Bionematicide in Brazil," accessed August 26, 2023, https://www.corteva.us/content/corteva/corporate/our-homepage/resources/media-center/corteva-and-stoller-exclusive-agreement-to-sell-bionematicide-in-brazil.html (PDF in author's possession).

25. United States Environmental Protection Agency, "Human Health Issues Related to Pesticides," accessed March 3, 2025, https://www.epa.gov/pesticide-science-and-assessing-pesticide-risks/human-health-issues-related-pesticides.

26. Stoller Safety Data Sheet: Mover. Revision May 26, 2021. The PDF of the 2021 revision (in author's possession) uses the phrases "may damage fertility or the unborn child" and "harmful to aquatic life." A revised 2023 version for the same product with the same chemical composition, available online and in author's possession as a PDF file, likewise cautions that the product "may damage fertility or the unborn child" but does not identify aquatic toxicity as a hazard. "Safety Data Sheet: Sugar Mover," Stoller, accessed March 3, 2025, https://stollerusa.com/wp-content/uploads/SUGAR-MOVER_Z-SUGARM_201_20231206_EN.pdf. Corteva acquired Stoller in 2023.

27. See Mnif et al., "Effect of Endocrine Disruptor Pesticides"; Stone, "Agricultural Intensification," 4; Tudi et al., "Agriculture Development, Pesticide Application, and Its Impact on the Environment"; Jedy-Agba et al., "Trend in Cervical Cancer Incidence."

28. Italics added for emphasis. For discussion of pesticide misuses and hazards, see Rother, "Pesticide Suicides"; Rother, "Pesticide Labels."

29. London, "Human Rights, Environmental Justice, and the Health of Farm Workers."

30. Agri-Africa, "Kulisha Africa" (2017 brochure, downloaded August 1, 2022; website since taken down).

31. Agri-Africa, "Kulisha Africa," 6.

32. Women exposed to industrial-strength pesticides experience increased risk of polycystic ovarian syndrome (Sharma et al., "Potential Environmental Toxicant Exposure"), a "marked reduction in fertility" (Fucic et al., "Reproductive Health Risks Associated with Occupational and Environmental Exposure to Pesticides," 6576), and higher rates of miscarriage than do women in the general population (Landeros et al., "Genotoxicity and Reproductive Risk in Workers Exposed to Pesticides" [Chile]; van Wendel de Joode et al., "Pesticide Exposure, Birth Size, and Gestational Age" [Costa Rica]).

33. This network includes scholars and researchers at Tumaini University and the University of Dar es Salaam; women delegates to the International Women's Day convention held in Moshi, Tanzania, March 8, 2023; and environmental researchers in the governmental and nongovernmental sectors.

34. A subject exceptionally well covered in Phillips, *Ethnography of Hunger.*

35. Klein, *Shock Doctrine.*

36. Chachage, Ericson, and Gibbon, *Mining and Structural Adjustment*; Nyamnjoh, "Globalization, Boundaries, and Livelihoods"; Shivji, "The Roots of the Agrarian Crisis in Tanzania"; Simsa'a, "Structural Adjustment Policies." See also Kepe, Wynberg, and Ellis, "Land Reform"; Manji, "Land Reform in the Shadow of the State"; the journals *Review of African Political Economy, Africa Development,* and *African Development Review*; and bibliographic listings available at codesria.org.

37. Shipton, *Mortgaging the Ancestors,* especially 2–3.

38. Narotzky, "Where Have All the Peasants Gone?"

39. Piemonte and Gironi, "Land-Use Change Emissions"; Posen et al., "Greenhouse Gas Mitigation for U.S. Plastics Production"; Yang et al., "Replacing Gasoline with Corn Ethanol Results in Significant Environmental Problem-Shifting."

40. Bataka, "Global Value Chains Participation and Gender Inequalities in Sub-Saharan Africa"; Lang, Ponte, and Vilakazi, "Linking Power and Inequality in Global Value Chains"; Lee et al., "Global Value Chains and Agrifood Standards."

41. It may seem odd that genetic modifications would lower rather than increase yields in the long run. Genetically modified crops enable farmers to increase glyphosate use. "However, glyphosate is becoming less effective as weed resistance mounts—14 glyphosate-resistant (GR) weed species have been documented in U.S. crop-production areas. GR weeds can reduce crop yields and increase weed-control costs, and recent surveys suggest that the amount of affected cropland is increasing." See Jorge Fernandez-Cornejo and Craig Osteen, "Managing Glyphosate Resistance May Sustain Its Efficacy and Increase Long-Term Returns to Corn and Soybean Production," Economic Research Service, US Department of Agriculture, May 4, 2015, https://www.ers.usda.gov/amber

-waves/2015/may/managing-glyphosate-resistance-may-sustain-its-efficacy-and-increase-long-term-returns-to-corn-and-soybean-production.

42. The International Agency for Research on Cancer classifies glyphosate as a probable human carcinogen. For evaluations of the "carcinogenic potential of this herbicide," see Chang et al., "Glyphosate Exposure and Urinary Oxidative Stress Biomarkers." Bassil and colleagues point specifically to MCPA, in "Cancer Health Effects of Pesticides." Brosnan et al. indicate MCPA is an ingredient of some Roundup-branded herbicides. See "Update on Roundup-Branded Herbicides for Consumers." Roh et al. report that "dicamba increased the risk of lung cancer and colon cancer . . . [and] was associated with non-Hodgkin lymphoma and multiple myeloma" and that "those in the highest quartile of dicamba exposure had increased risks of liver and intrahepatic bile duct cancer." "Pesticides and Cancer," 197. The Roundup Ready Xtend Technology commercial website (accessed June 12, 2024, https://www.roundupreadyxtend.com/stewardship/Pages/default.aspx) confirms that dicamba is an ingredient of Roundup Ready Xtend Technology. See also Sheila Kaplan, "Childhood Exposure to Common Herbicide May Increase the Risk of Disease in Young Adulthood," Berkeley Public Health, March 1, 2023, https://publichealth.berkeley.edu/news-media/research-highlights/childhood-exposure-to-common-herbicide-may-increase-the-risk-of-disease-in-young-adulthood/; and Pedroso et al., "Cancer and Occupational Exposure to Pesticides."

43. Monsanto merged with Bayer in 2017; the Monsanto Fund philanthropy was renamed the Bayer Fund shortly thereafter. Beginning in 2024, many Roundup-branded herbicides *in the residential market* may no longer contain glyphosate. Brosnan et al., "Update on Roundup-Branded Herbicides for Consumers." The company announced, however, that "there will be no change in the availability of the company's glyphosate formulations in the U.S. professional and agricultural markets." Quoted in Michelle Llamas, "Roundup Lawsuits," November 18, 2024, ConsumerNotice.org, https://www.consumernotice.org/legal/roundup-lawsuits/. Presumably there are no changes in the company's glyphosate (or dicamba or MCPA) formulations in African markets.

44. "Home," Bayer Fund, accessed June 11, 2024, https://www.fund.bayer.us/#home-header.

45. Bessire, *Running Out*; Blanchette, "Living Waste and the Labor of Toxic Health."

46. Broadway and Stull, "The Wages of Food Factories," 43; We Care, "Our Ethical Principles" (and especially "Animal Well-Being for Pigs"), accessed June 11, 2024, https://www.porkcares.org/ethical-principles/animal-well-being/.

47. Maro, quoted in Ebe Daems and Kweli Ukwethembeka Iqiniso, "Tanzanian Farmers Are Facing Heavy Prison Sentences If They Continue Their Traditional Seed Exchange," Grain.org, January 8, 2017, https://grain.org/en/article/5633-tanzanian-farmers-are-facing-heavy-prison-sentences-if-they-continue-their-traditional-seed-exchange.

48. See, for example, Cathleen Flahardy, "Organic Growers Appeal Case Against Monsanto," *Inside Counsel: Breaking News,* March 20, 2012, ProQuest (1020995555); Cathleen Flahardy, "Wheat Farmers Sue Monsanto," *Inside Counsel: Breaking News,* June 10, 2013, ProQuest (1366339548); Brian Bowling, "Farmers Sued for Saving Monsanto Wheat Seeds," *McClatchy— Tribune Business News,* July 14, 2011, ProQuest (876198661); Elizabeth Fraser and Anuradha Mittal, "Seeds of Change: Corporate Power, Grassroots Resistance, and the Battle over the Food System," *Dollars and Sense,* March–April 2015, https://www.dollarsandsense.org/archives/2015/0315 frasermittal.html; Mayer, "Aftermath of the Seed Wars," 681; Slater, "Poverty via Monopolization."

49. See Blanchette, *Porkopolis*; Hetherington, *Government of Beans*; Lamb, *Love for the Land*; Sullivan, *Unsettling Agribusiness*; Welker, *Kretek Capitalism*; and Zlolinski, *Made in Baja.*

50. Benson and Kirsch, "Capitalist Corporation."

51. Personal communication with secondary school graduates, March 2023, Kilimanjaro Region, Tanzania.

52. Ohnuki-Tierney, *Flowers That Kill.*

53. Compare Moore, "Work of 'Feeding the World.'" 175; and Shiva, *Stolen Harvest,* 103.

54. "Greenwashing," too, is a communicatively polysemous term, albeit one that parodies corporate sustainability programs by using the modifier "washing" to reveal companies' word "laundering." The quid pro quo of communicative opacity motivates action without actually addressing the underlying causes of climate change.

55. Indeed, their signage asserted that "smart farming" could control climate for various crops, whereas, at best, it can only reduce water resource use.

56. On illocutionary speech acts, see Niesen, "Speech Acts"; and Austin, *How to Do Things with Words.*

57. Tim Unwin, "Digital Technologies Are Part of the Climate Change Problem," ICTWorks, February 20, 2020, https://www.ictworks.org/digital-technologies-climate-change-problem/; Yunus Kemp, "Nuclear Energy: Amazon, Google to use SMRs to Power Data Centers, AI." ESI Africa, October 18, 2024, https://www.esi-africa.com/industry-sectors/smart-technologies/nuclear-energy-amazon-google-to-use-smrs-to-power-data-centres-ai/.

CHAPTER 3

1. The term *Goringhaicona* arose during precolonial times to refer to a Khoi group of farmers and others who left the Gorinhaiqua community and joined the Sonqua people who fished.

2. "Controversy over the Location of Amazon African Headquarters in Cape Town," *AfricaNews*, May 14, 2021, https://www.africanews.com/2021/05/14/controversy-over-the-location-of-amazon-african-headquarters-in-cape-town/. A traditional house is an alliance of extended Khoi families.

3. Leslie London, online videoconference interview with the author, July 7, 2023.

4. "Jobs vs Heritage: The Battle over Amazon's New Africa HQ," *Al Jazeera*, June 3, 2021, https://www.aljazeera.com/news/2021/6/3/amazons-africa-hq-on-ice-as-communities-push-for-heritage-status.

5. Some Capetonians speculated that the developer and Amazon chose this site for its beautiful views of Table Mountain; however, the developer never gave a reason.

6. Oliver Milman, "Indigenous Leaders Urge Businesses and Banks to Stop Supporting Deforestation," *The Guardian*, September 21, 2022, https://www.theguardian.com/environment/2022/sep/21/indigenous-leaders-amazon-rainforest-businesses-banks; Green, *Rock, Water, Life*; Gustafson, *Bolivia in the Age of Gas*; Walsh, *Made in Madagascar*.

7. See "Home: A/Xarra Restorative Justice Forum Members," Centre for African Studies, University of Cape Town, accessed March 3, 2025, https://humanities.uct.ac.za/african-studies/san-and-khoi-unit-axarra-restorative-justice-forum/axarra-restorative-justice-forum-members.

8. Tauriq Jenkins, interview with the author, March 3, 2022, Cape Town.

9. See, for example, John Eligon, "New Amazon Headquarters Sparks Feud Among Indigenous South Africans," *New York Times*, February 26, 2022, https://www.nytimes.com/2022/02/26/world/africa/south-africa-amazon.html; Alexandra Wexler, "Amazon Faces Headquarters Controversy—This Time in Africa," *Wall Street Journal*, September 23, 2021, https://www.wsj.com/articles/amazon-faces-headquarters-controversythis-time-in-africa-11632389400; Leah Wilson and Loni Prinsloo, "Amazon's New Africa Site Draws Ire in Indigenous People Protest, *Time* Magazine, June 16, 2021, https://time.com/6073659/amazon-africa-indigenous-protest/; Wendell Roelf, "Heritage Dispute Engulfs Site Chosen for Amazon's New African HQ," Reuters, June 3, 2021, https://www.reuters.com/world/africa/heritage-dispute-engulfs-site-chosen-amazons-new-african-hq-2021-06-03/; Isobel Asher Hamilton, "Some Indigenous Groups in South Africa Want to Stop Amazon Building a New HQ on the Site of a Historic Battleground," *Business Insider*, September 24, 2021, https://www.businessinsider.com/amazon-cape-town-hq-south-africn-indigenous-groups-oppose-2021-9?IR=T; Leslie London, Tauriq Jenkins, and Marc Turok for the Liesbeek Action Campaign, "The Liesbeek Action Campaign: 'Yes, Misinformation Must Stop but It Is Not Coming from Opponents of the Development," *Daily Maverick*, August 25, 2021, https://www.dailymaverick.co.za/article/2021-08-25-the-liesbeek-action-

campaign-yes-misinformation-must-stop-but-it-is-not-coming-from-opponents-of-the-development/

10. On deterritorialized legal protocols, compare Mbembe, "At the Edge of the World."

11. San ancestral territories embrace Botswana, Namibia, Angola, Zambia, Zimbabwe, Lesotho, and South Africa; Southern Khoi ancestral territories, South Africa's Western Cape and the coastal regions of the Eastern Cape. The Portuguese colonized Angola; the Germans, Namibia; and the Netherlands and Britain, South Africa.

12. Verbuyst, *Khoisan Consciousness*.

13. Quoted in Mellet, *The Lie of 1652*, 133.

14. The symbol ‖ indicates a phonemic click.

15. Quoted in Mellet, *The Lie of 1652*, 13.

16. John Dashe notes: "Though agricultural land makes up nearly 80 percent of South Africa's total area, blacks—who make up three-fourths of the population—control just 4 percent of individually-owned farmland, while whites—who comprise just 9 percent—own 72 percent of land." Dashe, "Land Reform in South Africa," Wilson Center (blog), November 23, 2021, https://www.wilsoncenter.org/blog-post/land-reform-in-south-africa). See also Zondi et al., "Discrimination Followed Us into Paradise."

17. The Group Areas Act determined race using subjective assessments. Some people of Khoi and San were labeled Black, others Colored.

18. Campbell, "Transnational White Supremacist Militancy Thriving in South Africa."

19. All currency conversions are made using Oanda.com.

20. Trevor Sacks, "Whistle-Blowers Lay Out Amazon/River Club Developers' Alleged Dirty Tricks," *Daily Maverick*, August 21, 2023, https://www.dailymaverick.co.za/opinionista/2023-08-21-whistle-blowers-lay-out-amazon-river-club-developers-alleged-dirty-tricks/. Sacks calls the transaction a sale though technically it was a transfer, not a sale.

21. London, personal communication with the author, January 2, 2024.

22. I have no reason to believe, however, that LLPT's contractors were aware that some of their employees were from other countries.

23. "Jobs vs Heritage."

24. Paramount Chief Aran, quoted in Shange, "Identity and Environmental Harmony," 138.

25. See the articles cited in note 9 of this chapter.

26. See the words of the LLPT's heritage impact assessment consultant in the first three minutes of "Riverclub Pt. 1," YouTube, posted by ed ang, February 8, 2019, https://youtu.be/ZNy-gtIXEbo. For additional documentation, see materials available on the Liesbeek Action Campaign site, http://liesbeek.org

(accessed January 6, 2025) and the Observatory Civic Association YouTube channel, accessed January 6, 2025, https://obs.org.za/oca-youtube-channel/.

27. South African Government, "National Heritage Resources Act 25 of 1999," https://www.gov.za/documents/national-heritage-resources-act, accessed September 14, 2024; Abdulqawi A. Yusuf, "Introductory Note" to "Convention Concerning the Protection of the World Cultural and Natural Heritage, Paris, 16 November 1972," Audiovisual Library of International Law, United Nations, accessed March 3, 2025, https://legal.un.org/avl/ha/ccpwcnh/ccpwcnh.html.

28. AFMAS Solutions, "River Club First Nations Report," November 2019, https://theriverclubct.co.za/wp/wp-content/uploads/2020/01/AFMAS-Solutions-FInal-River-Club-First-Nations-Report.pdf, 48, 87, 96, 97. For Jan van Riebeeck's journal, see Internet Archive, accessed June 20, 2024, https://archive.org/search?query=Jan+van+Riebeeck+Journal%2C+1619-1677.

29. See UNESCO's Intangible Cultural Heritage Convention and Committee updates, accessed March 3, 2025, https://www.unesco.org/en/intangible-cultural-heritage.

30. As quoted in the Founding Affidavit by Leslie London, to the High Court of South Africa (Western Cape Division, Cape Town), August 1, 2021, 53 (referencing the second heritage impact assessment, AFMAS Solutions, "River Club First Nations Report," 80; emphasis added).

31. Leslie London, email communication with the author, August 13, 2023.

32. Personal observation. On one occasion I emailed an operations manager, who relayed my observation to the project engineer, whose contact replied, "We do apologise this is not the norm." Field notes, October 22, 2021. Yet I heard late-night pounding multiple times.

33. See Liesbeek Action Campaign, accessed January 6, 2025, https://www.liesbeek.org/.

34. For discussion of Amazon Inc. and its territorial disputes, see Jesus and Bastos, "Insertion of Amazon Inc. in Brazil"; and Robins and Baumgardt, "Opening the Black Box."

35. A pseudonym, as are the names Joshua, Pangani, Fortuné, Amadou, and, later, Jaco. To my knowledge, Amazon's developer was not aware that these wage laborers were undocumented.

36. "Jeff Bezos and the Secretive World of Superyachts," *BBC News,* May 13, 2021, https://www.bbc.com/news/world-us-canada-57079327; Jedidah Tabalia, "Here Is the Cheapest Way to Build a House in South Africa," *Briefly,* July 22, 2020, https://briefly.co.za/70799-here-cheapest-build-a-house-south-africa.html. Tabalia reports that "statistics from house owners have revealed that building a beautiful 3-bedroom house takes in between $150,826 and $434,187." My estimate uses the lower figure, rounds numbers, and assumes two people per bedroom.

37. Jeff Rudin, "Jeff Bezos Is Neither an Altruist nor a Socialist, and Amazon's River Club Venture Is Not About Job Creation," *Daily Maverick*, September 6, 2021, https://www.dailymaverick.co.za/opinionista/2021-09-06-jeff-bezos-is-neither-an-altruist-nor-a-socialist-and-amazons-river-club-venture-is-not-about-job-creation/.

38. "Controversy over the Location of Amazon African Headquarters in Cape Town," *AfricaNews*, May 14, 2021, https://www.africanews.com/2021/05/14/controversy-over-the-location-of-amazon-african-headquarters-in-cape-town/.

39. Leslie London, online videoconference interview with the author, July 7, 2023.

40. See "Local Donors" link on "Donate," Liesbeek Action Campaign, accessed January 5, 2025, https://www.liesbeek.org/donate.

41. Leslie London, online videoconference interview with the author, July 7, 2023.

42. As paraphrased by Leslie London, in online videoconference interview with the author, July 7, 2023.

43. Shange, "Identity and Environmental Harmony," 146.

44. On data mining and cloud computing, see Rambabu et al., "Data Mining in Cloud Computing," and Abrera, "Data Privacy and Security." On AI and cloud computing, see Hong et al., "Multi-Hop Cooperative Computation Offloading for Industrial IoT-Edge-Cloud Computing Environments."

45. On digital data as a source of revenue growth, see Kantipudi et al., "Study of Recurring Revenue Growth for IT Infrastructure Providers"; Okeyo, "Customer-Centric Data Strategies"; and Jemiluyi and Jeke, "Tax Revenue Mobilization Effort."

46. "The Data Game: What Amazon Knows About You and How to Stop It," *The Guardian*, February 27, 2022, https://www.theguardian.com/technology/2022/feb/27/the-data-game-what-amazon-knows-about-you-and-how-to-stop-it.

47. Amazon calls its code of ethics "Our Positions." See https://www.aboutamazon.com/about-us/our-positions (accessed March 3, 2025.) Copy in author's possession.)

48. "AWS Investment in South Africa Results in Economic Ripple Effect," AWS, April 13, 2023, https://aws.amazon.com/blogs/publicsector/aws-investment-south-africa-results-economic-ripple-effect/; AWS Economic Development, "AWS Economic Impact Study," 2023, https://d1.awsstatic.com/WWPS/pdf/south-africa-eis-final-report-uk-english.pdf.

49. AWS Economic Development, "AWS Economic Impact Study," 7.

50. AWS Economic Development, "AWS Economic Impact Study," 18.

51. See John Eligon, "Amazon Builds on Indigenous South African Land, Sparking Fierce Feud," *New York Times*, February 27, 2022, A6.

52. See "The Data Game."

53. Shange, "Identity and Environmental Harmony," 155.

54. For example, "In Amazon's 'Hellscape,' Workers Face Insecurity and Crushing Targets," *Business and Human Rights Resource Center,* September 7, 2018, https://www.business-humanrights.org/en/latest-news/in-amazons-hellscape-workers-face-insecurity-and-crushing-targets/; "New York Labor Leaders: Amazon Has 'Record of Routinely Mistreating Workers,'" *The Guardian,* November 28, 2018, https://www.theguardian.com/technology/2018/nov/28/new-york-labor-leaders-amazon-workers.

55. "Amazon Illegally Threatened NYC Workers Ahead of Union Votes, Judge Finds," *Daily Maverick,* February 1, 2023, https://www.dailymaverick.co.za/article/2023-02-01-amazon-illegally-threatened-nyc-workers-ahead-of-union-votes-judge-finds/.

56. Lesley Green to the Chairperson and Committee of the Observatory Civic Association, June 22, 2021 (copy in author's possession).

57. Compare Shipton, *Mortgaging the Ancestors,* 232.

58. Wamalwa, "Embodied Memories."

59. Bam-Hutchison, "The Politics of Heritage"; du Plessis and Plaut, *Understanding South Africa,* 131–46; Modisane, "Reflections on Fire as Postcolonial Metaphor"; Shange, "Identity and Environmental Harmony," 144.

60. Mascia-Lees, *Gender and Difference in a Globalizing World,* 165.

61. Marable, "Globalization and Racialization," 2–3.

62. Shange "Identity and Environmental Harmony," 148.

63. Mbembe, "At the Edge of the World."

64. Khoisan, "Navigating a Minefield," 30, cited in Shange "Identity and Environmental Harmony," 145.

CHAPTER 4

1. Global Health Watch, 255; Schoemaaker, "History of Medicine in Sub-Saharan Africa"; Tilley, "Medicines, Empires, and Ethics in Colonial Africa."

2. The Bill & Melinda Gates Foundation changed its name to the Gates Foundation in 2024, following the couple's separation in 2021. Because my research spanned the years of this transition, I use the foundation's names interchangeably.

3. The Bill & Melinda Gates Foundation provides cash contributions, participates on the Global Fund's board, and supports its fundraising and programming efforts. See "Bill & Melinda Gates Foundation," The Global Fund, accessed March 3, 2025, https://www.theglobalfund.org/en/private-ngo-partners/resource-mobilization/bill-melinda-gates-foundation.

4. To attempt to verify Urassa's claim that Gates-funded clinics did not grant African scientists, doctors, and public health officials access to the data those companies compile, I contacted the Gates Foundation by email (October 31, 2024) and via their online contact form (also October 31, 2024; https://www

.gatesfoundation.org/about/contact/write-to-us), asking for its help connecting me with the appropriate person, office, or Gates entity. I received no reply.

5. According to "World's 100 Largest Philanthropic Foundations List," Arco Lab,, accessed September 12, 2024, https://www.arcolab.org/en/worlds-100-largest-philanthropic-foundations-list/. For net assets, see the Bill & Melinda Gates Foundation 2023 Form 990, ProPublica, accessed December 24, 2024, https://projects.propublica.org/nonprofits/organizations/562618866.

6. Erin Banco, Ashleigh Furlong, and Lennart Pfahler, "How Bill Gates and Partners Used Their Clout to Control the Global Covid Response—with Little Oversight," *Politico*, September 14, 2022, https://www.politico.com/news/2022/09/14/global-covid-pandemic-response-bill-gates-partners-00053969; "Total Number of Coronavirus (COVID-19) Vaccination Doses Administered in Tanzania as of June 19, 2022," *Statista*, accessed August 29, 2023, http://www.statista.com/statistics/1258567/total-number-of-covid-19-accinatio-doses-in-tanzania/; homepage, U.S. Embassy in Tanzania, accessed August 29, 2023, https://tz.usembassy.gov.

7. Jenna Ross, "How Does the Bill and Melinda Gates Foundation Invest Its Money?" *Visual Capitalist*, May 4, 2021, https://www.visualcapitalist.com/how-does-the-bill-and-melinda-gates-foundation-invest-its-money/; "Buffett's Berkshire Bets on Big Pharma, Invests in Four Drugmakers," Reuters, November 16, 2020, https://www.reuters.com/article/us-investment-funds-berkshire/buffetts-berkshire-invests-in-four-big-drugmakers-idINKBN27W2TS; Angus Liu, "Buffett's Berkshire Bets Big on AbbVie, Bristol Myers, Merck, Pfizer as COVID-19 Drives Healthcare Investment," *Fierce Pharma*, November 17, 2020, https://www.fiercepharma.com/pharma/warren-buffett-s-berkshire-bets-big-abbvie-bristol-myers-merck-pfizer-as-covid-drives.

8. "Pfizer: Our Impact on Innovation," Pfizer, accessed March 3, 2025, https://www.pfizer.com/about/responsibility/global-impact/the-gavi-alliance.

9. Tanzanian colleagues in my network independently verified this fact (field notes, February 2024).

10. Gimbel et al., "Donor Data Vacuuming." Linsey McGoey also criticizes the Gates Foundation's global health involvement. She argues that the foundation's emphasis on data for vaccine development overshadows more comprehensive public health initiatives that could benefit the countries receiving aid. See McGoey, *No Such Thing as a Free Gift.*

11. Again, I tried to verify this with the Gates Foundation, contacting them twice, but received no reply.

12. Moderna imposes similar requirements. Massachusetts-based Moderna Inc. received support from the Global Fund and in 2022 launched a "first-in-Africa clinical trial of mRNA HIV vaccine development." "IAVI and Moderna Launch First-In-Africa Clinical Trial of MRNA HIV Vaccine Development Program," news release, Moderna, May 18, 2022, https://investors.modernatx.com

/news/news-details/2022/IAVI-and-Moderna-Launch-First-in-Africa-Clinical-Trial-of-mRNA-HIV-Vaccine-Development-Program/default.aspx.

13. For discussion of how intellectual property laws resulted in unequal access to COVID-19 vaccines, see Sekalala et al., "Decolonising Human Rights."

14. For a time, Moderna ignored the question of whether scientists in South Africa were decoding the Moderna vaccine formula in order to make the vaccine in Cape Town, but that oversight was temporary.

15. Folayan and colleagues, in "Considerations for Stakeholder Engagement," indicate, "The norms, values, and practices of collectivist societies in Sub-Saharan Africa and the low research literacy pose challenges to the conduct of clinical trials" (44).

16. Banco, Furlong, and Pfahler, "How Bill Gates and Partners Used Their Clout."

17. Blunt, "The Gates Foundation, Global Health, and Domination"; Storeng, "The GAVI Alliance and the 'Gates Approach' to Health System Strengthening"; "Global Vaccine Community Must Bring Price of New Vaccines," *Doctors Without Borders*, April 18, 2013, https://www.doctorswithoutborders.org/latest/global-vaccines-community-must-bring-price-new-vaccines-down.

18. Quoted in Banco, Furlong, and Pfahler, "How Bill Gates and Partners Used Their Clout."

19. Soonest Nathaniel, "Expect Dead Bodies in the Street of African Countries, Melinda Gates Warns," *ChannelsTV,* April 13, 2020, https://www.channelstv.com/2020/04/13/covid-19-expect-dead-bodies-in-the-street-of-african-countries-melinda-gates-warns/.

20. Jonathan Grossman, in *The Art of Alibi*, defines "alibi" as an "excuse story" that rests on tacit cultural agreements (143, 148).

21. Malloy, "Research Material and Necromancy," 431; Lowes and Montero, "Legacy of Colonial Medicine"; Tilley, "Medicine, Empires, and Ethics in Colonial Africa"; Weindling, "The Dangers of White Supremacy" (Namibia experiments).

22. Mechanic, "Apartheid Medicine," 41; Crenner, "The Tuskegee Syphilis Study and the Scientific Concept of Racial Nervous Resistance."

23. During World War II, Farben manufactured the cyanide-based pesticide that killed millions of people, mainly Jews, in Nazi-occupied Germany. Bartop, "Zyklon B."

24. Vaughan, "Research Enclave in 1940s Nigeria." Vaughn notes that the scientists planned to "control" the experiment by choosing a low-population density region and vaccinating people, but that, too, was experimental because the vaccine strain was grown from chick embryos and had not been field-tested in humans. See also Birn, "Backstage," 130, which reports that the Rockefeller Foundation referred to much of Africa and the southern United States as "backward."

25. Part 2, Article 7: Crimes Against Humanity, Rome Statute of the International Criminal Court, 1998, https://www.icc-cpi.int/sites/default/files/RS-Eng.pdf.

26. "Bill Gates Conspiracy Theories Echo through Africa," *France 24*, May 28, 2020,https://www.france24.com/en/20200528-bill-gates-conspiracy-theories-echo-through-africa.

27. Lenzer, "Secret Report Surfaces Showing That Pfizer Was at Fault in Nigerian Drug Tests." See also Peterson, *Speculative Markets*.

28. Ghinai et al., "Listening to the Rumours"; Njeru et al., "Did the Call for Boycott by the Catholic Bishops Affect the Polio Vaccination Coverage in Kenya in 2015?"

29. Cunningham, "Partially Treated"; Howard W. French, "AIDS Research in Africa: Juggling Risks and Hopes." *New York Times*, October 9, 1997, 1; Wendland, "Research, Therapy, and Bioethical Hegemony."

30. Nombulelo Shange, professor of anthropology, University of the Free State, personal communication with the author, November 14, 2023. For information about COVID-19 vaccine trials in South Africa, see Shabir A. Madhi, "COVID-19 Vaccine Trial in South Africa: Everything You Need to Know," *The Conversation*,July8,2020,https://theconversation.com/covid-19-vaccine-trial-in-south-africa-everything-you-need-to-know-142305.

31. Anna Clark, "IUDs to Prevent HIV in Kenya?" *The Nation*, May 6, 2011, https://www.thenation.com/article/archive/iuds-prevent-hiv-kenya/; Lydia Guterman, "Project Prevention Feels It Is Crucial to Educate HIV/AIDS Positive Women on Long Term Birth Control," *News Medical Life Sciences*, December 2, 2010, https://www.news-medical.net/news/20101202/Project-Prevention-feels-it-is-crucial-to-educate-HIVAIDS-positive-women-on-long-term-birth-control.aspx.

32. "Children Requiring a Caring Kommunity" (grant maker tax period 2021), Cause IQ, www.causeiq.com/organizations/children-requiring-a-caring-kommunity,330731572/funding, accessed June 24, 2024. The organization works primarily in the United States and operated previously in the United Kingdom. Abbass et al., "Ethical Issues in Providing and Promoting Contraception to Women with Opioid Use Disorder."

33. "Candid: Foundation Directory," Amazon Grantmaker Profile, accessed August 29, 2023, https://fconline.foundationcenter.org/fdo-grantmaker-profile?key=AMAZ022. Amazon canceled the program in February 2023. Kaitlyn Radde, "Amazon Ends Charity Donation Program AmazonSmile," NPR, January 19, 2023, https://www.npr.org/2023/01/19/1149993013/amazon-amazonsmile-charity-donation-program.

34. See Płotka and Rezmer, "Project Prevention's Cases of Paid Sterilization."

35. Derkas, "Organization Formerly Known as Crack."

36. Brett Davidson, "Preventing Project Prevention," *Open Society Foundations,* https://www.opensocietyfoundations.org/voices/preventing-project-

prevention, accessed June 29, 2024; "The Kenyan High Court Rules Forced Sterilization of Woman with HIV Violates Her Human Rights," Sigrid Rausing Trust, March 3, 2023, https://www.sigrid-rausing-trust.org/story/the-kenyan-high-court-rules-forced-sterilization-of-woman-with-hiv-violates-her-human-rights/; Kasiva, "Robbed of Choice"; H. Kibira, "Kenya: Women Seek Justice over Sterilisation," *The Star* (Nairobi), August 23, 2012, http://allafrica.com/stories /201208240201.html.

37. "Return of a Prodigal Son: The Ruling Party Anoints a Crown Prince," *The Economist,* December 22, 2012; "McDonald's South Africa Chain Bought by Cyril Ramaphosa," *BBC News*, March 17, 2011.

38. "President Cyril Ramaphosa: Official Launch of Nant-SA Vaccine Manufacturing Campus," South African Government, January 19, 2022, https://www .gov.za/speeches/president-cyril-ramaphosa-official-launch-nant-sa-vaccine-manufacturing-campus-19-jan-0. Other vaccine investments on the continent included building a Moderna plant in Kenya. "Moderna Signs Agreement for First mRNA Factory in Africa," Open Access Government, March 9, 2022, https://www.openaccessgovernment.org/moderna-first-mrna-factory-in-africa/131187/. See also "The Access to Advanced Health Institute [AAHI] Announces Leadership Change Reinforcing Commitment to Support Underserved Communities in Africa," AAHI, September 9, 2024. https://www.aahi.org/press-release/the-access-to-advanced-health-institute-announces-leadership-change-reinforcing-commitment-to-support-underserved-communities-in-africa/. Market research conducted before NantWorks's South Africa investment estimated the country's pharmaceutical annual sales at US$4 billion in 2022, with that number expected to reach US$5.9 billion by 2025.

39. "President Cyril Ramaphosa."

40. South Africa has the largest income distribution inequality globally. See *World Inequality Report 2022*, World Inequality Lab, 37, accessed June 22, 2024, https://wir2022.wid.world. For 2023 data, see "20 Countries with the Biggest Inequality in Income Distribution Worldwide in 2023, Based on the Gini Index," Statista, March 2024, https://www.statista.com/statistics/264627/ranking-of-the-20-countries-with-the-biggest-inequality-in-income-distribution/.

41. The RDP subsidized housing for South African citizens earning less than R3,500 (US$214) per household per month in 2022 rands.

42. South African Government, "South African Government Social Listening Report." November 5, 2021 (copy in author's possession).

43. South African Government, "South African Government Social Listening Report," November 12, 2021 (copy in author's possession). The report that day read: "Pfizer profiting from vaccine sales. The news that Pfizer has made billions in profits from their Covid vaccine has not been well received, with more negative comments . . . describing the company as 'modern day drug dealers,' accusing the

company of being 'a money scheme' and that 'covid was created' for that purpose."
The link to the Social Listening Report has been discontinued as have the links
within the report.

44. I say "COVID-like" symptoms because, like many people, Amadou and
Fortuné preferred not to get tested, fearing the diagnosis would be a death sentence. Again, to my knowledge, Amazon's developer was not aware these men
were undocumented laborers.

45. In 2020, "a US$15 million grant toward the [COVID vaccine] trial was
awarded to Novavax by the Bill & Melinda Gates Foundation. 2,665 healthy
adults and nearly 250 medically stable, HIV-positive adults" were enrolled in
South Africa. Makoni, "Covid-19 Vaccine Trials in Africa," e79. The trial discussed in Makoni's article is not the trial I discussed with Amadou and Fortuné.

46. "South Africa: Insurance and Compensation," ClinRegs, National Institute of Allergy and Infectious Disease, updated December 2023, https://
clinregs.niaid.nih.gov/country/south-africa#insurance_&_compensation.

47. I have no evidence that the manufacturer, the trial administrators, or the
government agencies involved violated any public health research protocols or
that healthcare providers in South Africa were aware of Amadou's and Fortuné's
undocumented status. I did not ask and Amadou did not share his health status
regarding HIV.

48. "IAVI and Moderna Launch First-in-Africa Clinical Trial."

49. Again, I have no direct evidence that they did have such knowledge in this
trial.

50. "IAVI and Moderna Launch First-in-Africa Clinical Trial."

51. Rothman, *Biomedical Empire.*

52. Storeng quoted in Banco, Furlong, and Pfahler, "How Bill Gates and Partners Used Their Clout." See also Stein, Katerini, and de Bengy Puyvallée, "Global
Health Nonsense."

53. Banco, Furlong, and Pfahler, "How Bill Gates and Partners Used Their
Clout"

54. "The Rockefeller Foundation Commits Nearly USD 35 Million to Covid-
19 Response Efforts in Africa" news release, Rockefeller Foundation, February
3, 2021, https://www.rockefellerfoundation.org/news/the-rockefeller-foundation-
commits-nearly-usd-35-million-to-covid-19-response-efforts-in-africa/.

55. "Awarded Grant," Ford Foundation, accessed August 29, 2023, https://
www.fordfound.org/work/our-grants/awarded-grants/awarded-grant/core-sup-
port-for-the-africa-cdc-continent-wide-covid-19-response-aimed-at-preventing-
transmission-de/137772; "Annual Report, FY 2019–2020," Carnegie Corporation of New York, March 2021, https://media.carnegie.org/filer_public/74
/d4/74d4a0b8-77b0-4524-8e1c-b48a41ad21dd/carnegie_ar_fy2019-20-fin
.pdf; "Annual Report, FY2020–2021," Carnegie Corporation of New York, March

2022, https://media.carnegie.org/filer_public/5b/88/5b88dc48-76e9-4443-8075-1e092ce83b04/carnegie_ar_fy2020-21-fin.pdf; "Annual Report, FY2021–2022," Carnegie Corporation of New York, March 2023, https://media.carnegie.org/filer_public/15/e8/15e8a194-3adb-4eb2-a7b5-8029f31a3570/carnegie_ar_fy2021-22-fin.pdf; "Collaborating against COVID-19: A Timeline," Bill & Melinda Gates Foundation, accessed June 29, 2024, https://www.gatesfoundation.org/ideas/a-timeline-of-gates-foundations-fight-against-covid-19.

56. See "Collaborating Against COVID-19: A Timeline," Bill & Melinda Gates Foundation, accessed March 3, 2025, https://www.gatesfoundation.org/ideas/a-timeline-of-gates-foundations-fight-against-covid-19.

57. Malpani quoted in Banco, Furlong, and Pfahler, "How Bill Gates and Partners Used Their Clout." See also Burki, "Fresh Questions over Gates Foundation Governance."

58. Rothman, *Biomedical Empire*, 33; Tilley, *Africa as a Living Laboratory*, 219.

59. For accounts of this era, see the works of Hunt, *A Colonial Lexicon of Birth Ritual, Medicalization, and Mobility;* Jochelson, *Colour of Disease*; and Echenberg, *Black Death, White Medicine.*

60. Ladson-Billings, "Through a Glass Darkly"; Strong, Odendaal, and Kelly, "Education for Subordination."

61. Jane Wakefield, "How Bill Gates Became 'Voodoo Doll' of Covid-19," *BBC News*, June 6, 2020, https://www.bbc.com/news/technology-52833706.

62. Boaz, *Voodoo*.

63. Banco, Furlong, and Pfahler, "How Bill Gates and Partners Used Their Clout."

64. The Gates Family Trust (now the Gates Trust) holds the personal assets of Bill Gates. They are managed by Cascade Asset Management Company (https://cascadeassetmanagement.com/faqs/), and invested in (among other companies) Berkshire Hathaway, which invests in Pfizer. See Ross, "How Does the Bill and Melinda Gates Foundation Invest Its Money?"

65. Katharina Buchholz, "The World's Biggest Players in Pharma," *Statista*, June 15, 2022, https://www.statista.com/chart/10149/top-ten-in-big-pharma/ (see, especially, the infographic); "Pfizer Reports Fourth-Quarter and Full-Year 2020 Results and Releases 5-Year Pipeline Metrics," *Businesswire*, February 2, 2021, https://www.businesswire.com/news/home/20210202005425/en/PFIZER-REPORTS-FOURTH-QUARTER-AND-FULL-YEAR-2020-RESULTS-AND-RELEASES-5-YEAR-PIPELINE-METRICS; "Moderna Reports Fourth Quarter and Fiscal Year 2020 Financial Results and Provides Business Updates," Moderna, February 25, 2021, https://investors.modernatx.com/news/news-details/2021/Moderna-Reports-Fourth-Quarter-and-Fiscal-Year-2020-

Financial-Results-and-Provides-Business-Updates/default.aspx; "Moderna Reports $18.5bn Total Revenue in Full-Year 2021," *Pharmaceutical Technology,* February 25, 2022, https://www.pharmaceutical-technology.com/news /moderna-reports-revenue-2021/.

66. On the cost of sustainable water projects, see African Union Development Agency–NEPAD, *2nd PIDA Priority Action Plan (2021–2030).* The equivalency in pharmaceutical factories is adjusted for inflation. See African Union, *Pharmaceutical Manufacturing Plan for Africa.*

67. See Sanjana Bhardwaj, "I Joined 1,800 Maternal Health Experts in Cape Town; What I Heard Gave Me Hope for Moms and Newborns," Bill & Melinda Gates Foundation, June 1, 2023, https://www.gatesfoundation.org/ideas /articles/maternal-newborn-health-innovation-policy-imnhc-2023.

68. Musk's increased by 851 percent to US$234 billion, and Bezos's by 46% to US$165.1 billion. Florian Zandt, "The U.S. Billionaires Profiting the Most from the Pandemic," *Statista,* March 15, 2022, https://www.statista.com/chart /22068/change-in-wealth-of-billionaires-during-pandemic/ (see, especially, infographic).

69. Katharina Buchholz, "The Biggest Private Coronavirus Donations," *Statista,* May 7, 2020, https://www.statista.com/chart/21640/biggest-private-coronavirus-donations/ (see, especially, infographic).

70. See "Data Explorer," The Global Fund, accessed January 6, 2025, https:// data.theglobalfund.org/.

71. Banco, Furlong, and Pfahler, "How Bill Gates and Partners Used Their Clout."

72. "Bill & Melinda Gates Foundation: Full Text of 'Full Filing' for Fiscal Year ending Dec. 2021," ProPublica, May 9, 2023, https://projects.propublica.org /nonprofits/organizations/562618866/202243159349100839/full.

73. "Covid-19 Vaccines and Corruption Risks: Preventing Corruption in the Manufacture, Location, and Distribution of Vaccines," UNODC (United Nations Office on Drugs and Crime), accessed March 3, 2025, https://www.unodc.org /documents/corruption/COVID-19/Policy_paper_on_COVID-19_vaccines_and_ corruption_risks.pdf; Kevin Johnson, "'A Brazen Scheme': 47 Charged with Siphoning $250M from COVID-19 Child Meal Program," *USA Today,* September 20, 2022, https://www.usatoday.com/story/news/politics/2022/09/20 /covid-19-child-meal-program-fraud-charges/10435117002/.

74. "Where Are Africa's Billions? News," Transparency International, July 11, 2019, https://www.transparency.org/en/news/where-are-africas-billions; "Lack of Transparency over Vaccine Trials, Secretive Contracts, and 'Science by Press Release' Risk Success of Global COVID-19 Response," Transparency International, May 25, 2021, https://www.transparency.org/en/press/covid-19-vaccines-lack-of-transparency-trials-secretive-contracts-science-by-press-release-risk-success-of-global-response.

CHAPTER 5

1. Proper names of people, the school, and the community (Vineyard Valley) are pseudonyms. Names of publicly traded companies and publicly profiled donors are not.

2. Field notes, Vineyard Valley, March 2022.

3. Statistics South Africa, statssa.gov.za; field notes, March 2022.

4. Osuafor, "Alcohol and Drug Use as Factors for High-School Learners' Absenteeism."

5. The Michael & Susan Dell Foundation is a nonprofit private family foundation separate from Dell Technologies. Owning 345.07 million shares in 2024, Dell CEO Michael Dell was the largest shareholder of Dell Technologies; Susan Dell and Vanguard are significant additional shareholders. In this chapter, I refer to the Dell Foundation as "Dell" or "the foundation" and Dell Technologies by that name. Eddie Pan, "5 Investors Betting Big on Dell Technologies (DELL) Stock," InvestorPlace, March 1, 2020, https://investorplace.com/2024/03/5-investors-betting-big-on-dell-technologies-dell-stock/.

6. Department of Basic Education South Africa, "School Realities," December 2022, https://www.education.gov.za/Portals/0/EMIS/School%20Realities%20December%202022.pdf?ver=2022-12-12-112304-000; "2021 Estimates of National Expenditure: Vote 16—Basic Education," National Treasury, Republic of South Africa, accessed June 24, 2024, https://www.treasury.gov.za/documents/national%20budget/2021/ene/Vote%2016%20Basic%20Education.pdf.

7. There were thirteen collaboration schools in 2023. "DGMT Welcomes Western Cape High Court Ruling to Uphold Collaboration Schools," DGMT (D. G. Murray Trust), July 21, 2023, https://dgmt.co.za/dgmt-welcomes-western-cape-high-court-ruling-to-uphold-collaboration-. Thirteen is a tiny fraction of the schools in the province, but the Basic Education Department approved expanding the number of collaboration schools to 15 percent of the total. Herbert, "Shareholder Schools," 27.

8. For discussions of South African collaboration schools, see Herbert, "Shareholder Schools"; and Feldman, "Public-Private Partnerships in South African Education."

9. For Dell's form 990 for 2015, see "Nonprofit Explorer: Texas—Michael & Susan Dell Foundation," ProPublica, accessed December 2, 2024, https://projects.propublica.org/nonprofits/organizations/364336415.

10. YearBeyond, accessed July 18, 2023, https://www.yearbeyond.org/; "Injini, Africa's EdTech Accelerator," Injini, accessed July 18, 2023, https://www.injini.africa/.

11. For Dell's 2021 Expenditure Responsibility Statement and form 990 for 2015, see "Nonprofit Explorer: Texas—Michael & Susan Dell Foundation."

12. School employee, interview with the author, March 2022.

13. Principal of Starling Vocational Technical School, personal communication with the author, March 2022.

14. Field notes, Vineyard Valley, March 2022.

15. A pseudonym that retains the spirit.

16. See Peter Leonard, "Beyond Data Privacy: Data 'Ownership' and Regulation of Data-Driven Business," ABA (American Bar Association), January 27, 2020, https://www.americanbar.org/groups/science_technology/publications /scitech_lawyer/2020/winter/beyond-data-privacy-data-ownership-and-regulation-datadriven-business/.

17. "What Is Data Mining?," Purdue University, https://business.purdue.edu /master-of-business/online-masters-in-business-administration/posts/what-is-data-mining.php, accessed March 3, 2025.

18. Bhattacharyya, *Futures of Racial Capitalism*; Zuboff, "Surveillance Capitalism." See also Maguire and Low, *Trapped*, which ethnographically links surveillance to the social engineering of public space.

19. Hook, "Schooling as Plantation," S100.

20. Strong and Kelly, "Youth Leadership for Development," 217. See also Hunter, *Race for Education*.

21. Williamson, "Big EdTech," 158.

22. "What Is Data Mining?"

23. Nicholls, "Euergetism."

24. Mill, *On Liberty*, 14.

25. Rudyard Kipling, "The White Man's Burden" (1899), Kipling Society, accessed December 2, 2024, https://www.kiplingsociety.co.uk/poem/poems_ burden.htm.

26. See "Exempt Organization Types," IRS (US Internal Revenue Service). accessed March 3, 2025, https://www.irs.gov/charities-non-profits/exempt-organization-types; "Guide to the Taxation of Special Trusts (Issue 3)," SARS (South African Revenue Service), September 8, 2020, https://www.sars.gov.za /wp-content/uploads/Ops/Guides/LAPD-IT-G20-Guide-to-the-Taxation-of-Special-Trusts.pdf.

27. DGMT, "Annual Report, 2020," 66, accessed December 24, 2024, https:// dgmt.co.za/wp-content/uploads/2021/04/DGMT-2020-ANNUAL-REPORT-final-digital.pdf. The equivalent of US$24,046,000 in April 2020 (Oanda.com).

28. "How We Fund Grants," Michael & Susan Dell Foundation, accessed December 24, 2024, https://www.dell.org/how-we-fund/grants. The equivalent of USD 2,454,066 in April 2022 (Oanda.com).

29. "How Venture Philanthropy Works," *Giving with Impact* (podcast, Stanford Social Innovation Review), January 29, 2020, https://ssir.org/podcasts /entry/how_venture_philanthropy_works_and_its_role_in_effective_charity.

30. Varoufakis, *Technofeudalism*; Wark, *Capital Is Dead*.

31. Rotberg, *The Founder*.

32. "Other Carnegie Organizations," Carnegie Corporation of New York, accessed March 3, 2025, https://www.carnegie.org/about/our-history/other-carnegie-organizations/. For the calculated worth in 2024 dollars, see "Inflation Calculator," Saving.org, accessed December 2, 2024, https://www.saving.org/inflation/.

33. Cappy, "The Politics of Partnership." See also "Special Feature: Carnegie in South Africa—First Inquiry into Poverty," Carnegie Corporation Oral History Project, Columbia University Libraries Oral History Research Office, accessed March 3, 2025, http://www.columbia.edu/cu/lweb/digital/collections/oral_hist/carnegie/special-features/.

34. Rhodes's legacy and the value of his scholarship programs are now challenged. See Bond, "In South Africa, 'Rhodes Must Fall'"; and Ntloedibe, "Where Are Our Heroes and Ancestors?"

35. Saltman, *Gift of Education*, 5.

36. Field notes, June 2022.

37. Charumbira, "'A School Said to Resemble a Luxury Hotel'"; Celean Jacobson, "Oprah Winfrey to Open School for Girls in SA," *Mail and Guardian*, January 2, 2007; John Donnelly, "Outside Oprah's School, a Growing Frustration," *McClatchy-Tribune Business News*, January 20, 2007; Burges-Wilkerson, Fuller, and Frederick, "Say It Isn't So Lady 'O'"; Rebecca Davis, "First Matriculants Leave Oprah's School," *Daily Maverick* (Cape Town), December 2, 2011.

38. Ntaka, "Double Consciousness," 51; Du Bois, *Souls of Black Folk*; Fanon, *Black Skin, White Masks*; Haffajee, *What If There Were No Whites in South Africa?*

39. Refilwe, quoted in Ntaka, "Double Consciousness," 41.

40. Ntaka, "Double Consciousness," 44.

41. Bongeka, quoted in Ntaka, "Double Consciousness," 43, 44.

42. Ntaka, "Double Consciousness," 43.

43. Ntaka, "Double Consciousness," 45.

44. According to a Henley on Klip resident. Field notes, June 2022.

45. Budabin and Richey, *Batman Saves the Congo*, 163–64.

46. "About Basic Education," Department of Basic Education, Republic of South Africa, accessed March 3, 2025, https://www.education.gov.za/AboutUs/AboutDBE.aspx.

47. Ferguson, "Declarations of Dependence."

48. Danielsen, "Denunciations of Dependence," 48.

49. Douglas, "No Free Gifts," vii.

50. "Nonprofit Explorer: Texas—Michael & Susan Dell Foundation."

51. Kieth Lewin, "Peak Aid and Time for Something Different: Sustainable Financing for Education," UKFIET: The Education and Development Forum, August 23, 2019, https://www.ukfiet.org/2019/peak-aid-and-time-for-something-different-sustainable-financing-for-education/.

52. Klees, "New Philanthropy."

53. Dolan, Huang, and Gordon, "Ambiguity of Mutuality"; Hook, "Education Reform in Times of Crisis."

54. Harvey, "'New' Imperialism."

55. Polanyi, *Great Transformation*, 76.

56. Lehman and James, "Charitable Bequest Importance Among Donors to Different Types of Charities."

57. Douglas, "No Free Gifts," xiv.

58. Veselinovic Milena, "Why Corruption Is Holding Africa Back," CNN, updated January 8, 2016, https://www.cnn.com/2015/12/24/africa/africa-corruption-transparency-international/index.html.

CONCLUSION

1. Robinson, "Black Marxism." See also Harris, "Whiteness as Property."

2. Ramones and Merry, "Capitalist Transformation and Settler Colonialism"; Sahlins, "Cosmologies of Capitalism."

3. Li, "Indigeneity, Capitalism, and the Management of Dispossession"; West, *Dispossession and the Environment*; Harvey, "'New' Imperialism."

4. Dharia, *Industrial Ephemeral*.

5. See, for example, Marber, "Globalization and Its Contents"; and Johnson, "Globalization."

6. See, for example, Stiglitz, *Globalization and Its Discontents*; and Wedel, *Shadow Elite*.

7. A point Krasner makes in "Globalization and Sovereignty."

8. A point Ferguson elaborates in *Global Shadows*.

Bibliography

Abbass Nadia, Tani Malhotra, Brooke Bullington, and Kavita Shah Arora. "Ethical Issues in Providing and Promoting Contraception to Women with Opioid Use Disorder." *Journal of Clinical Ethics* 33, no. 2 (Summer 2022): 112–23.

Abowd, Thomas. "Scarcity Amid Abundance: Navigating the Waters of Neoliberal Austerity in Detroit." *City and Society* 32, no. 2 (2024).

Abrera, Joseph. "Data Privacy and Security in Cloud Computing: A Comprehensive Review." *Journal of Computer Science and Information Technology* 1, no. 1 (2024): 1–9. https://doi.org/10.61424/jcsit.v1i1.58.

Adu Sarfo, Emmanuel, and Rabbi Tweneboah. "Mineral Wealth Paradox: Health Challenges and Environmental Risks in African Resource-Rich Areas." *BMC Public Health* 24, no. 724 (March 2024). https://doi.org/10.1186/s12889-024-18137-1.

Agbiboa, Daniel Egiegba. *They Eat Our Sweat: Transport Labor, Corruption, and Everyday Survival in Urban Nigeria.* Oxford: Oxford University Press, 2022.

African Union. *Pharmaceutical Manufacturing Plan for Africa: Business Plan.* Addis Ababa, Ethiopia, 2012. https://au.int/sites/default/files/pages/32895-file-pmpa_business_plan.pdf.

African Union Development Agency–NEPAD. *2nd PIDA Priority Action Plan (2021–2030): Projects Prospectus.* Johannesburg, South Africa, 2023.

https://www.nepad.org/publication/2nd-pida-priority-action-plan-2021-2030-projects-prospectus.

Albertus, Michael. "Why Land Reform Matters in South Africa's Election." *Foreign Policy*, May 27, 2024. https://foreignpolicy.com/2024/05/27/south-africa-election-anc-land-reform-matters/.

Alessandri, Todd, Sylvia Sloan Black, and William E. Jackson III. "Black Economic Empowerment Transactions in South Africa: Understanding When Corporate Social Responsibility May Create or Destroy Value." *Long Range Planning* 44 (2011): 229–49. https://doi.org/10.1016/j.lrp.2011.02.002.

Arndt, Lucas. "Linking Wealth and Power: Direct Political Action of Corporate Elites and the Wealthiest Capitalist Families in the United States and Germany." *CRIS Papers* 5, no. 1 (October 2023): 1–30. https://doi.org/10.25647/osc.papers.05.

Atinkut Asmare, Birtukan, Bernhard Freyer, and Jim Bingen. "Women in Agriculture: Pathways of Pesticide Exposure, Potential Health Risks, and Vulnerability in Sub-Saharan Africa." *Environmental Sciences Europe* 34, no. 89 (September 2022): 1–14. https://doi.org/10.1186/s12302-022-00638-8.

Austin, John L. *How to Do Things with Words: The William James Lectures.* Oxford: Oxford University Press, 1962.

Axelrod, Joshua. "Corporate Honesty and Climate Change: Time to Own Up and Act." NRDC (Natural Resource Defense Council), February 26, 2019. https://www.nrdc.org/bio/josh-axelrod/corporate-honesty-and-climate-change-time-own-and-act.

Ballestero, Andrea. *A Future History of Water.* Durham, NC: Duke University Press, 2019.

Bakhtin, Mikhail M. "Discourse in the Novel." In *The Dialogic Imagination: Four Essays,* translated by Caryl Emerson and Michael Holquist and edited by Michael Holquist, 259–422. Austin: University of Texas Press, 1981.

Bam, June, and Rafaël Verbuyst. "Indigenous History, Activism, and the Decolonizing University: Challenges, Opportunities, and the Struggle over the Khoisan Past in Post-Apartheid South Africa." In *Professional Historians in Public: Old and New Roles Revisited,* edited by Berber Bevernage and Lutz Raphael, 213–41. Boston: De Gruyter, 2023. https://doi.org/10.1515/9783111186047-009.

Bam-Hutchison, J. "The Politics of Heritage in Africa: Economies, Histories, and Infrastructures. *Anthropology Southern Africa* 40, no. 3 (2017): 238–40.

Barman, Emily. "The Social Bases of Philanthropy." *Annual Review of Sociology* 43 (2017): 271–90. http://www.jstor.org/stable/44863233.

Bartop, Paul. "Zyklon B." In The Holocaust: An Encyclopedia and Document Collection, edited by Paul R. Bartrop and Michael Dickerman, vol. 1, 742–43. Santa Barbara, CA: ABC-CLIO, 2017.

Bassil K. L. C. Vakil, M. Sanborn, D. C. Cole, J. S. Kaur, and K. J. Kerr. "Cancer Health Effects of Pesticides: Systematic Review." *Canadian Family Physician* 53, no. 10 (October 2007): 1704–11. PMID: 17934034; PMCID: PMC2231435.

Bataka, Hodabalo. "Global Value Chains Participation and Gender Inequalities in Sub-Saharan Africa: Importance of Women Education." International Economics 178 (August 2024). https://doi.org/10.1016/j.inteco.2024.100483

Beckert, Jens. "Varieties of Wealth: Toward a Comparative Sociology of Wealth Inequality." *Socio-Economic Review* (December 2023). https://doi.org/10.1093/ser/mwad068.

Benson, Peter, and Stuart Kirsch. "The Capitalist Corporation." In *The International Encyclopedia of Anthropology,* edited by Hilary Callan. New York: John Wiley, 2018.

Bessire, Lucas. *Running Out: In Search of Water on the High Plains.* Princeton, NJ: Princeton University Press, 2021.

Bhattacharyya, Gargi. *The Futures of Racial Capitalism.* Hoboken, NJ: Polity Press, 2024.

Biehl, João, and Torben Eskerod. "Conclusion: Global Public Health." In *Will to Live: AIDS Therapies and the Politics of Survival,* 373–406. Princeton, NJ: Princeton University Press, 2007. http://www.jstor.org/stable/j.ctv1wmz48h.22.

Birn, A.-E. "Backstage: The Relationship between the Rockefeller Foundation and the World Health Organization, Part I: 1940s–1960s." *Public Health* 128, no. 2 (2014): 129–40.

Biswas, Asit K., and Cecilia Tortajada. "Water Crisis and Water Wars: Myths and Realities." *International Journal of Water Resources Development* 35, no. 5 (2019): 727–31. https://doi.org/10.1080/07900627.2019.1636502.

Blancato, Filippo Gualtiero. "The Cloud Sovereignty Nexus: How the European Union Seeks to Reverse Strategic Dependencies in its Digital Ecosystem." *Policy and Internet* 16, no. 1 (2024): 12–32. https://doi.org/10.1002/poi3.358.

Blanchette, Alex. "Living Waste and the Labor of Toxic Health on American Factory Farms." *Medical Anthropology Quarterly* 33, no. 1 (2019): 80–100. https://doi.org/10.1111/maq.12491.

Blanchette, Alex. *Porkopolis: American Animality, Standardized Life, and the Factory Farm.* Durham, NC: Duke University Press, 2020.

Blunt, Gwilym David. "The Gates Foundation, Global Health, and Domination: A Republican Critique of Transnational Philanthropy." *International Affairs* 98, no. 6 (November 2022): 2039–56. https://doi.org/10.1093/ia/iiac022.

Boafo, Yaw Agyeman, O. Saito, S. Kato, C. Kamiyama, K. Takeuchi, and M. Nakahara. "The Role of Traditional Ecological Knowledge in Ecosystem Services Management: The Case of Four Rural Communities in Northern

Ghana." *International Journal of Biodiversity Science, Ecosystem Services, and Management* 12, nos. 1–2 (2016): 24–38. https://doi.org/10.1080/21513 732.2015.1124454.

Boaz, Danielle N. *Voodoo: The History of a Racial Slur*. Oxford: Oxford University Press, 2023.

Boccaletti, Giulio. *Water: A Biography*. New York: Penguin Random House, 2021.

Bond, Patrick. "In South Africa, 'Rhodes Must Fall' (while Rhodes' Walls Rise)." *New Global Studies* 13, no. 3 (2019): 335–50.

Bornstein, Erica. "The Impulse of Philanthropy." *Cultural Anthropology* 24, no. 4 (2009): 622–51. http://www.jstor.org/stable/25619800.

Brause, Holly. "From Paralyzing to Actionable Futures: Facilitating Farmer Participation in Water Conservation Through a Multiscalar Horizoning Work Approach." *Culture, Agriculture, Food and Environment* 2024: 1–8.

Brennan, James R. "Blood Enemies: Exploitation and Urban Citizenship in the Nationalist Political Thought of Tanzania, 1958–75." *Journal of African History* 47, no. 3 (November 2006): 389–413. https://doi.org/10.1017 /s0021853706001794.

Broadway, Michael J., and Donald D. Stull. "The Wages of Food Factories." *Food and Foodways* 18, nos. 1–2 (April 2010): 43–65. https://doi.org/10.1080 /07409711003708413.

Brosnan, Jim, Natalie Bumgarner, Rebecca Bowling, Gregg Breeden, and Celeste Scott. "Update on Roundup-Branded Herbicides for Consumers." Institute of Agriculture, the University of Tennessee, May 2023. https:// uthort.tennessee.edu/wp-content/uploads/sites/228/2024/05/Update-on -Roundup-Branded-Herbicides.pdf.

Budabin, Alexandra and Lisa Ann Richey. *Batman Saves the Congo: How Celebrities Disrupt the Politics of Development*. Minneapolis: University of Minnesota Press, 2021.

Burden-Stelly, Charisse. "Modern U.S. Racial Capitalism." *Monthly Review* 72, no. 3 (2020): 8–20. https://doi.org/10.14452/mr-072-03-2020-07_2.

Burges-Wilkerson, Barbara, Barbara K. Fuller, and Nathaniel Frederick. "Say It Isn't So Lady 'O': A Sex Scandal at the Oprah Leadership Academy for Girls." *Journal of Critical Incidents* 8 (2015): 59–62.

Burki, Talha. "Fresh Questions over Gates Foundation Governance." *The Lancet* 399, no. 10324 (February 5, 2022): P508. https://www.thelancet.com /journals/lancet/article/PIIS0140-6736(22)00226-4/fulltext#%20.

Burns, Carol J., and Daland R. Juberg. "Cancer and Occupational Exposure to Pesticides: An Umbrella Review." *International Archives of Occupational and Environmental Health* 94, no. 5 (July 2021): 945–57. https://doi.org /10.1007/s00420-020-01638-y.

Butt, Waqas. "Technics of Labor: Productivism, Expertise, and Solid Waste Management in a Public-Private Partnership." *Anthropology of Work Review* 41, no. 2 (2020): 108–18.

Byala, Sara. *Bottled: How Coca-Cola Became African.* New York: Oxford University Press, 2023.

Callander, Steven, Dana Foarta, and Takuo Sugaya. "Market Competition and Political Influence: An Integrated Approach." *Econometrica* 90, no. 6 (November 11): 2723–53.

Campbell, John. "Transnational White Supremacist Militancy Thriving in South Africa." *Foreign Affairs*, September 17, 2020.

Canhan, Hugo ka. *Riotous Deathscapes.* Durham, NC: Duke University Press, 2023.

Canfield, Matthew C. *Translating Food Sovereignty: Cultivating Justice in an Age of Transnational Governance.* Redwood City, CA: Stanford University Press, 2023.

Cappy, Christina. "The Politics of Partnership: The Phielps-Stokes Fund and the Carnegie Corporation in South Africa in the Early Twentieth Century." Master's thesis, University of Wisconsin–Madison, March 2012.

Carse, Ashley, Townsend Middleton, Jason Cons, Jatin Dua, Gabriela Valdivia, and Elizabeth Cullen Dunn. "Chokepoints: Anthropologies of the Constricted Contemporary." *Ethnos* 88, no. 2 (May 2020): 193–203.

Chachage, C. S. L., Magnus Ericsson, and Peter Gibbon. *Mining and Structural Adjustment: Studies on Zimbabwe and Tanzania.* Uppsala: Scandinavian Institute of African Studies, 1993.

Chakravarty, Paula, and Denise Ferreira da Silva, DF. "Accumulation, Dispossession, and Debt: The Racial Logic of Global Capitalism—An Introduction." *American Quarterly* 64, no. 3 (September 2012): 361–85. https://doi.org/10.1353/aq.2012.0033.

Chancel, Lucas, Thomas Piketty, Emmanuel Saez, and Gabriel Zucman. "World Inequality Report 2022." Paris: World Inequality Lab. https://wir2022.wid.world/.

Chang, Junning, William S. Symes, Felix Lim, and L. Roman Carrasco. "International Trade Causes Large Net Economic Losses in Tropical Countries via the Destruction of Ecosystem Services." *Ambio* 45, no. 4 (March 2016): 387–97. https://doi.org/10.1007/s13280-016-0768-7.

Chang, Vicky C., Gabriella Andreotti, Maria Ospina, Christine G. Parks, Danping Liu, Joseph J. Shearer, Nathaniel Rothman, Debra T. Silverman, Dale P. Sandler, Antonia M. Calafat, Laura E. Beane Freeman, and Jonathan N. Hofmann. "Glyphosate Exposure and Urinary Oxidative Stress Biomarkers in the Agricultural Health Study." *Journal of the National Cancer Institute*, 115, no. 4 (April 2023): 394–404. https://doi.org/10.1093/jnci/djac242.

Charumbira, Ruramisai. "'A School Said to Resemble a Luxury Hotel': Historicizing African Women's Quest for Education Before Oprah's School." *History Compass* 7, no. 3 (May 2009): 624–43.

Chirau, Takunda J., Joyce Shirinde, and Cheryl McCrindle. "Access to Healthcare by Undocumented Zimbabwean Migrants in Post-Apartheid South Africa." *African Journal of Primary Health Care and Family Medicine* 16, no. 1 (2024). https://doi.org/10.4102/phcfm.v16i1.4126.

Chitonge, Horman, Orleans Mfune, Bridget Umar, Gear Kajoba, Diana Banda, and Lungisile Ntsebeza. "Silent Privatization of Customary Land in Zambia: Opportunities for a Few, Challenges for Many." *Social Dynamics* 43, no. 1 (January 2017): 82–102. https://doi.org/10.1080/02533952.2017.1356049.

Coomes, Oliver T., Shawn J. McGuire, Eric Garine, Sophie Caillon, Doyle McKey, Elise Demeulenaere, Devra Jarvis, et al. "Farmer Seed Networks Make a Limited Contribution to Agriculture? Four Common Misconceptions." *Food Policy* 56 (October 2015): 41–50. https://doi.org/10.1016/j.foodpol.2015.07.008.

Cooper, Elizabeth, Erdmute Alber, and Wandia Njoya, eds. *The Education Alibi: Tracing Education's Entanglements across Contemporary Africa.* Ann Arbor: University of Michigan Press, 2025.

Cooper, Elizabeth, Erdmute Alber, and Wandia Njoya. "Introduction." In *The Education Alibi: Tracing Education's Entanglements across Contemporary Africa*, edited by Elizabeth Cooper, Erdmute Alber, and Wandia Njoya. Ann Arbor: University of Michigan Press, 2025.

Cousins, Ben. "Land Reform in South Africa: The Politics of Expropriation Without Compensation." In *Land Tenure Challenges in Africa: Confronting the Land Governance Deficit*, edited by Horman Chitonge and Ross Harvey, 99–119. Cham, Switzerland: Springer International, 2022.

Crane, Johanna Tayloe. *Scrambling for Africa: AIDS, Expertise, and the Rise of American Global Health Science.* Ithaca, NY: Cornell University Press, 2013.

Crenner, Christopher. "The Tuskegee Syphilis Study and the Scientific Concept of Racial Nervous Resistance." *Journal of the History of Medicine and Allied Sciences* 67, no. 2 (April 2012): 244–80. https://doi.org/10.1093/jhmas/jrr003.

Cunningham, Brooke. "Partially Treated: AIDS, Inequality, and Ethics—The Controversy over the Short Course AZT Trials." Doctoral dissertation, University of Pennsylvania, 2006.

Dahl, Robert A. "Can International Organizations Be Democratic? A Sceptic's View." In *The Global Transformations Reader*, edited by David Held and Anthony McGrew, 530–41. Malden, MA: Polity Press, 2003.

Danielsen, Lotte. "Denunciations of Dependence: Race, Gender, and the Double Bind of Domestic Work in the Eastern Cape." *Focaal: Journal of Global and Historical Anthropology* 90 (June 2021): 47–57. https://doi.org/10.3167/fcl.2021.900105.

Decker, Corrie, and Elisabeth McMahon. *The Idea of Development in Africa: A History*. Cambridge: Cambridge University Press, 2020.

Decker, Stephanie. "Corporate Political Activity in Less Developed Countries: The Volta River Project in Ghana, 1958–66." *Business History* 53, no. 7 (December 2011): 993–1017. https://doi.org/10.1080/00076791.2011.618223.

Decoteau, Claire Laurier. *Ancestors and Antiretrovirals: The Biopolitics of HIV/AIDS in Post-Apartheid South Africa*. Chicago: University of Chicago Press, 2013.

Derkas, Erika. "The Organization Formerly Known as Crack: Project Prevention and the Privatized Assault on Reproductive Wellbeing." *Race, Gender, and Class* 19, nos. 34 (2012): 179–95. http://www.jstor.org/stable/43497495.

Dharia, Namita. *The Industrial Ephemeral: Labor and Love in Indian Architecture and Construction*. Oakland: University of California Press, 2022.

DiBartolomeis, Michael, Susan Kegley, Pierre Mineau, Rosemarie Radford, and Kendra Klein. "An Assessment of Acute Insecticide Toxicity Loading (AITL) of Chemical Pesticides Used on Agricultural Land in the United States." *PLoS ONE* 14, no. 8 (2019): e0220029.

Dietrich, Simone. *States, Markets, and Foreign Aid*. Cambridge: Cambridge University Press, 2021.

Dolan, Catherine, Julia Qermezi Huang, and Colin Gordon. "The Ambiguity of Mutuality: Discourse and Power in Corporate Value Regimes." *Dialectical Anthropology* 45, no. 1 (2021.): 9–27. https://doi.org/10.1007/s10624-019-09569-y

Douglas, Mary. "Foreword: No Free Gifts." In *The Gift: The Form and Reason for Exchange in Archaic Societies* (1954), by Marcel Mauss, ix–xxiii. New York: Routledge, 1990.

Drew, Georgina. "Coca-Cola and the Moral Economy of Rural Development in India." *South Asia: Journal of South Asian Studies* 44, no. 3 (2021): 477–97.

Du Bois, W. E. Burghardt. *The Souls of Black Folk: Essays and Sketches*. 2nd edition. Chicago: A. C. McClurg & Co., 1903. Online, Open Library, Internet Archive. https://openlibrary.org/books/OL24179917M/The_Souls_Of_Black_Folk.

Du Plessis, Anja. *South Africa's Water Predicament: Freshwater's Unceasing Decline*, 109–41. Cham, Switzerland: Springer International, 2023.

Du Plessis, Carien, and Martin Plaut. *Understanding South Africa*. London: C. Hurst, 2019.

Dugard, J. (2021). "Water Rights in a Time of Fragility: An Exploration of Contestation and Discourse around Cape Town's 'Day Zero' Water Crisis." *Water*, 73, no. 22 (2021). https://www.doi.org/10.3390/wl 3223247

Echenberg, Myron. *Black Death, White Medicine: Bubonic Plage and the Politics of Public Health in Colonial Senegal, 1914–1945*. Oxford: James Currey, 2002.

Erikson, Susan. "Betting on Pandemic: Op-Ed." *Medical Anthropology* 39. no. 5 (April 2020): 380–81. https://doi.org/10.1080/01459740.2020.1746302.

Fanon, Frantz. *Black Skin, White Masks*. London: Pluto Press, 1986.

Farmer, Paul. *Pathologies of Power: Health, Human Rights, and the New War on the Poor*. Berkeley: University of California Press, 2009.

Fassin, Didier. "The Politics of Conspiracy Theories: On AIDS in South Africa and a Few Other Global Plots." *Brown Journal of World Affairs* 17, no. 2 (2011): 39–50. http://www.jstor.org/stable/24590791.

Fucic, Aleksandra, Radu C. Duca, Karen S. Galea, Tihana Maric, Kelly Garcia, Michael S. Bloom, Helle R. Andersen, and John E. Vena. 2021. "Reproductive Health Risks Associated with Occupational and Environmental Exposure to Pesticides." *International Journal of Environmental Research and Public Health* 18 (12): 6576. https://doi.org/10.3390/ijerph18126576.

Feldman, Jennifer Ann. "Public-Private Partnerships in South African Education: Risky Business or Good Governance?" *Education as Change* 24, no.1 (April 2020): 1–18.

Ferguson, James. "Declarations of Dependence: Labor, Personhood, and Welfare in Southern Africa." *Journal of the Royal Anthropological Institute* 19, no. 2 (June 2013): 223–42.

Ferguson, James. *Global Shadows: Africa in the Neoliberal World Order*. Durham, NC: Duke University Press, 2006.

Ferguson, James. "The Uses of Neoliberalism." *Antipode* 41, no. S1 (March 2010): S166–S184. https://doi.org/10.1111/j.1467-8330.2009.00721.x.

Folayan, Morenike Oluwatoyin, Brandon Brown, Bridget Haire, Chinedum Peace Babalola, and Nicaise Ndembi. "Considerations for Stakeholder Engagement and COVID -19 Related Clinical Trials' Conduct in Sub-Saharan Africa." *Developing World Bioethics* 21, no. 1 (March 2021): 44–50. https://doi.org/10.1111/dewb.12283.

Foster, Robert J. "Corporations as Partners: 'Connected Capitalism' and the Coca-Cola Company." *PoLAR: Political and Legal Anthropology Review* 37, no. 2 (2014): 246–58.

Freidberg, S. "Metrics and Mētis: Work and Practical Knowledge in Agri-Food Sustainability Governance." *Agriculture and Human Values* 40 (2023): 245–57. https://doi.org/10.1007/s10460-022-10351-0.

Fuhrer, Jeff. *The Myths That Made Us: How False Beliefs About Racism and Meritocracy Broke Our Economy (and How to Fix It)*. Cambridge, MA: MIT Press, 2023.

Fuller, Richard, Philip J. Landrigan, Kalpana Balakrishnan, et al. "Pollution and Health: A Progress Update." *The Lancet Planetary Health* 6, no. 6 (June 2022): e535-e547. https://doi.org/10.1016/S2542-5196(22)00090-0.

Gajadhur, Revantha, and Angelo Nicolaides. "A Reflection on Corporate Social Responsibility in Africa Contrasted with the UAE and Some Asian Nations." *Athens Journal of Law* 8, no. 2 (April 2022): 157–72.

Gathii, James Thuo, and Ntina Tzouvala. "Racial Capitalism and International Economic Law: Introduction." *Journal of International Economic Law* 25, no. 2 (June 2022): 199–206. https://doi.org/10.1093/jiel/jgac025.

Gerrard, Michael B. "Public-Private Partnerships." *Finance and Development* 38, no. 3 (September 2021). https://www.imf.org/external/pubs/ft/fandd/2001 /09/gerrard.htm.

Ghinai Isaac, Chris Willott, Ibrahim Dadari, Heidi J. Larson. "Listening to the Rumours: What the Northern Nigeria Polio Vaccine Boycott Can Tell Us Ten Years On." *Global Public Health*. 8, no. 10 (2013): 1138–50. https://doi.org /10.1080/17441692.2013.859720.

Gill, Lesley. "The Limits of Solidarity: Labor and Transnational Organizing Against Coca-Cola." *American Ethnologist* 36, no. 4 (November 2009): 667–80. https://doi.org/10.1111/j.1548-1425.2009.01202.x.

Gimbel, S., B. Chilundo, N. Kenworthy, C. Inguane, D. Citrin, R. Chapman, et al. "Donor Data Vacuuming: Audit Culture and the Use of Data in Global Health Partnerships." *Medicine Anthropology Theory* 5, no. 2 (2018). https:// doi.org/10.17157/mat.5.2.537.

Giridharadas, Anand. *Winners Take All: The Elite Charade of Changing the World*. New York: Alfred A. Knopf, 2018.

Githiria, Joseph Muchiri, and Moshood Onifade. "The Impact of Mining on Sustainable Practices and the Traditional Culture of Developing Countries." *Journal of Environmental Studies and Sciences* 10 (May 2020): 394–410. https://doi.org/10.1007/s13412-020-00613-w.

Global Health Watch. *Global Health Watch 2: An Alternative World Health Report*. New York: Zed Books, 2008.

Go, Julian. "The Imperial Origins of American Policing: Militarization and Imperial Feedback in the Early 20th Century." *American Journal of Sociology* 125, no. 5 (March 2020): 1193–254. https://doi.org/10.1086/708464.

Govindrajan, Radhika. *Animal Intimacies : Interspecies Relatedness in India's Central Himalayas*. Chicago: University of Chicago Press, 2018.

Graeber, David. *Direct Action: An Ethnography*. Oakland: AK Press, 2009.

Gramsci, Antonio. "State and Civil Society." In *Selections from Prison Notebooks*, edited by Quintin Hoare, Geoffrey Nowell-Smith, and Geoffrey Nowell-Smith. London: Lawrence and Wishart, 2005. muse.jhu.edu/book/34838.

Grant, Ruth W., and Robert O. Keohane. "Accountability and Abuses of Power in World Politics." *American Political Science Review* 99, no. 1 (February 2005): 29–43. https://doi.org/10.1017/s0003055405051476.

Green, Lesley. *Rock, Water, Life: Ecology and Humanities for a Decolonial South Africa*. Durham, NC: Duke University Press, 2020.

Grossman, Jonathan. *The Art of Alibi: English Law Courts and the Novel.* Baltimore: Johns Hopkins University Press, 2002.

Guest, Kenneth J. *Cultural Anthropology: A Toolkit for a Global Age.* 4th edition. New York: W. W. Norton, 2023.

Gustafson, Bret. *Bolivia in the Age of Gas.* Durham, NC: Duke University Press, 2020.

Gustafsson, Maria-Therese, Almut Schilling-Vacaflor, and Andrea Lenschow. "The Politics of Supply Chain Regulations: Towards Foreign Corporate Accountability in the Area of Human Rights and the Environment?" *Regulation and Governance* 17, no. 4 (October 2023): 853–69. https://doi.org/10.1111/rego.12526.

Haffajee, Ferial. *What If There Were No Whites in South Africa?* Johannesburg: Pan Macmillan SA, 2015.

Hamisi, Nyaso Malilo, Baozhen Dai, and Masud Ibrahim. "Global Health Security amid COVID-19: Tanzanian Government's Response to the COVID-19 Pandemic." *BMC Public Health* 23, no. 1 (January 2023). https://doi.org/10.1186/s12889-023-14991-7.

Hansen, Kathryn. "Deluge in South Africa." NASA Earth Observatory, April 13, 2022. https://earthobservatory.nasa.gov/images/149720/deluge-in-south-africa.

Harnish, Allison, Lisa Cliggett, and Thayer Scudder. "Rivers and Roads: A Political Ecology of Displacement, Development, and Chronic Liminality in Zambia's Gwembe Valley." *Economic Anthropology* 6, no. 2 (March 2019). https://doi.org/10.1002/sea2.12151.

Harris, Cheryl. "Whiteness as Property." *Harvard Law Review* 106, no. 8 (1993): 1707–91.

Hartmann, Thom. *Unequal Protection: How Corporations Became "People" and How You Can Fight Back.* Oakland: Berrett-Koehler, 2010.

Harvey, David. "The 'New' Imperialism: Accumulation by Dispossession." *Socialist Register* 49 (2004): 63–87.

Harvey, David. *The New Imperialism.* Oxford: Oxford University Press, 2003.

Harvey, David. *A Brief History of Neoliberalism.* Oxford: Oxford University Press, 2007.

Hay, Iain. "Economic Wealth and Political Power in the Second Gilded Age." In *Geographies of the Super-Rich,* edited by Iain Hay and Choon-Piew Pow, 26–42. Northampton, MA: Edward Elgar, 2013.

Hetherington, Kregg. *The Government of Beans: Regulating Life in the Age of Monocrops.* Durham, NC: Duke University Press, 2020.

Hengeveld, Maria. "Girl Incorporated: Corporate Empowerment Programmes for Women Workers; What Drives Them and Who Benefits?" PhD diss., University of Cambridge, 2022. https://doi.org/10.17863/CAM.95258.

Herbert, Amelia Simone. "Shareholder Schools: Racial Capitalism, Policy Borrowing, and Marketized Education Reform in Cape Town, South Africa." *Comparative Education Review* 67, no 51 (February 2023): S1, S66–S88. https://doi.org/10.1086/722271.

Hites, Sándor. "Between Social Duty and the Greed of Giving: On Philanthrocapitalism and Gift-Patriotism." *Comparative Literature Studies* 56, no. 3 (2019): 469–86. https://doi.org/10.5325/complitstudies .56.3.0469.

Hong, Zicong, Wuhui Chen, Huawei Huang, Song Guo, and Zibin Zheng. "Multi-Hop Cooperative Computation Offloading for Industrial IoT-Edge-Cloud Computing Environments." *IEEE Transactions on Parallel and Distributed Systems* 30, no. 12 (2019): 2759–74.

Hook, Tyler. "Educational Reform in Times of Crisis: The Dual Missions of Corporatized Education in Liberia." In *The Education Alibi: Tracing Education's Entanglements across Contemporary Africa*, edited by Elizabeth Cooper, Erdmute Alber, and Wandia Njoya. Ann Arbor: University of Michigan Press, 2025.

Hook, Tyler. "Schooling as Plantation: Racial Capitalism and Plantation Legacies in Corporatized Education Reform in Liberia." *Comparative Education Review* 67, no. S1 (2023): S89–S109.

Hunt, Nancy Rose. *A Colonial Lexicon of Birth Ritual, Medicalization, and Mobility in the Congo*. Durham, NC: Duke University Press, 1999.

Hunter, Mark. *Race for Education: Gender, White Tone, and Schooling in South Africa*. Cambridge: Cambridge University Press, 2019.

Iheka, Cajetan. *Naturalizing Africa: Ecological Violence, Agency, and Postcolonial Resistance in African Literature*. Cambridge: Cambridge University Press, 2018.

International Agency for Research on Cancer. *IARC Monographs on the Evaluation of Carcinogenic Risks to Humans*. Vol. 112, *Some Organophosphate Insecticides and Herbicides*. Geneva: World Health Organization, 2017.

Jackson, Jean E. "'I Am a Fieldnote': Fieldnotes as a Symbol of Professional Identity." In *Fieldnotes: The Makings of Anthropology*, edited by Roger Sanjek, 3–33. Ithaca, NY: Cornell University Press, 1990.

Jedy-Agba, Elima, Walburga Yvonne Joko, Biying Liu, Nathan Gyabi Buziba, Margaret Borok, Anne Korir, Leo Masamba, et al. "Trends in Cervical Cancer Incidence in Sub-Saharan Africa." *British Journal of Cancer* 123, no. 1 (July 2020): 148–54.

Jemiluyi, Olufunmilayo Olayemi, and Leward Jake. "Tax Revenue Mobilization Effort in Southern African Development Community (SADC) Bloc: Does ICT Matter?" *Cogent Economics and Finance* 11, no. 1 (2023). https://doi.org /10.1080/23322039.2023.2172810.

Jesus, Fernando Soares de, and José Messias Bastos. "Insertion of Amazon Inc. in Brazil: Logistical Operations, Disputes, and Territorial Strategies." *GEOUSP* (Universidade de São Paulo) 28 (2024): e210038.

Jochelson, Karen. *The Color of Disease: Syphilis and Racism in South Africa, 1880–1940*. Basingstoke, UK: Palgrave, 2001.

Johnson, D. Gale. "Globalization: What It Is and Who Benefits." *Journal of Asian Economics* 13, no. 4 (2002): 427–39.

Kantipudi, Veera V. S., A. Seetharaman, and K. Maddulety. "Study of Recurring Revenue Growth for IT Infrastructure Providers." Paper presented at 8th International Symposium on Multidisciplinary Studies and Innovative Technologies (ISMSIT), Ankara, Turkey, 2024. https://doi.org/10.1109/ISMSIT63511.2024.10757305.

Kaplan, Martha. "Fijan Water in Fiji and New York: Local Politics and a Global Commodity." *Cultural Anthropology : Journal of the Society for Cultural Anthropology* 22, no. 4 (2007): 685–706. https://search-ebscohost-com.ezproxy.library.wisc.edu/login.aspx?direct=true&db=anl&AN=606459&site=ehost-live&scope=site.

Kar, Sohini. 2018. *Financializing Poverty: Labor and Risk in Indian Microfinance*. Stanford, CA: Stanford University Press, 2018.

Kasiva, Frances. "Robbed of Choice: Forced and Coerced Sterilization Experiences of Women Living with HIV in Kenya." African Gender Media Initiative. Nairobi: University of Nairobi Department of Obstetrics and Gynaecology, 2012.

Kepe, Thembela, Rachel Wynberg, and William Ellis. "Land Reform and Biodiversity Conservation in South Africa: Complementary of in Conflict?" *International Journal of Biodiversity Science and Management* 1, no. 1 (March 2005): 3–16.

Khoisan, Zenzile Khoisan. "Navigating a Minefield to Assert Agency." *New Agenda: South African Journal of Social and Economic Policy* 2020, no. 78 (December 2020): 26–30.

Kimambo, Niwaeli E., Jessica L'Roe, Lisa Naughton-Treves, and Volker C. Radeloff. "The Role of Smallholder Woodlots in Global Restoration Pledges: Lessons from Tanzania. " *Forest Polity and Economics* 111 (June 2020). https://doi.org/10.1016/j.forpol.2020.102144.

Klees, Steven J. "New Philanthropy: A Critique." In *New Philanthropy and the Disruption of Global Education*, edited by Marina Avelar and Lara Patil, 45–47. Geneva: Network for International Policies and Cooperation in Education and Training, 2020.

Klein, Naomi. *The Shock Doctrine: The Rise of Disaster Capitalism*. London: Penguin Books, 2007.

Krasner, Stephen D. "Globalization and Sovereignty." In *States and Sovereignty in the Global Economy*, edited by David A. Smith, Dorothy J. Solinger, and Steven C. Topic, 34–52. London: Routledge, 1999.

Kumar, Ravi, ed. *Education, State, and Market: Anatomy of Neoliberal Impact*. Deli: Akar Books, 2014.

Kwayu, Aikande C. "Taxing the Rich: Interfaith Activism in Tanzania's Mining Sector." In *Religious Activism in the Global Economy: Promoting, Reforming, or Resisting Neoliberal Globalization?*, edited by Sabine Dreher and Peter J. Smith, 209–27. Lanham, MD: Rowman and Littlefield, 2016.

Ladson-Billings, Gloria. "Through a Glass Darkly: The Persistence of Race in Education Research and Scholarship." *Educational Researcher* 41, no. 4 (May 2012): 115–20. http://www.jstor.org/stable/41477775.

Lamb, Brooks. *Love for the Land: Lessons from Farmers Who Persist in Place*. New Haven, CT: Yale University Press.

Landeros Natalia, Soledad Duk, Carolina Márquez, Bábara Inzunza, Ian S. Acuña-Rodríguez, and Liliana A. Zúñiga-Venegas. "Genotoxicity and Reproductive Risk in Workers Exposed to Pesticides in Rural Areas of Curicó, Chile: A Pilot Study." *International Journal of Environment Research on Public Health* 19, no. 24 (December 2022): 16608.

Lang, Julianne, Stefano Ponte, and Thando Vilakazi. "Linking Power and Inequality in Global Value Chains." *Global Networks* 23, no. 4 (2023): 755–71. https://doi.org/10.1111/glob.12411.

Lansing, Stephen. *Priests and Programmers*. Princeton, NJ: Princeton University Press, 2009.

Latour, Bruno. 2000. "When Things Strike Back: A Possible Contribution of 'Science Studies' to the Social Sciences." *British Journal of Sociology* 51, no. 1 (2000): 107–23. https://doi.org/10.1080/000713100358453.

Lee, Joonkoo, Gary Gereffi, and Janet Beauvais. "Global Value Chains and Agrifood Standards: Challenges and Possibilities for Smallholders in Developing Countries." *Proceedings of the National Academy of Sciences* 109, no. 31 (2010): 12326–31. https://doi.org/10.1073/pnas.0913714108.

Lehman, Jennifer, and James Russell. "Charitable Bequest Importance Among Donors to Different Types of Charities." *International Journal of Nonprofit and Voluntary Sector Marketing* 25, no. 2 (May 2020): 1–8. https://doi.org/10.1002/nvsm.1657.

Lenzer, Jeanne. "Secret Report Surfaces Showing That Pfizer Was at Fault in Nigerian Drug Tests." *British Medical Journal* 27, no. 332 (7552) (May 2006): 1233. https://doi:10.1136/bmj.332.7552.1233-a.

Levine, Susan. *Medicine and the Politics of Knowledge*. Pretoria: HSRC (Human Sciences Research Council) Press, 2013.

Li, Tania Murray. "Indigeneity, Capitalism, and the Management of Dispossession." *Current Anthropology* 51, no. 3 (2010): 385–414. https://doi.org/10.1086/651942.

Li, Tania Murray, and Pujo Semedi. *Plantation Life: Corporate Occupation in Indonesia's Oil Palm Zone*. Durham, NC: Duke University Press, 2021.

Livingston, Julie. *Self-Devouring Growth: A Planetary Parable As Told from Southern Africa*. Durham, NC: Duke University Press, 2019.

Lofchie, Michael F. *The Political Economy of Tanzania: Decline and Recovery*. Philadelphia: University of Pennsylvania Press, 2014.

London, Leslie. "Human Rights, Environmental Justice, and the Health of Farm Workers in South Africa." *International Journal of Occupational and Environmental Health* 9, no. 1 (November 2013): 59–68.

Louwyck, A., A. Vandenbohede, G. Heuvelmans, M. Van Camp, and K. Walraevens. "The Water Budget Myth and Its Recharge Controversy: Linear vs. Nonlinear Models." *Groundwater* 61 (2023): 100–110. https://doi.org.ezproxy.library.wisc.edu/10.1111/gwat.13245.

Low, Setha. *Why Public Space Matters*. New York: Oxford University Press, 2023.

Lowes, Sara, and Eduardo Montero. "The Legacy of Colonial Medicine in Central Africa." *American Economic Review* 111, no. 4 (April 2021): 1284–1314. https://www.jstor.org/stable/27027713.

Luhrmann, Tanya M. "Anthropology as Spiritual Discipline." *American Ethnologist* 51, no. 1 (February 2024): 24–27.

Lyatuu, Danieli J. *Watch Your Steps! Proverbs from Kilimanjaro*. Neuendettelsau, Germany: Erlanger Verlag, 2008.

Lyimo, Emanuel P., Susan F. Rumisha, Irene R. Mremi, Chacha D. Mangu, Coleman Kishamawe, Mercy G. Chiduo, Lucas E. Matemba, Veneranda M. Bwana, Isolide S. Massawe, and Leonard E. G. Mboera. "Cancer Mortality Patterns in Tanzania: A Retrospective Hospital-Based Study, 2006–2015." *JCO Global Oncology* 6 (November 2020): 224–32. https://doi.org/10.1200/jgo.19.00270.

Madhi, Shabir A. "COVID-19 Vaccine Trial in South Africa: Everything You Need to Know." *The Conversation*, July 8, 2020. https://theconversation.com/covid-19-vaccine-trial-in-south-africa-everything-you-need-to-know-142305.

Mahase, Elisabeth. "Covid-19: Oxford Team Begins Vaccine Trials in Brazil and South Africa to Determine Efficacy." *British Medical Journal* 369 (2020): 1–2. https://www.jstor.org/stable/27238013.

Makey, Leane, Meg Parsons, Karen Fisher, Alyssce Te Huna, Mina Henare, Vicky Miru, Millan Ruka, and Mikaera Miru. "(Un) Heard Voices of Ecosystem Degradation: Stories from the Nexus of Settler-Colonialism and Slow Violence." *Sustainability* 14, no. 22 (2022): 14672.

Makoni, Munyaradzi. "Covid-19 Vaccine Trials in Africa." *The Lancet Respiratory Medicine* 8 (November 2020): e79–e80. https://doi.org/10.1016/S2213-2600(20)30401-X.

Malloy, Patrick. "Research Material and Necromancy: Imagining the Political-Economy of Biomedicine in Colonial Tanganyika." *International Journal of*

African Historical Studies 47, no. 3 (2014): 425–43. http://www.jstor.org /stable/24393437.

Manji, Ambreena. "Land Reform in the Shadow of the State: The Implementation of New Land Laws in Sub-Saharan Africa." *Third World Quarterly* 22, no. 3 (2001): 327–42.

Maquire, Mark, and Setha M. Low. *Trapped: Life Under Security Capitalism.* Redwood City, CA: Stanford University Press, 2024.

Mascia-Lees, Francis E. *Gender and Difference in a Globalizing World: Twenty-First-Century Anthropology.* Long Grove, IL: Waveland Press, 2010.

Marable, Manning. "Globalization and Racialization." *ZNet Classics* (blog), August 13, 2004. https://znetwork.org/znetarticle/globalization-and-racialization-by-manning-marable/.

Marber, Peter. "Globalization and Its Contents." *World Policy Journal* 21, no. 4 (April 2005): 29–37. https://doi.org/10.1215/07402775-2005-1010.

Marcoux, Shannon. "Coca-Cola's Cape Town Crisis: Examining Companies' Water Rights Obligations in a Changing Climate." *Business and Human Rights Journal* 7, no. 2 (June 2022): 298–302. https://doi.org/10.1017/bhj .2021.64.

Marx, Karl. *Capital.* Volume 1. 1867. Marxists Internet Archive. Accessed November 13, 2024. https://www.marxists.org/archive/marx/works/download /pdf/Capital-Volume-I.pdf.

Masquelier, Adeline. "Water Spirits in Water-Less Places: The Case of Madame Sabot." In *Sacred Waters,* edited by Henry John Drewal, 75–85. Bloomington: Indiana University Press, 2008.

Massuel, Sylvain, and Jeanne Riaux. "Groundwater Overexploitation: Why is the Red Flag Waved? Case Study on the Kairouan Plain Aquifer." *Hydrogeology Journal* 25, no. 6 (September 2017): 1607–20. https://doi.10.1007 /s10040-017-1568-2.

Maxted, N., L. Guarino, L. Myer, and E. A. Chiwona. "Towards a Methodology for On-Farm Conservation of Plant Genetic Resources." *Genetic Resources and Crop Evolution* 49, no. 1 (2002): 31–46. https://doi.org/10.1023/a: 1013896401710.

Mayer, Zach. "The Aftermath of the Seed Wars: How Farmers' Inability to Control the Seed They Harvest Has Created a Dangerous Consolidation of the Seed Industry." *University of Missouri Kansas City Law Review* 91 (2022): 681–700.

Mbembe, Achille. "At the Edge of the World: Boundaries, Territoriality, and Sovereignty in Africa." *Public Culture* 12, no. 1 (Winter 2000): 259–84. https://doi.org/10.1215/08992363-12-1-259.

McGoey, Linsey. *No Such Thing as a Free Gift: The Gates Foundation and the Price of Philanthropy.* New York: Verso, 2015.

McNamee, Stephen J., and Robert K. Miller Jr. *The Meritocracy Myth.* Lanham, MD: Rowman and Littlefield, 2004.

Mechanic, David. "Apartheid Medicine." *Society* 10, no. 3 (1973): 36–44.

Meena, Bartholomew. *Mount Kilimanjaro: Our Pride.* Dar es Salaam: E&D Vision, 2015.

Mellet, Patric Tariq. *The Lie of 1652: A Decolonised History of Land.* Cape Town: Tafelberg, 2020.

Merry, Sally Engle. "Measuring the World: Indicators, Human Rights, and Global Governance." *Current Anthropology* 52, no. S3 (2011): S83–S95. https://doi.org/10.1086/657241.

Mill, John Stuart. *On Liberty.* 1859. Reprint, Kitchener, Ontario: Batoche Books, 2001.

Mintz, Sidney W. *Worker in the Cane: A Puerto Rican Life History.* New York: W. W. Norton, 1974.

Mintz, Sidney W. *Sweetness and Power: The Place of Sugar in Modern History.* New York: Viking, 1985.

Mnif, Wissem, Aziza Ibn Hadj Hassine, Aicha Bouaziz, Aghleb Bartegi, Olivier Thomas, and Benoit Roig. "Effect of Endocrine Disruptor Pesticides: A Review." *International Journal of Environmental Research and Public Health* 8, no. 6 (2011): 2265–2303. https://doi.org/10.3390/ijerph8062265.

Modisane, Litheko. "Reflections on Fire as Postcolonial Metaphor of Rupture." *Social Dynamics* 2–4 (2024). https://doi.org/10.1080/02533952.2024.2320548.

Mokoena, Amanda. "Questioning Day Zero: Rights, Provision, and Water Inequality in South Africa." *Human Organization* 82, no. 3 (Fall 2023): 223–34.

Moll, Tessa. "Medical Mistrust and Enduring Racism in South Africa." *Journal of Bioethical Inquiry* 18, no 1 (January 2021): 117–20. https://doi.org/10.1007/s11673-020-10072-1.

Moore, Ilona. "The Work of 'Feeding the World': From India's Green Revolution to the Paradox of Plenty." Doctoral dissertation, University of Minnesota, 2014.

Morgan, Stephen, Jarrad Farris, and Michael E. Johnson. "Foreign Direct Investment in Africa: Recent Trends Leading Up to the African Continental Free Trade Area." *USDA Economic Research Service Bulletin*, no. 242 (October 2022): 1–34.

Morris, Christopher. *Biotraffic: Medicines and Environmental Governance in the Afterlives of Apartheid.* Oakland: University of California Press, 2024.

Morris, Christopher. "Royal Pharmaceuticals: Bioprospecting, Rights, and Traditional Authority in South Africa." *American Ethnologist* 43, no. 3 (2016): 525–39.

Mosse, David. *Cultivating Development: An Ethnography of Aid Policy and Practice.* London: Pluto Press, 2008.

Mtei, Edwin. *From Goatherd to Governor: The Autobiography of Edwin Mtei.* Dar es Salaam: Mkuki na Nyota, 2009.

Muehlebach, Andrea. *A Vital Frontier: Water Insurgencies in Europe.* Durham, NC: Duke University Press, 2023.

Musacchio, Laura R. "Key Concepts and Research Priorities for Landscape Sustainability." *Landscape Ecology* 28, no. 6 (2013): 995–98. https://doi.org/10.1007/s10980-013-9909-6.

Narotzky, Susana. "Where Have All the Peasants Gone?" *Annual Review of Anthropology* 45, no. 1 (2016): 301–18. https://doi.org/10.1146/annurev-anthro-102215-100240.

Nash, June C. "Consuming Interests: Water, Rum, and Coca-Cola from Ritual Propitiation to Corporate Expropriation in Highland Chiapas." *Cultural Anthropology* 22, no. 4 (2007): 621–39.

Nash, June C. *We Eat the Mines and the Mines Eat Us: Dependency and Exploitation in Bolivian Tin Mines.* New York: Columbia University Press, 1979.

Ndong Ntoutoume, Achille Gildas. "Challenges of CSR in Sub-Saharan Africa: Clarifying the Gaps Between the Regulations and Human Rights Issues." *International Journal of Corporate Social Responsibility* 8, no. 2 (2023). https://doi.org/10.1186/s40991-023-00079-3.

Nicholls, Matthew. "Euergetism." In *Encyclopedia of Political Theory*, edited by Mark Bevir, 458–61. Thousand Oaks, CA: Sage, 2005.

Niesen, Peter. "Speech Acts." In *The Habermas Handbook*, edited by Hauke Brunkhorst, Regina Kreide, and Christina LaFont, 56–58. New York: Columbia University Press, 2018.

Nielsen, Kristian S., Kimberly A. Nicholas, Felix Creutzig, Thomas Dietz, and Paul C. Stern. "The Role of High-Socioeconomic-Status People in Locking In or Rapidly Reducing Energy-Driven Greenhouse Gas Emissions." *Nature Energy* 6 (September 2021): 1011–16. https://doi.org/10.1038/s41560-021-00900-y.

Nilsson, Eva. "The Instrumentalization of CSR by Rent-Seeking Governments: Lessons from Tanzania." *Business and Society* 62, no. 6 (2023), 1173–1200. https://doi.org/10.1177/00076503221123744.

Njeru Ian, Yusuf Ajack, Charles Muitherero, Dickens Onyango, Johnny Musyoka, et al. "Did the Call for Boycott by the Catholic Bishops Affect the Polio Vaccination Coverage in Kenya in 2015? A Cross-Sectional Study." *Pan African Medical Journal* 24 (June 2016): 120. https://doi.org/10.11604/pamj.

Ntaka, Noxolo. "Double Consciousness: A Comparative Approach to Interpreting the Experiences of Black Female Pupils in a Predominantly Black,

Well-Resourced, and Historically White School in South Africa." MA thesis, University of the Witwatersrand, Johannesburg, 2019.

Ntloedibe, France Nkokomane. "Where Are Our Heroes and Ancestors? The Spectre of Steve Biko's Ideas in *Rhodes Must Fall* and the Transformation of South African Universities." *African Identities* 17, no. 1 (2019): 64–79. https://doi.org/10.1080/14725843.2019.1654851.

Nyamnjoh, Francis B. "Globalization, Boundaries, and Livelihoods: Perspectives on Africa." *Philosophia Africana* 6, no. 2 (August 2003): 1–18.

Ohnuki-Tierney, Emiko. *Flowers That Kill: Communicative Opacity in Political Spaces*. Redwood City, CA: Stanford University Press, 2015.

Okeyo, Maxwell. "Customer-Centric Data Strategies to Drive Revenue Growth." Master's thesis, Aga Khan University, East Africa, 2024.

Orlove, Ben, and Steven C. Caton. "Water Sustainability: Anthropological Approaches and Prospects." *Annual Review of Anthropology* 39, no. 1 (2010): 401–15. https://doi.org/10.1146/annurev.anthro.012809.105045.

Orock, Rogers Tabe Egbe. "Less-Told Stories About Corporate Globalization: Transnational Corporations and CSR as the Politics of (Ir)responsibility in Africa. *Dialectical Anthropology* 37 (2013): 27–50. https://doi.org/10.1007/s10624-013-9293-2.

Ortner, Sherry B. "Dark Anthropology and Its Others." *HAU: Journal of Ethnographic Theory* 6, no. 1 (June 2016): 47–73. https://doi.org/10.14318/hau6.1.004.

Osuafor, Godswill N. "Alcohol and Drug Use as Factors for High-School Learners' Absenteeism in the Western Cape." *South African Journal of Psychiatry* 27 (December 2021): a1679. https://doi.org/10.4102/sajpsychiatry.v27i0.1679.

Owusu, Alex Barimah, Paul W. K. Yankson, and Stephen Frimpong. "Smallholder Farmers' Knowledge of Mobile Telephone Use: Gender Perspectives and Implications for Agricultural Market Development." *Progress in Development Studies* 18, no. 1 (2017): 36–51.

Pallangyo, P., Z. S. Mkojera, N. R. Hemed, et al. "Obesity Epidemic in Urban Tanzania: A Public Health Calamity in an Already Overwhelmed and Fragmented Health System." *BMC Endocrine Disorders* 20, no. 147 (2020). https://doi.org/10.1186/s12902-020-00631-3.

Panetta, Claire. "'Digging in the Water'? Grassroots Urbanism, the Egyptian State, and the Politics of Heritage-Making in Post-Revolution Cairo." *International Journal of Heritage Studies* 26, no. 12 (2020): 1221–39. https://doi.org/10.1080/13527258.2020.1747102.

Paredes Nachón, Francisco Javier, Cristina López-Duarte, and Marta M. Vidal-Suárez. "The Impact of Official Development Aid Flows on Business Internationalisation." *Business Strategy and Development* 7, no. 2 (2024): e388.

Pedroso, Thays Millena Alves, Marcelino Benvindo-Souza, Felipe de Araújo Nascimento, Júlia Woch, Fabiana Gonçalves dos Reis, and Daniela de Melo e Silva. "Cancer and Occupational Exposure to Pesticides: A Bibliometric Study of the Past 10 Years." *Environmental Science and Pollution Research* 29, no. 12 (March 2022): 17464–75. https://doi.org/10.1007/s11356-021-17031-2.

Perramond, Eric. *Unsettled Waters: Rights, Law, and Identity in the American West*. Oakland: University of California Press, 2019.

Peters, Pauline. "Conflicts over Land and Threats to Customary Tenure in Africa." *African Affairs* 112, issue 449 (October 2013): 543–62.

Peterson, Kristin. *Speculative Markets: Drug Circuits and Derivative Life in Nigeria*. Durham, NC: Duke University Press, 2014.

Phillips, Kristin D. *An Ethnography of Hunger: Politics, Subsistence, and the Unpredictable Grace of the Sun*. Bloomington: Indiana University Press, 2018.

Piemonte, Vincenzo, and Fausto Gironi. 2010. "Land-Use Change Emissions: How Green Are the Bioplastics?" *Environmental Progress and Sustainable Energy* 30, no. 4 (2010): 685–91. https://doi.org/10.1002/ep.10518.

Pigou, Piers. "Land Reform in South Africa: Fact and Fiction." International Crisis Group, 2018.Płotka, Bartosz, and Kamila Rezmer. "The Human Rights Relativized: Project Prevention's Cases Of Paid Sterilization." *CBU International Conference Proceedings* 7 (2019): 591–94.

Polanyi, Karl. *Great Transformation: The Political and Economic Origins of Our Time*. Boston: Beacon Press, 2001.

Posen, I. Daniel, Paulina Jaramillo, Amy E. Landis, and W. Michael Griffin. "Greenhouse Gas Mitigation for U.S. Plastics Production: Energy First, Feedstocks Later." *Environmental Research Letters* 12, no. 3 (2017): 034024. https://doi.org/10.1088/1748-9326/aa60a7.

Powers, Theodore, and Jimmy Pieterse. "Vacillating Vaccines: Responses to Covid-19 in the United States and South Africa." *Anthropology Southern Africa* 47, no. 1 (August 2023): 6–19. https://doi.org/10.1080/23323256.2023.2226706.

Pradhan, Uma. *Simultaneous Identities: Language, Education, and the Nepali Nation*. New York: Cambridge University Press, 2020.

Pyysiäinnen, Jarkko, Darren Halpin, and Andrew Guilfoyle. "Neoliberal Governance and 'Responsibilisation' of Agents: Reassessing the Mechanisms of Responsibility-Shift in Neoliberal Discursive Environments." *Distinction: Journal of Social Theory* 18, no. 2 (October 2017): 215–35. https://doi.org/10.1080/1600910X.2017.1331858.

Rahman, K. Sabeel, and Kathleen Thelen. "The Rise of the Platform Business Model and the Transformation of Twenty-First-Century Capitalism." *Politics and Society* 47, no. 2 (June 2019): 177–204. https://doi.org/10.1177/0032329219838932.

Raimundo, Ines. "Food Insecurity in the Context of Climate Change in Maputo City, Mozambique." In *Climate Change and Food Security: Africa and the Caribbean*, edited by Elizabeth Thomas-Hope, 172–80. New York: Routledge, 2017.

Rajan, Kaushik Sunder. *Pharmocracy: Value, Politics, and Knowledge in Global Biomedicine*. Durham, NC: Duke University Press, 2017.

Ramones, Ikaika and Engle Merry Sally. "Capitalist Transformation and Settler Colonialism: Theorizing the Interface." *American Anthropologist* 123, no. 4 (December 2021): 741–52. https://doi.org/10.1111/aman.13655.

Rambabu, M., S. Gupta, and R. S. Singh. "Data Mining in Cloud Computing: Survey." In *Innovations in Computational Intelligence and Computer Vision*, edited by M. K. Sharma, V. S. Dhaka, T. Perumal, N. Dey, and J. M. R. S. Tavares. Advances in Intelligent Systems and Computing 1189. Singapore: Springer, 2021. https://doi.org/10.1007/978-981-15-6067-5_7.

Ramutsindela, Maano. *Transfrontier Conservation in Africa: At the Confluence of Capital, Politics, and Nature*. Cambridge: CABI (Commonwealth Agricultural Bureau International), 2007.

Republic of South Africa, Department of Water and Sanitation. National Assembly: Minister of Water and Sanitation Written Reply to Question 19. 2022.

Reyes-García, Victoria. "Traditional Crop Management." In *The International Encyclopedia of Anthropology*, edited by Hilary Callan. New York: John Wiley, 2020.

Ricciardi, Vincent, Navin Ramankutty, Zia Mehrabi, Larissa Jarvis, and Brenton Chookolingo. "How Much of the World's Food Do Smallholders Produce?" *Global Food Security* 17 (June 2018): 64–72. https://doi.org/10.1016/j.gfs.2018.05.002.

Riebeck, Jan van. *Journal, 1619–1677*. Cape Town: A. A. Balkema, 1952. https://archive.org/details/riebeecksjourna00archgoog/page/n116/mode/2up.

Ritchie, Hannah. "Food Production Is Responsible for One-Quarter of the World's Greenhouse Gas Emissions." OurWorldInData, 2019. https://ourworldindata.org/food-ghg-emissions.

Ritchie, Hannah, Pablo Rosado and Max Rose. "Environmental Impacts of Food Production." Our World in Data, 2022. Accessed March 3, 2025. https://ourworldindata.org/environmental-impacts-of-food.

Robbins, Joel. "Beyond the Suffering Subject: Toward an Anthropology of the Good." *Journal of the Royal Anthropological Institute* 19, no. 3 (2013): 447–62. http://www.jstor.org/stable/42001631.

Robbins, Ocean. "Monocropping: A Disastrous Agricultural System." *Food Revolution Network*, March 18, 2022. https://foodrevolution.org/blog/monocropping-monoculture/.

Roberts, Susan M. "Development Capital: USAID and the Rise of Development Contractors." *Annals of the Association of American Geographers* 104, no. 5 (2014): 1030–51.

Robins, Steven and Laurin Baumgardt. "Opening the Black Box of Urban Development: Cultural Heritage Activism at the Amazon Megaproject in Cape Town." *Theoria* 71, no. 179 (March 2024): 24–47. https://doi.org/10. 3167/th.2024.7117802.

Robinson, Cedric J. 2000. *Black Marxism: The Making of the Black Radical Tradition.* Chapel Hill: University of North Carolina Press, 2000.

Roh, Taehyun, Anisha Aggarwal, Nishat Tasnim Hasan, Alka Upadhyay, and Nusrat Fahmida Trisha. "Pesticides and Cancer." In *Environmental Oncology,* edited by E. H. Bernicker, 177–211. Cham, Switzerland: Springer, 2023.

Roll, Kate, Catherine Dolan, and Dinah Rajak. "Remote (Dis)engagement: Shifting Corporate Risk to the 'Bottom of the Pyramid.'" *Development and Change* 52, no. 4 (2021): 878–901.

Rossi, Martin A. "The Impact of Individual Wealth on Posterior Political Power." *Journal of Economic Behavior and Organization* 106 (October 2014): 469–80. https://doi.org/10.1016/j.jebo.2014.08.006.

Rotberg, Robert I. *The Founder: Cecil Rhodes and the Pursuit of Power.* New York: Oxford University Press, 1988.

Rother, Hanna-Andrea. "Pesticide Labels: Protecting Liability or Health?—Unpacking 'Misuse' of Pesticides." *Current Opinion in Environmental Science and Health* 4 (August 2018): 10–15. https://doi.org/10.1016/j.coesh. 2018.02.004.

Rother, Hanna-Andrea. "Pesticide Suicides: What More Evidence Is Needed to Ban Highly Hazardous Pesticides?" *Lancet Global Health* 9, no. 3 (2021): e225–e226. https://doi.org/10.1016/s2214-109x(21)00019-x.

Rothman, Barbara Katz. *The Biomedical Empire: Lessons Learned from the COVID-19 Pandemic.* Redwood City, CA: Stanford University Press, 2021.

Rudnyckyj, Daromir. "Reconsidering Reciprocity and Capitalism." *Ethnography* 24, no. 3 (June 2023): 450–53.

Sachs, Jeffrey D. *Common Wealth: Economics for a Crowded Planet.* New York: Penguin Press, 2008.

Sahlins, Marshall. "Cosmologies of Capitalism: The Trans-Pacific Sector of 'the World System.'" *Proceedings of the British Academy* 74 (March 1988): 1–51.

Saltman, Kenneth J. *The Gift of Education: Public Education and Venture Philanthropy.* New York: Palgrave, 2010.

Sampat, Bhaven N. "The Impact of Publicly Funded Biomedical and Health Research: A Review." In *Measuring the Impacts of Federal Investments in Research: A Workshop Summary,* edited by Stephen Merrill and Steve Olson, 153–92. Washington, DC: National Academies Press, 2011.

Sanders, Bernie. *It's OK to Be Angry About Capitalism.* New York: Crown, 2023.

Sandel, Michael J. *Tyranny of Merit: What's Become of the Common Good?* New York: Farrar, Straus and Giroux, 2020.

Sargent, Adam. "Working against Labor: Struggles for Self in the Indian Construction Industry." *Anthropology of Work Review* 41, no. 2 (2020): 76–85.

Sawyer, Suzana. "Corporations." In *The Wiley Blackwell International Encyclopedia of Anthropology,* edited by Hilary Callan, 2. Malden, MA: John Wiley, 2018.

Scheper-Hughes, Nancy. "The Primacy of the Ethical: Propositions for a Militant Anthropology." *Current Anthropology* 36, no. 3 (1995): 409–40.

Schoemaaker, Lyn. "History of Medicine in Sub-Saharan Africa." In *The Oxford Handbook of the History of Medicine,* edited by Mark Jackson, 266–84. Oxford: Oxford University Press, 2012.

Sekalala, Sharifah, Lisa Forman, Timothy Hodgson, Moses Mulumba, Hadijah Namyalo-Ganafa, and Benjamin Mason Meier. "Decolonising Human Rights: How Intellectual Property Laws Result in Unequal Access to the COVID-19 Vaccine." *British Medical Journal Global Health* 6, no. 7 (July 2021): e006169. https://doi.org/10.1136/bmjgh-2021-006169.

Shange, Nombulelo Tholithemba. "Identity and Environmental Harmony as Practised by Table Mountain Doctors: A Struggle over Land and African Healing Systems." Doctoral dissertation, University of the Free State, Bloemfontein, South Africa, 2023.

Sharma, Priya, Nisha Bilkhiwal, Pragya Chaturvedi, Sachin Kumar, and Preeti Khetarpal. "Potential Environmental Toxicant Exposure, Metabolizing Gene Variants, and Risk of PCOS: A Systematic Review." *Reproductive Toxicology* 103 (August 2021): 124–32. https://doi.org/10.1016/j.reprotox.2021.06.005

Sharp, Lesley A., and Nancy N. Chen. "Introduction: Bioinsecurity and Human Vulnerability." In *Bioinsecurity and Vulnerability,* edited by Nancy N. Chen and Lesley A. Sharp, xi–xxxiv. Santa Fe: School for Advanced Research Press, 2014.

Shipton, Parker. *Mortgaging the Ancestors: Ideologies of Attachment in Africa.* New Haven, CT: Yale University Press, 2009.

Shiva, Vandana. *The Stolen Harvest: The Hijacking of the Global Food Supply.* Lexington: University of Kentucky Press, 2016.

Shivji, Issa G. "The Roots of the Agrarian Crisis in Tanzania: A Theoretical Perspective." *Eastern Africa Social Science Research Review* 3, no. 4 (January 1987).

Simatele, Mulala D., Eromose E. Ebhuoma, Henry B. Tantoh, and Felix K. Donkor. "Asset Vulnerability Analytical Framework and Systems Thinking as a Twin Methodology for Highlighting Factors That Undermine Efficient Food Production." *Jambá: Journal of Disaster Risk Studies* 11, no. 1 (January 2019): 1–12. https://doi.org/10.4102/jamba.v11i1.597.

Simsa'a, Layla El Awad. "Structural Adjustment Policies and Women in the Rural Areas in Africa: A Review of Some Major Issues." *Africa Development* 23, nos. 3–4 (1998): 135–47.

Slater, Elizabeth. "Poverty via Monopolization: The Impact That Intellectual Property Rights and Federal Subsidies Have on Farm Poverty." *Journal of Intellectual Property Law* 29, no. 1 (Fall 2021): 209–32.

Smith, Daniel Jordan. 2022. *Every Household Its Own Government: Improvised Infrastructure, Entrepreneurial Citizens, and the State in Nigeria.* Princeton, NJ: Princeton University Press, 2022.

Smith, James H. *The Eyes of the World: Mining the Digital Age in the Eastern DR Congo.* Chicago: University Of Chicago Press, 2021.

South African Government. "Blue Drop National Report," Department of Water and Sanitation, 2023. https://ws.dws.gov.za/IRIS/releases/BDN_2023_Report.pdf. Accessed March 3, 2025.

South African Government. "Living Heritage." Department of Sport, Arts and Culture. Accessed August 27, 2023. http://www.dac.gov.za/content/living-heritage. Page discontinued.

South African Government. "President Cyril Ramaphosa: Official Launch of Nant-SA Vaccine Manufacturing Campus." January 19, 2022. https://www.gov.za/speeches/president-cyril-ramaphosa-official-launch-nant-sa-vaccine-manufacturing-campus-19-jan-0.

South African Government. "South African Government Social Listening Report," November 5, 12, 2021. https://sacoronavirus.co.za/2021/11/11/south-africa-covid-19-and-vaccine-social-listening-report-12-november-2021-report-26/ https://sacoronavirus.co.za/category/academic-articles/page/2/ (As of February 19, 2024, the site is no longer updated; copies of the reports in the author's possession).

South African Government. "Vote 16: Basic Education," *2021 Estimates of National Expenditure,* 251–68. https://www.treasury.gov.za/documents/national%20budget/2021/ene/Vote%2016%20Basic%20Education.pdf.

South African Government. "About Basic Education." Department of Basic Education: Republic of South Africa, 2021. Accessed April 24, 2024. https://www.education.gov.za/AboutUs/AboutDBE.aspx.

South African High Court. "The Second Heritage Impact Assessment," as quoted in the Founding Affidavit by Leslie London to the High Court of South Africa (Western Cape Division, Cape Town), August 1, 2021.

Stackpole, Thomas. "Content Moderation Is Terrible by Design." *Harvard Business Review,* November 9, 2022.

Stambach, Amy Elizabeth. *Lessons from Mount Kilimanjaro.* New York: Routledge, 2000.

Stambach, Amy Elizabeth, and Joseph Pesambili. "'Why Are They Already Digging Our Graves?': Understanding the Emotional Responses to Covid-19

Vaccine Hesitancy in Tanzania and South Africa." *Anthropological Quarterly,* 98, no. 1 (January 2025): 285–313.

Stambach, Amy Elizabeth, and Aikande Clement Kwayu. "Witness to a Passing." *Hau: The Journal of Ethnographic Theory* 11, no. 2 (Autumn 2021): 412–27. https://doi.org/10.1086/716216.

Stein, Felix, Katerini Tagmatarchi Storeng, and Antoine de Bengy Puyvallée. "Global Health Nonsense." *British Medical Journal* 372, no. 12 (December 2022): o2932. https://doi.org/10.1136/bmj.o2932.

Stiglitz, Joseph E. *Globalization and Its Discontents.* New York: W. W. Norton, 2002.

Stone, Glenn Davis. "Agricultural Intensification." In *The International Encyclopedia of Anthropology,* edited by Hilary Callan. New York: John Wiley, 2018.

Storeng, Katerini T. "The GAVI Alliance and the 'Gates Approach' to Health System Strengthening." *Global Public Health* 9, no. 8 (August 2014): 865–879. https://doi.org/10.1080/17441692.2014.940362.

Strang, Veronica. "The Taniwha and the Crown: Defending Water Rights in Aotearoa / New Zealand." *Wiley Interdisciplinary Reviews: Water* 1, no. 1 (December 2013): 121–31. https://doi.org/10.1002/wat2.1002.

Strang, Veronica. *Water: Nature and Culture.* London: Reaktion Books, 2015.

Strang, Veronica. "Water Rights." In *The International Encyclopedia of Anthropology,* edited by Hilary Callan, 3–7. New York: John Wiley, 2018.

Strong, Krystal, and Christiana Kallon Kelly. "Youth Leadership for Development: Contradictions of Africa's Growing Leadership Pipeline." *Journal of Modern African Studies* 60, no. 2 (June 2022): 217–38. https://doi.org/10.1017/S0022278X22000064.

Strong, Krystal, Rehana Odendaal, and Christiana Kallon Kelly. "Education for Subordination: Youth and the Afterlives of Coloniality and Racialization in Africa." In *World Yearbook of Education 2023: Racialization and Educational Inequality in Global Perspective,* edited by Janelle Scott and Monisha Bajaj, 103–18. New York: Routledge, 2023.

Sullivan, LaShandra. *Unsettling Agribusiness: Indigenous Protests and Land Conflict in Brazil.* Lincoln: University of Nebraska Press, 2023.

Suris, Jeffrey S. *Networking Futures: The Movements Against Corporate Globalization.* Durham, NC: Duke University Press, 2008.

Sy, Aida, and Tony Tinker. "From Exxon *Valdez* to Oriental Nicety: African Environmental Issues, Accounting, and Corporate Responsibilities." *African Journal of Economic and Sustainable Development* 2, no. 3 (2013): 189–203. https://doi.org/10.1504/ajesd.2013.056990.

Tarusarira, Joram. "Climate Security and Religion in Africa: Towards Sustainable Development Goals." In *The Palgrave Handbook of Religion, Peace-*

building, and Development in Africa, edited by S. M. Kilonzo, E. Chitando, and J. Tarusarira, J., 125–42. New York: Palgrave Macmillan, 2023.

Tax, Sol. "Action Anthropology." *Current Anthropology* 16, no. 4 (December 1975): 514–17.

Teaiwa, Martina. *Consuming Ocean Island: Stories of People and Phosphate from Banaba.* Bloomington: Indiana University Press, 2015.

Terranova, Tiziana. "Free Labor: Producing Culture for the Digital Economy." *Social Text* 18, no. 2 (Summer 2000): 33–58.

Tett, Gillian. *Fool's Gold: The Inside Story of J. P. Morgan and How Wall Street Greed Corrupted Its Bold Dream and Created a Financial Collapse.* New York: Free Press, 2010.

Tilley, Helen. "Medicine, Empires, and Ethics in Colonial Africa." *AMA Journal of Ethics* 18, no. 7 (July 2016): 743–753. https://doi.org/10.1001/journalofet hics.2016.18.7.mhst1-1607.

Tilley, Helen. *Africa as a Living Laboratory: Empire, Development, and the Problem of Scientific Knowledge, 1870–1950.* Chicago: University of Chicago Press, 2011.

Trouillot, Michel-Rolph. "Culture on the Edges: Creolization in the Plantation Context." In *Trouillot Remixed: The Michel-Rolph Trouillot Reader,* edited by Yarimar Bonilla, Greg Beckett, and Mayanthi L. Fernando, 194–214. Durham, NC: Duke University Press, 2021.

Tudi, Muyesaier, Huada Daniel Ruan, Li Wang, Jia Lyu, Ross Sadler, Des Connell, Cordia Chu, and Dung Tri Phung. "Agriculture Development, Pesticide Application, and Its Impact on the Environment." *International Journal of Environmental Research and Public Health* 18, no. 2 (2021). https://doi.org/10.3390/ijerph18031112.

United Republic of Tanzania. "The National Irrigation Act, 2013." Accessed March 3, 2025. https://www.nirc.go.tz/uploads/publications/sw1585297337 -ActNo-4-2013-Irrigation%20Act%20Tanzania.pdf.

United States Environmental Protection Agency. "Enhanced Aquifer Recharge Research." Updated January 9, 2024. https://www.epa.gov/water-research /enhanced-aquifer-recharge-research.

University of Cape Town. "A/Xarra Restorative Justice Forum." Faculty of Humanities. Updated 2024. https://humanities.uct.ac.za/african-studies /san-and-khoi-unit-axarra-restorative-justice-forum/axarra-restorative- justice-forum-members.

United Nations Educational, Scientific, and Cultural Organization (UNESCO). "Imminent Risk of a Global Water Crisis, Warns the UN World Water Development Report 2023." https://www.unesco.org/en/articles/imminent- risk-global-water-crisis-warns-un-world-water-development-report- 2023

United Nations Office for Disaster Risk Reduction. "South Africa: Flooding in KwaZulu-Natal and Eastern Cape 2022." PreventionWeb. Accessed June 10, 2024. https://www.preventionweb.net/collections/south-africa-flooding-kwazulu-natal-and-eastern-cape-2022.

United States Embassy in Tanzania. "Homepage." Accessed March 3, 2025. https://tz.usembassy.gov.

Van Koppen, Barbara, Barbara Schreiner, and Patience Mukuyu. "Redressing Legal Pluralism in South Africa's Water Law." *Journal of Legal Pluralism and Unofficial Law* 53, no. 3 (November 2021), 383–96. https://doi.org/10.1080/07329113.2021.2016266

Van Wendel de Joode, Berna, Joge Peñaloza-Castañeda, Ana Mora, Andrea Corrales-Vargas, Brenda Eskenazi, Jane A. Hoppin, and Christian H. Lindh. "Pesticide Exposure, Birth Size, and Gestational Age in the ISA Birth Dohort, Costa Rica." *Environmental Epidemiology* 8, no. 2 (April 2024): e290. https://doi.org/10.1097/EE9.0000000000000290

Vaughan, Megan. "A Research Enclave in 1940s Nigeria: The Rockefeller Foundation Yellow Fever Research Institute at Yaba, Lagos, 1943–49." *Bulletin of the History of Medicine* 92, no. 1 (Spring 2018): 172–205. https://www.jstor.org/stable/26495362.

Varoufakis, Yanis. *Technofeudalism: What Killed Capitalism*. Brooklyn, NY: Melville House, 2023.

Velásquez, Teresa A. "Producing Ethical Water: Anti-Mining Activism and Conflicts over Municipal Water Provisioning in Cuenca, Ecuador." *Journal of Latin American and Caribbean Anthropology* 27 (2022): 575–86.

Verbuyst, Rafael. *Khoisan Consciousness*. Leiden, Netherlands: Brill, 2022.

Verger, Antoni, Christopher Lubienski, and Gita Steiner-Khamsi, eds. *World Yearbook of Education 2016: The Global Education Industry*. New York: Routledge, 2016.

Walsh, Andrew. *Made in Madagascar: Sapphires, Ecotourism, and the Global Bazaar*. Toronto: University of Toronto Press, 2012.

Wamalwa, Kevin. "Embodied Memories: Rethinking Victimhood and Villainy in the Aftermath of the Sabaot Land Defense Forces' Violence in Mt. Elgon, Kenya." PhD diss., University of Wisconsin–Madison, 2024.

Warikandwa, Tapiwa V., and Patrick C. Osode. "Indigenisation Jurisprudence and the Renewed Fight Against 'Fronting' to Advance Broad-Based Black Economic Empowerment in South Africa: An Appraisal of the Broad-Based Black Economic Empowerment Amendment Act of 2013." In *Social and Legal Theory in the Age of Decoloniality: (Re-)Envisioning Pan-African Jurisprudence in the 21st Century*, edited by Tapiwa V. Warikandwa, Artwell Nhemachena, and Samuel K. Amoo, 367–98. Oxford: Langaa RPCIG, 2018. https://doi.org/10.2307/j.ctvh9vwf3.14.

Wark, McKenzie. *Capital Is Dead: Is This Something Worse?* New York: Verso, 2019.

Weindling, Paul. "The Dangers of White Supremacy: Nazi Sterilization and Its Mixed-Race Adolescent Victims." *American Journal of Public Health* 112, no. 2 (February 2022): 248–54. https://doi.org/10.2105/AJPH.2021.306593.

Welker, Marina. *Kretek Capitalism: Making, Marketing, and Consuming Clove Cigarettes in Indonesia.* Oakland: University of California Press, 2024.

Wendland, Claire L. "Research, Therapy, and Bioethical Hegemony: The Controversy over Perinatal AZT Trials in Africa." *African Studies Review* 51, no. 3 (December 2008): 1–23. https://doi.org/10.1353/arw.0.0084.

Williamson, Ben. "Big EdTech." *Learning, Media, and Technology* 47, no. 2 (2022): 157–62. https://doi.org/10.1080/17439884.2022.2063888.

Winter, S., and C. D. Morris. "Mistbelt Grassland Fragmentation in the Umvoti Conservancy, KwaZulu-Natal, South Africa." *South African Journal of Botany* 67, no. 2 (2001): 303–11. https://doi.org/10.1016/s0254-6299(15)31133-9.

Wedel, Janine R. *Shadow Elite: How the World's New Power Brokers Undermine Democracy, Government, and the Free Market.* New York: Basic Books, 2009.

Weeks, Sindiso Mnisi. "South African Legal Culture and Its Dis/Empowerment Paradox." In *The Oxford Handbook of Law and Anthropology*, edited by Maria-Claire Foblets, Mark Goodale, Maria Sapignoli, and Olaf Zenker, 56–72. Oxford: Oxford University Press, 2022.

West, Paige. *Dispossession and the Environment: Rhetoric and Inequality in Papua, New Guinea.* New York: Columbia University Press, 2016.

Wingfield, Matthew. "'Working Time' in Environmental Activism: Engaging 'Slow Violence' in the Philippi Horticultural Area." *Anthropology Southern Africa* 45, no. 4 (December 2022): 219–30. https://doi.org/10.1080/23323256.2022.2141810.

Wittfogel, Karl A. *Oriental Despotism: A Comparative Study of Total Power.* New Haven, CT: Yale University Press, 1957.

Woodhouse, Philip. "New Investment, Old Challenges: Land Deals and the Water Constraint in African Agriculture." *Journal of Peasant Studies* 39, nos. 3–4 (April 2012): 777–94.

Wutich, Amber, and Melissa Beresford. "The Economic Anthropology of Water." *Economic Anthropology* 6, no. 2 (June 2019): 168–82. https://doi.org/10.1002/sea2.12153.

Yang, Yi, Junghan Bae, Junbeum Kim, and Sangwon Suh. "Replacing Gasoline with Corn Ethanol Results in Significant Environmental Problem-Shifting." *Environmental Science and Technology* 46, no. 7 (2012): 3671–78. https://doi.org/10.1021/es203641p.

Zhao, Q., W. Xiong, Y. Xing, et al. "Long-Term Coffee Monoculture Alters Soil Chemical Properties and Microbial Communities." *Scientific Reports* 8, no. 6116 (April 2018). https://doi.org/10.1038/s41598-018-24537-2.

Zigon, Jarrett. *How Is It Between Us? Relational Ethics and Care for the World.* Chicago: HAU Books, 2024.

Zlolinski, Christian. *Made in Baja: The Lives of Farmworkers and Growers Behind Mexico's Transnational Agricultural Boom.* Oakland: University of California Press, 2019.

Zondi, Thobeka, Samela Mtyingizane, Ngqapheli Chunu, Steven Gordon, Benjamin Roberts, and Jare Struwig. "Discrimination Followed Us into Paradise: A Quantitative Analysis of Self-Reported Racial Discrimination." In *Paradise Lost: Race and Racism in Post-Apartheid South Africa*, edited by Gregory Houston, Modimowaarwa Kanyane, and Yul Derek Davids, 179–99. Leiden, Netherlands: Brill, 2022.

Zuboff, Shoshana. "The Age of Surveillance Capitalism." In *Social Theory Re-Wired*, edited by Wesley Longhover and Daniel Winchester, 203–13. New York: Routledge, 2003. https://doi.org/10.4324/9781003320609.

Index

Page numbers followed by *fig.* and *map* indicate figures and maps, respectively. Notes are indicated by *n* followed by the note number.

Founded in 1893,
UNIVERSITY OF CALIFORNIA PRESS
publishes bold, progressive books and journals
on topics in the arts, humanities, social sciences,
and natural sciences—with a focus on social
justice issues—that inspire thought and action
among readers worldwide.

The UC PRESS FOUNDATION
raises funds to uphold the press's vital role
as an independent, nonprofit publisher, and
receives philanthropic support from a wide
range of individuals and institutions—and from
committed readers like you. To learn more, visit
ucpress.edu/supportus.

www.ingramcontent.com/pod-product-compliance
Lightning Source LLC
Chambersburg PA
CBHW020852270326
41928CB00006B/673